D1458398

THE RAILWAY RACE TO THE NORTH

The West Coast train, hauled by Caledonian 4-4-0 No. 70, passes the 'winning post' at Kinnaber Junction, while its defeated East Coast rival, behind a Holmes 4-4-0 of the North British, waits to follow it to Aberdeen.

[*From a painting by Jack Hill*]

THE RAILWAY RACE
TO THE NORTH

By

O. S. NOCK
B.Sc., M.I.C.E., M.I.Mech.E., M.I.Loco.E.

LONDON:

Ian Allan Ltd

Made and printed in England by
STAPLES PRINTERS LIMITED
at their Rochester, Kent, establishment

Contents

		PAGE
I	THE SEEDS ARE SOWN	9
II	THE YEARS OF MANOEUVRE	13
III	THE RIVALS AND THEIR PROSPECTS	23
IV	THE 'EIGHTY-EIGHT'	34
V	LOCOMOTIVE PERFORMANCE IN 1888	49
VI	UNEASY TRUCE	61
VII	1895 – BUILDING UP	74
VIII	NEARING THE CLIMAX	90
IX	THE AMAZING FINISH	105
X	THE AFTERMATH	122
XI	LOCOMOTIVE PERFORMANCE IN 1895	132

APPENDICES:

I	L.N.W.R. RECORDS OF ENGINE WORKING	152
II	EAST COAST TRAFFIC CIRCULARS	162

Preface

WHEN Mr Ian Allan and his co-director Mr G. Freeman Allen first put to me the idea of a book about the Race to the North the prospect, though exciting in itself, seemed rather bleak when it came to practical possibilities. What was there new to be written about it? At best could one hope for more than a modern re-hash of 'Kinnaber', with a reappraisal of the locomotive work involved? However, a little canvassing among friends in the railway service brought some heartening results; the editors of *The Railway Gazette*, *The Railway Magazine*, and the *British Railways Magazine* kindly published letters from me asking for information, anecdotes, and reminiscences, and although in volume the result was, perhaps, less than I had hoped, some of the material that did come to light was of first-class importance. In this I am indebted above all others to Mr E. G. Marsden and Mr R. F. Harvey, for the information they put at my disposal. The correspondence and telegrams between the East Coast General Managers during the critical weeks of July and August 1895, which I have been able to include in Chapters VIII, IX and X, throw a vivid light upon the attitude and policy of what may be called the unwilling participants in the struggle. Unfortunately nothing of a similar kind has been preserved on the West Coast side, though the policy of Euston and Buchanan Street from July 15th onwards now seems clear enough.

Among others who have helped me with information I should like to mention particularly Mr C. J. Alcock, who has not only written me many letters on the subject, but has met me and told in his inimitable way of the sights he saw at Euston in those exciting days. Then there is also Mr George Perry, who has passed on to me his personal memories of one of the leading drivers who took part, and I am no less indebted to Locomotive Inspector Bob Steadman, of Gateshead, for much interesting information from the North Eastern side.

From such reminiscences, from letters, from newspaper comment, and from the occasional touches of local colour in the factual writing of such enthusiasts as Rous-Marten, the Rev. W. J. Scott, and Norman D. Macdonald I have been able to build up something of a picture of the scene against which the race was run; a scene in which business men still wore gilled shirts and gold seals, in which a man making a privileged trip on an engine would not think to discard his tall hat, and in which the telegram was the fastest means of communication. Yet in such an age both sides showed an amazing speed in organizing their resources to produce unparalleled feats of running at the shortest of short notices. Men were travelling faster than ever before, by any medium; night by night the record was going higher and higher, until the final West Coast achievement, with its average of 63·2 m.p.h. over a distance of 540 miles, set up a British record that has not yet been broken. Although the whole affair, together with the earlier skirmish in 1888, could be dismissed as a stunt, and far removed from practical business, both sides won fame and honour in the process, and without any doubt gathered in a wealth of experience.

The spirit that animated the contests of 1888 and 1895 is not dead, even now. One could understand a healthy rivalry between the East and West Coast routes in grouping days, when the streamlined engines of Sir Nigel Gresley and Sir William Stanier were vying with each other for the British maximum speed record; but even after nationalization the sparks of 1895 are not finally down. After the great run of the 'Caledonian' from Carlisle to Euston on September 5th, 1957, when the overall average speed for the 299 miles was 70½ m.p.h. start to stop, one found *The Railway Gazette* commenting, rather apprehensively: '. . . it is to be hoped that inter-Regional rivalry will not lead to a revival of the races to Scotland at the end of the last century. On the other hand, occasional very fast runs are a stimulus to mechanical and operating staffs, and serve a useful purpose if they result in appreciable improvements in the time-tables.'

Be that as it may, this backward look to the great days of 1888 and 1895, with the research involved, has been an exhilarating task, and I must thank once again all those who have contributed to it, by their letters, their telephone calls, and by their pictures, some of which we have been able to reproduce.

O. S. NOCK.

20 Sion Hill,
Bath.
August 1958.

I

The Seeds are Sown

'I CHALLENGE them,' thundered George Hudson, 'to leave London with twenty carriages, and I will beat them to York!'

He was speaking at a general meeting of the Midland Railway, at Derby, in 1845. Ten years had passed since that famous visit to Whitby, when Hudson had met George Stephenson and learned that the North Midland Railway was to be built. Nearly ten years had passed since he had persuaded his fellow citizens in York to build their line not to Leeds, but to join the North Midland near Normanton. His great conception of a network of lines covering most of the country under one management – his management! – had developed more rapidly than anyone could have foreseen, but in this new proposal of 1845 for a direct line between London and York was something that cut right across his interests. In Hudson's eyes railway communication between London and York was already established; there was no need for a second route. He was no quiet schemer, or intriguer, though to be sure he had agents stationed far and wide, and it was surprising how much trouble they did cause. He went bald-headed for his opponents, with bombast and threats galore; but nothing he could do or utter shook the steadfast resolve of the 'London & York' promoters.

Much as he disliked the thought of strenuous competition for its own sake, he must have realized 'deep down inside' that once the London & York direct line was established his own route would pass into a secondary position. A glance at the map is sufficient to show its disadvantages. It might pass through a succession of large towns, where important traffic could be collected – Rugby, Leicester, Derby, Chesterfield and Normanton – but the very density of the traffic would mean congestion and slow running. On the other hand, the London & York should have the advantage of a clear, as well as a straight, road. So Hudson fought with might and main to block the passage of the London & York Bill at every stage through Parliament, and lost no opportunity of ridiculing or belittling the whole project. At the same Midland meeting he roared: 'These juvenile promoters would have spent every shilling of their capital by the time they had arrived at Grantham.' The people of Lincolnshire wanted railway communication, and before the loop line of the London & York could be built Hudson had cut clean across their path with a line to Lincoln from Nottingham. The London & York was to pass through Peterborough; again Hudson was there first, with a cross-country branch from Leicester. Having crossed their main route at two vital points, Hudson sought to undermine their position in London. Through his vast and ever-increasing authority and stature he secured a seat on the board of the Eastern Counties Railway, and the merest glance at a map is enough to make the most sanguine wonder how a new and wholly independent line could survive against such a colossus.

The London & York had as its leader and outstanding personality, one Edmund Denison, a man of the toughest fibre and highest integrity. He was the last to be intimidated by threats, or influenced by mere bombast. It so happened he was at Derby on the day of the Midland meeting of 1845, and sure enough he came face to face with Hudson on the station platform. Flushed by the tumultuous enthusiasm with which his rhetoric had been received by the Midland shareholders, Hudson sailed up to Denison and taunted him with the same cut about juvenile promoters spending all their money before the job was finished; he went one better by adding that the London & York would not have had enough to get to Grantham if they had got their money honestly. It was enough. Denison called Hudson a blackguard to his face, and when the 'Railway King', realizing he had gone too far, sought to explain that he meant his remarks only as a jest, Denison turned his back on him with the words: 'Go away, Hudson, I've done with you.' And one has only to study the portraits of Denison and to note the set of his jaw to realize that those were indeed his final words.

Hudson's tactics might delay the passage of the London & York Bill, but they could not prevent it, and ultimately the new railway was duly authorized, and took the title of Great Northern Railway. In its early days it was aptly referred to as the 'Ishmael of railways'. Every established concern, and some too that had scarcely got into their stride, were against it. Even so it may be a little difficult at this stage to see how the fierce rivalries of pioneer days – rivalries, moreover, between the Midland and the Great Northern – have very much to do with the Race to the North, as it was run in 1895. But there was a group of very influential diehards in the railway world of the day who clung to the view that Euston was the one and only admissible gateway to the North. Even after public demand had influenced Parliament towards the passage of the London & York Bill the diehards strove by every means in their power to 'contain' the

Great Northern in its own territory – nay, to encircle it; for Hudson succeeded in gaining control of the Eastern Counties Railway, as well as of the entire line to the north-east from Rugby to Newcastle. The London & Birmingham, though lying outside the Hudson 'empire', was ready enough to play his game so far as the Great Northern was concerned, for their connection off the Midland brought in a good deal of business.

It is interesting to speculate upon how the course of railway history might have flowed if Hudson's integrity had been on the same level as his drive, his business acumen, and his force of personality. There is no need for me to retell the tale of how his phaeton career came to an end; but the fact of his passing from the scene made no change in the attitude of earlier railways towards the Great Northern, in fact the efforts to restrict and minimize its activities were re-doubled. Leadership of the confederacy, as it came to be called, passed naturally to the strongest personality in the group – to Captain Mark Huish, the General Manager of the London & North Western; so formidable, indeed, was the array of railway strength that he marshalled under the banner of Euston Square that many a young and struggling railway administration would have given up the battle for the right of trading freely, and sought terms for amalgamation, or some other line of less resistance. The long-drawn-out negotiations of the period 1850–3 were nothing more nor less than an attempt to strangle the Great Northern, by a series of 'arrangements' for pooling of traffic, division of receipts, and other artificial means of preventing the development of its own business. It was not surprising in face of all that had gone before that the Great Northern Railway, its Board of Directors, its principal officers, and men in quite humble positions grew to look with great care and suspicion upon its older neighbours.

But never was the Great Northern Railway shaken in its resolve to fight things out to the very end. True, there were times when the entire onus, both of strategy and tactics, seemed to rest on the shoulders of Edmund Denison. He was 'C.-in-C.', brigadier and platoon commander rolled into one. It was not that support was lacking from the Board or from the senior executives, but that Seymour Clarke, the General Manager, while the ablest of traffic superintendents, was the worst of negotiators. His straightforward outlook and innate honesty were no match for the wiles of his con-temporaries; time and time again he was outwitted and misled into making a bad bargain, and more than once Denison had to persuade the Board to repudiate an agreement he had concluded. A lesser man than Denison would have sacked his General Manager, and equally a lesser man than Clarke might have resigned in a huff; but Clarke was an apt pupil, and in course of time he came to acquire much of the foresight, resilience, and sagacity in negotiation that so distinguished his great chairman.

The Great Northern Railway came into existence facing challenges of all kinds. Three years before its first trains ran it had been challenged to a speed contest, not that any such incentive was needed to spur its engineers and traffic men into brilliant action. Encompassed by a ring of hostile concerns, the only way it could make headway was by the speed and comfort of its services. The others might, in its early days, force upon it agreements over rates and fares, but there was not, in those pioneer days, any move from the Euston Square 'confederacy' towards dictating any upper limit of speed. There had been a mild flutter in 1848 after the completion of the Caledonian line between Edinburgh, Glasgow and Carlisle. When, for the first time, a man could travel by train all the way from London to Edinburgh the West Coast companies took $15\frac{1}{2}$ hours over the job: 10 a.m. from Euston, and an arrival in Edinburgh at 1.30 a.m. next morning. The Great Northern main line was not then completed, and the rival London–Edinburgh train also started from Euston. North of Rugby its route followed the Hudson chain of companies – Midland, York and North Midland, York, Newcastle and Berwick; the bridges over the Tyne and Tweed were not yet completed, and through passengers had to be conveyed by road over these short sections. Despite this seemingly crippling handicap the East Coast companies were able to book their 9.30 a.m. service from Euston into Edinburgh at 10.35 p.m., an advantage of $2\frac{1}{2}$ hours over the West Coast. At that time, of course, the 'East Coast' route was only truly East Coast north of York, whereas with the opening of the Trent Valley direct line from Rugby to Stafford the West Coast route in 1848 was the same as it is today. In the summer of that year the West Coast made a great improvement, with a train from Euston at 9 a.m. which took only 12 hours to Edinburgh. The East Coast reply to this was an acceleration of the service connecting with the 9.30 a.m. from Euston to reach Edinburgh at 9.55 p.m. despite the inconvenience over the Tyne and the Tweed. At this stage the Great Northern, as a going concern, had not yet entered the picture. It was a case of one branch of the Euston Square confederacy running in mild competition with the other. There is not a great deal of significance about the times maintained, except to observe that at this time the London & North Western seemed strongly disinclined to hurry!

II

The Years of Manoeuvre

THE completion of the Great Northern main line in 1852 brought a great change in the railway operating strategy of this country. The distance from Kings Cross to York was thirty miles shorter than by the 'Hudson' route, and the journey time a full hour less. So much for Hudson's bombast of 1845! But although it was now possible to reach Edinburgh in eleven hours from Kings Cross, against twelve from Euston, the West Coast partners could afford to regard the difference with equanimity, if not a little unholy joy. Two years earlier, by the notorious 'Octuple Agreement', traffic between London and places north of York had been divided between eight companies, on a pooling basis. These eight were the West Coast allies, London & North Western, Lancaster & Carlisle, and Caledonian; the Hudson group, Midland, York & North Midland, and the York, Newcastle & Berwick; the North British; and the Great Northern. The terms dictated by the Euston Square confederacy gave the Great Northern no share at all in the traffic from London to Glasgow, Perth and Aberdeen, and a very poor share of that to the Tees-side towns, Newcastle, Berwick and Edinburgh. In 1850, of course, the Great Northern had only the Lincolnshire loop line open, and was no more than beginning to build up its traffic. The confederacy argued that the pooling scheme should be based on what each company was then doing; its leader, Captain Huish, was astute enough to realize the eventual capacity of the Kings Cross direct route, and by this artificial barrier of pooling receipts he sought to minimize its effectiveness.

Faced with the alternative of a ruinous competition in fares before his new company had fairly got into its stride, and before even the direct main line was completed, Edmund Denison consented. Even though he was able to get the agreement confined to a period of five years it was bad enough, after the main line was opened in 1852, to be hamstrung by an artificial restriction of this kind for the three years remaining in which the agreement had still to run.

Despite the Euston Square confederacy and despite the Octuple Agreement, the Great Northern soon began to be talked about as 'the favourite line to the North', and even before the direct main line was opened Queen Victoria chose it as her route to Scotland on her autumn visit to Balmoral in 1851. None of this favour from royalty and the travelling public served to improve the regard of Euston Square for its new competitor. The rivalry became more deep-seated than ever. At the same time, the years 1853–5 saw the begin-nings of a general change in the railway alliances of this country. Although by the terms of the Octuple Agreement some traffic between London and York continued to go via Rugby and Derby, in the public eye there was now only one way, and that from Kings Cross. Inevitably two of the Hudson companies, the York & North Midland, and the York, Newcastle & Berwick, began to draw away from the North Western and the Midland, and to team up with the Great Northern; and when these two companies joined with the Leeds Northern to amalgamate in 1854 and form the North Eastern Railway, the true East Coast *entente* was well on the way to establish-ment. Very soon the combined strength of the Great Northern and the North Eastern acting together was felt in the realm of railway politics, and in readiness for the ending of the Octuple Agreement, in 1855, the two companies made a resolute attempt to break into the territory north of Edinburgh. A local quarrel in Scotland gave them their opportunity, and Kings Cross and York 'cashed in' with a speed and success that Mark Huish and his associates might have envied.

Up to this time the Edinburgh & Glasgow Railway, though remaining independent of English railway politics, had been very much inclined towards the Euston Square confederacy. At one time Huish had made strenuous efforts to get them to join; but in sym-pathy they came within the same fold as the Caledonian. When a serious dispute arose, in 1854, between these two Scottish companies, the Great Northern and the North Eastern at once approached the Edinburgh & Glasgow, and secured access not only to Glasgow, but over two more independent lines to Perth and Aberdeen. The accompanying map shows how this was done. It was a piece of 'invasion' all the more daring and successful in that the Scottish lines north of Falkirk were, in sentiment, closely allied to the Caledonian. For the Great Northern and the North Eastern, how-ever, the situation was still very much on a razor edge since their access to Edinburgh lay over the metals of the North British. There must have been many times between 1850 and 1880 when Kings Cross and York could never be sure whether to treat the North British as friend or foe. Huish had done his best to get the N.B.R. into the confederacy, which would thus have blocked the Great

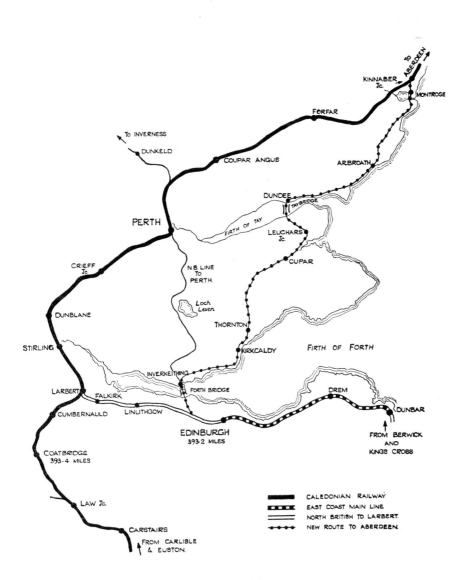

To ABERDEEN

KINNABER Jc.

MONTROSE

FORFAR

To INVERNESS

DUNKELD

COUPAR ANGUS

ARBROATH

DUNDEE

TAYBRIDGE

FIRTH OF TAY

PERTH

LEUCHARS Jc.

N.B. LINE TO PERTH.

CUPAR

CRIEFF Jc.

Loch Leven

DUNBLANE

THORNTON

STIRLING

KIRKCALDY

FIRTH OF FORTH

INVERKEITHING

LARBERT

FALKIRK

FORTH BRIDGE

DREM

CUMBERNAULD

LINLITHGOW

DUNBAR

EDINBURGH
393·2 MILES

FROM BERWICK
AND
KINGS CROSS

COATBRIDGE
393·4 MILES

LAW Jc.

CARSTAIRS

FROM CARLISLE
& EUSTON.

CALEDONIAN RAILWAY
EAST COAST MAIN LINE
NORTH BRITISH TO LARBERT
NEW ROUTE TO ABERDEEN.

Northern at Berwick; but the Scottish company pursued a strongly independent line, standing over the pivot point of the see-saw as it were, seeking to establish a series of 'bridgeheads' in England, ready to come down with all weight and influence on the winning side! The North British stood to gain by the new service from Kings Cross to Perth and Aberdeen, but then they gave the Great Northern and North Eastern a severe jolt in 1862, showing how unstable were the relations between the East Coast associates. It was in 1862 that the Waverley route from Edinburgh to Carlisle was completed, and the North British thereupon switched the bulk of their London traffic to it, cutting out the Great Northern and North Eastern and handing over to the North Western at Carlisle!

It is no wonder that Kings Cross and York never knew where they stood with the North British, and when another development arose in that same year, between the North Eastern and the North British, there was a startling sequel. It was in 1862 that the proposal to incorporate the Newcastle & Carlisle in the North Eastern was made. At once there was a storm of protest, in the forefront of which was the North British. The latter company had made several attempts to secure direct and independent access to Newcastle, and the North Eastern Board knew well that this was one of the most cherished ambitions of the North British. By the long branch line running south from Riccarton Junction in the Cheviots they had reached Hexham, and in the storm of 1862 the North Eastern conceived the idea of buying off their opposition to the merger by offering them running powers over the Newcastle & Carlisle line from Hexham into Newcastle. It was evidently not put quite so baldly as that; in fact, the bargain was one of the hardest ever driven by the North Eastern. Whether or not Kings Cross also had a hand in it one cannot say, but in all probability it was realized that the North British folks were prepared to sell their souls to get into Newcastle. So the North Eastern offered them running powers from Hexham in exchange for North Eastern running powers *from Berwick to Edinburgh*. As the late E. L. Ahrons once wrote, it was a case of selling one's birthright for a mess of pottage! And the North British fell for it – not only so, but they withdrew all opposition to the amalgamation of the Newcastle & Carlisle with the North Eastern. Those running powers from Berwick to Edinburgh were, in later years, to put the Great Northern and North Eastern in an immensely strong position in the operation of the Anglo-Scottish train services, and at this time in history it is astonishing to think how the astute North British management of the eighteen-sixties could have been so misled into pursuing the illusory

NORTH WESTERN EXPRESSES   *Above:* A 'Teutonic' with a mixture of bogie and six-wheeled stock.

Below: A 'Jumbo', with a characteristically mixed rake.

[*Locomotive Publishing Co*

Left: No. 491, one of the Drummond 'Waverley' Class, after removal of name.

NORTH BRITISH
4-4-0s

Below: Holmes type No. 634, sister engine to those participating in the race.

[Locomotive Publishing Co

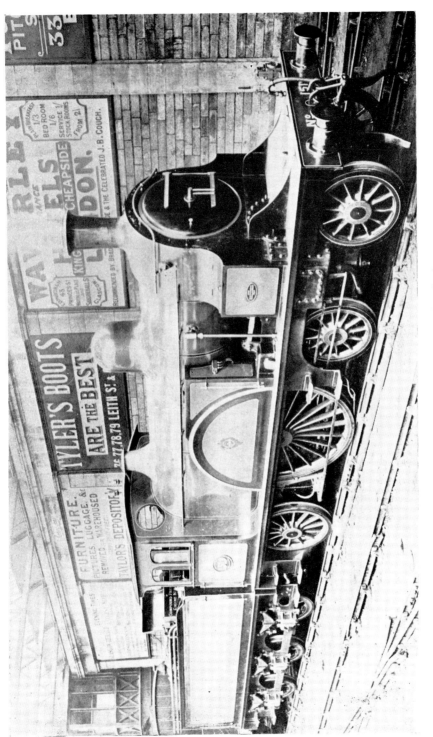

North Eastern Railway two-cylinder compound 4-2-2 No. 1519 ('J' Class) in Waverley Station, Edinburgh.

[Rev. T. B. Parley

G.N. EXPRESS LOCOMOTIVES
OF THE PERIOD

Above: 2-2-2 No. 234 at Kings Cross.

[*H. Gordon Tidey*

Below: 4-2-2 No. 550, as fitted with the simple, non-automatic vacuum brake.

[*Locomotive Publishing Co*

crown of entry into Newcastle. It brought them little except the lengthening of a barely remunerative branch line service.

Among railway directors, and equally among the higher ranks of the administrative staff, there were no delusions about the inter-company rivalries in mid-Victorian times. For many years the London & North Western, the Midland, the Great Northern, and the Manchester, Sheffield & Lincolnshire were constantly sparring for position. There was much hard bargaining at managerial con-ferences; there were intrigue and manoeuvre, and occasionally out-right clashes, as when a Great Northern engine went into Nottingham (Midland) for the first time, and when the Great Northern and Manchester, Sheffield & Lincolnshire together began a fast and highly competitive service from London to Manchester. Of the shareholders it must be said that very few had any interest in rail-ways as such; it was the dividends that mattered, and where a railway was not doing well its management was, often as not, trying to find a more prosperous concern with which it could amalgamate! This is about the only feasible explanation for the feints and somersaults in policy pursued at this time by the management of the Manchester, Sheffield & Lincolnshire Railway. With the workaday staff of the railway, however, it was very different. The traditions of service were rapidly built up. There was a 'something' about it that captured the minds and souls of those who ran the trains. There was pride in the job, and a pride in the company they served, and to these men there gradually filtered through something of the old spirit of rivalry that had permeated the higher councils of the railways since their very inception.

With nothing in the way of popular journalism to spread the news, no wireless, no television, details of an accident would pass by word of mouth. It would be contrary to human nature if the facts did not become distorted or exaggerated in the process, and it would only need a highly coloured version of the Nottingham affair of August 1852, or of the earliest trains from Kings Cross arriving in Man-chester in 1857, to change pride in one's own company to scorn, or even hatred of the others. It is true that neither of these famous cases of violence had anything to do with the eventual race to the North; but on the other hand the proximity of the London termini of the rival railways meant that staff were recruited from the same districts. In the taverns of St Pancras, Holloway, and Camden Town it would have been surprising if men from the Great Northern, the Midland, and the North Western had not come face to face, and it needs no expert in the homely dialect of Cockaigne to attempt a

B

reconstruction of the banter in many a 'pub' when the news about Nottingham or Manchester had found its way through.

'Strewth, Bill, d'y'ear what those Nor'-West scabs did at Manchester on Toosdy?'

'No, Tom.'

'Well, yer see, our bloke was running in, nice as yer please, when 'e sees their blokes shoving a trolley on to the line!'

'Coo!'

'Yes, an' arter e'd clapped on 'is brakes an' stopped – lucky 'e did stop! – they left the ruddy thing there and went off. Well, 'e and 'is mate goes up to shift it, and then a crowd o' Nor'-West scabs comes up, and sez to 'im, "You git aht. You ain't comin' in 'ere!"'

' "No, that you ain't!" ' A great dark man had come up behind them and stood threatening. "You keep yer ruddy noses aht o' Manchester. You ain't wanted."

Roars of laughter from the Great Northern men.

'An 'oo's goin' ter keep us aht? You, Matey?'

'Keep aht, I sez, you an' yer dirty pals from Sheffield. Muck, Sludge and Lightning!* That's it, muck!!'

The argument, such as it was, ended promptly with a resounding sock on the jaw from one of the Kings Cross men, and there is no need to describe in detail the uproar that followed, nor how it ended. But although a tavern brawl may not necessarily lead to a railway race, there were plenty among the rank and file on both sides who were ready enough to join whole-heartedly, in their own way, in the disputes that raged for so many years at the highest levels of the railway hierarchy. The Midland, the Great Northern and the North Western came into close proximity at Leeds; the Midland was established in Peterborough and Lincoln; and the Great Northern was gradually forcing its way into the Derbyshire coalfield. Rumour, that most disconcerting and deadly means of communication, exaggerated the smallest incident, and although the Great Northern depots of Peterborough and Grantham were miles apart from the North Western strongholds of Rugby and Crewe there were times when feelings began to run high.

With the policy of encirclement and protectionism consistently pursued from Euston, and the determination of Kings Cross to maintain and constantly improve its place in the sun, it seemed that sooner or later a severe contest would be inevitable. Men sensed that

* The blunt northerners often referred to the M.S. & L. as the 'Muck, Sludge and Lightning'.

it was coming. In a small way the situation was not unlike the international scene in Europe during Edwardian times, when many men in this country felt that sooner or later there would have to be a reckoning with Imperial Germany. It was discussed in every club in London. How the clash would eventually come was then obscure. So it was, too, in the early 'seventies between the Great Northern and the London & North Western. One surveys the railway scene of the period, visiting the potential storm centres one by one. At Manchester, if the North Western liked to exert themselves in running, the Great Northern and its partner the Manchester, Sheffield & Lincolnshire would stand no chance; the Great Northern held an easy supremacy at Peterborough, Lincoln and York, and the Midland would have to fight hard to compete seriously at Leeds and even at Sheffield. Farther afield, of course, there were Edinburgh, and even Perth; but such a contest would involve not only the two hereditary enemies at Kings Cross and Euston, but also their northern associates, and the onlooker could not be certain how they would react. Most doubtful of all was the attitude of the North British, traditionally more inclined towards the West Coast alliance than towards its own natural friends.

Then suddenly, in March 1872, there came an announcement from Derby that had repercussions in every railway board-room in the British Isles: as from April 1st, 1872, the Midland was going to admit third-class passengers to all its trains. Hitherto the best expresses on most lines had been available only to first- and second-class passengers. The Great Northern, following the opening of the Midland line to St. Pancras in 1868, had taken third-class passengers on certain crack expresses that were in strong competition with the Midland, and they followed the challenge of 1872 by putting third-class coaches on to all their trains, with the one exception of the 'Flying Scotsman'. But this exception was accompanied by a characteristic gesture from Kings Cross. A new train was put on for Edinburgh at 10.10 a.m. providing for all three classes a service identical in speed to the 'Scotsman', while the 10 a.m. itself, 'to maintain the special character of the East Coast route to Scotland', was accelerated by a full hour. Thus first- and second-class passengers by this famous train received a very substantial 'extra' for their money. The journey time from London to York was now 4 hours 15 minutes, an average speed, including stops, of 44 m.p.h.; as yet, however, the speed over the northern section of the route was not quite up to the same high standard. After the luncheon interval of 25 minutes at York, a time of 4 hours 50 minutes was required for

the remaining 205 miles on to Edinburgh. Nevertheless the acceleration of 1872 was a big step forward, and it can be attributed in no
small measure to the effect of Midland competition.

It might be wondered why the 'Flying Scotsman' should have
been singled out for preferential treatment, since it was not subject
to Midland competition of any kind at that period; but long experience in the arena of railway warfare had taught the Great Northern
management to keep a weather eye open for all eventualities, and by
that prosperous summer of 1872 construction was well advanced
of the Midland Railway's own independent line to Scotland, the
far-famed 'Settle & Carlisle'. It was fairly certain, in view of strong
North British interest in this project, that Derby would join forces
with Waverley in running a through service between St Pancras
and Edinburgh, and once the Settle & Carlisle was finished both
Euston and Kings Cross would be faced with a new, and potentially
formidable competitor. One can sense clearly that the Great Northern and North Eastern, well established as the favourite route to
the North, sought to consolidate their excellent position – not by
imposing schemes of traffic pooling or other artificial restrictions on
their rivals, but by the sheer excellence of their service to the public.

The acceleration of the 'Flying Scotsman', in response to the
Midland decision to admit third-class passengers to all trains, was a
very adequate rejoinder; but the Midland had a still more sensational
shot in its locker. On October 7th, 1874, it was announced from
Derby that from New Year's Day, 1875, they intended to abolish
second class altogether, and to reduce their first-class fares to the
existing second-class level, then $1\frac{1}{2}d$ per mile. This time there was an
intervening period between the Midland announcement and the
date at which the astonishing change was to come into effect, and
all the northern railways joined in making the strongest representa-
tions. For once Euston and Kings Cross were in complete agreement.
It was not so much the abolition of the second class, as the big
reduction of the first-class fares that was objected to. The Great
Northern and the North Western protested that such a change should
not be made by one company without a general conference. But the
Midland stood firm, and whether they liked it or not, the others had
to bring down their first-class fares. Otherwise the Midland would
have scooped all the traffic. Neither the Great Northern nor the
North Western went to the extent of abolishing second class at this
stage; neither did the Great Northern yet yield to admitting third-
class passengers to the 'Flying Scotsman'. But to both East and
West Coast routes the Midland challenge was now more serious

than ever, particularly as it was expected that the Settle & Carlisle line would be open in 1876. As if to anticipate a challenge in speed from the new Midland route, another half-hour was taken off the schedule of the 'Flying Scotsman' in the summer of 1876.

The years of manoeuvre were now drawing to a close. Curiously enough the East Coast accelerations had so far evoked little response from Euston. The West Coast expresses, jogging along at an easier pace and carrying a high proportion of the third-class business, paid well enough. It seemed that while the policy of the Great Northern was to give an ever-improving service, that of the North Western was to give the slowest that the public would stand. Economy was the watchword at Euston, and the slower the trains ran the less would be the working expenses. Engines were small, and their finish was rough and austere, while the drive for economy went to the extent of dimming the gas lamps on the arrival side at Euston, and only turning them full on when trains were actually coming in. Senior officers, going to conferences with other railways, were briefed to resist any attempts to acceleration. In the late 'seventies the timing of the 10 a.m. Scotch express from Euston was:

Section	Miles	Min.	Av. speed m.p.h.
Willesden-Rugby . . .	77·2	103	44·8
Rugby-Crewe . . .	75·4	96	47·2
Crewe-Preston . . .	51·0	67	45·8
Preston-Carlisle . . .	90·0	130	41·6

The overall time to Carlisle was then $7\frac{1}{2}$ hours, showing an average speed of 39·8 m.p.h., but in addition to the stops at Willesden, Rugby and Crewe this time included an interval of half an hour for lunch at Preston. In 1883, however, the North Western really bestirred itself and decided to accelerate the Scotch express by ten minutes; they achieved this not by any improvement in the running speed – for that would have cost money – but by knocking ten minutes off the luncheon interval! At this time the rival train from Kings Cross was booked to run the 105·5 miles to Grantham non-stop in 129 minutes, an average speed of 49·5 m.p.h.

That luncheon interval was at one time a test of stamina and forti-tude for those who left their seats in the train and made for the station dining-rooms. Neele has described the scene at Preston in its early days: 'The dining arrangements at first were of the rough-and-ready order, a hot and perspiring woman stood at the top of the table doing the carving, which required some energetic work on her part to supply the customers, all anxious to lose none of their allotted time.' In later years, however, when the L.N.W.R. had taken the arrangements into its own hands there was a great improvement. Some of the directors who had observed the working of roadside restaurants at French railway stations brought their influence to bear, and the commodious dining-room built on the island platform was frequently crowded on both sides, as the timetables were arranged so as to bring both the down and up Scotch expresses to Preston at the same time, and get patrons fed in one big party.

In the early 'eighties few among those who were to play leading parts in the open rivalry that was to break upon an unsuspecting public realized how quickly the sands were running out. The public as a whole knew nothing of the disputes and rivalries at managerial level, and when the contest in speed did begin it was hailed by the Press with all the 'ballyhoo' of a popular sporting event. As in the years of tension before the outbreak of war between two strongly armed groups of nations, when the geography of the frontiers is examined, strategic points and battlegrounds are discussed, so as a prelude to the railway races the rival routes must be studied, the locomotives compared, and the *dramatis personae* viewed against the rather sombre background of the times.

III

The Rivals and their Prospects

For a single chapter it is now necessary to anticipate events. If a contest in speed was actually to develop between the great trunk lines running north from London it was over the four hundred-odd miles to Edinburgh that the East and West Coast routes seemed most evenly matched, though the unbounded enterprise of the Midland made it necessary to consider it as a possible third competitor, despite the handicap of a longer route. In the early 'eighties, however, a contest in speed hardly seemed likely at all. It takes two runners at least to make a race, and in 1883 the Great Northern had not even stirred its own partner to really serious efforts. Meanwhile the North Western showed even more reluctance than the North Eastern to accelerate its principal passenger train services. The great organization based upon Euston was then under the iron discipline and virtual dictatorship of that tremendous Chairman, Richard Moon. In his opinion, an average speed of 40 m.p.h., start to stop, was quite fast enough for an express train; anything more led to unnecessary expense. That was the guiding principle laid down, and timetables, locomotive design, and every other feature of operation were based fundamentally upon it.

By the close of the year 1884 the North Western had five varieties of express passenger locomotive in regular main line service. These were the 'Lady of the Lake' 2-2-2 singles; the Ramsbottom 6 ft 7 in 'Newton' class 2-4-0s; the Webb 'Precedents'; and the three-cylinder compounds of the 'Experiment' and 'Dreadnought' classes. The 'Ladies' and the 'Newtons' were earlier products of the Crewe 'small-engine' policy; both good designs up to a point, but designs that must be judged against the rather leisurely background of contemporary London & North Western running. For upwards of twenty years the 'Ladies' had filled a special niche in the haulage of the Irish Mails throughout between Euston and Holyhead. The Post Office contract demanded an average speed of 42 m.p.h. and the North Western was often hard put to it to maintain booked time; every endeavour was made to keep the loads of these trains down to an absolute minimum, and ordinary third-class tickets were not available. For very many years all London & North Western third-class tickets had an inscription printed on them: 'Not available by the

Irish Mail'. Despite their diminutive size and dimensions, the 'Ladies' gained a reputation for fast running, with a curious result to be recorded later. The other Ramsbottom express locomotive class, the 'Newtons', was in process of being superseded by the Webb 'Precedents', and in the event of anything special being required it is unlikely that a 'Newton' would have been put on the job.

The Webb compounds represented a whole-hearted and sustained attempt to cut down running costs, and were entirely in keeping with the policy dictated by the high command at Euston. On theoretical grounds there was every reason to expect some economy, but in working out the details of the design so many extraneous features of doubtful quality were included that the advantage of compound expansion of the steam was completely obscured and swamped. Charles Rous-Marten, one of the most erudite and experienced of nineteenth-century observers, once wrote of the 'Experiment' class:

'It took a tremendous lot of hard flogging to get much over 50 or 55 miles an hour out of them. Anything over 60, even down the most tempting descent, was rare. I tried them with all sorts of expresses, sometimes travelling on the footplate, sometimes behind them. Setting aside one failure through a slight mishap to the machinery, I found the work consistently respectable, but never brilliant.'

Such a class could obviously be counted out, so far as any forthcoming speed contest was concerned, and the 'Dreadnoughts', of 1884, were not much better so far as speed was concerned. They were much more powerful, and on the whole more reliable, but even they did not often exceed 70 m.p.h. Furthermore they were heavy on maintenance and on coal, thus hardly measuring up to the standards of economy that were demanded at the time.

Whatever ideas Webb may have cherished about his three-cylinder compounds, the real mainstay of the North Western express services was the 'Precedent' class of 2-4-os, first introduced in 1874. It is no exaggeration to say that the design not only was outstanding in its day but remains one of the most outstanding in the whole history of the steam locomotive on British Railways. To outward appearances, though neat and compact, a 'Precedent' was not specially distinctive; it was the design of the cylinders and valves that gave to the engines the astonishing turn of speed that later became so characteristic of them. I have previously discussed the technical details at some length in my book *The Premier Line*, and so it will be enough to say here that the valve design was such as to permit a very free and unrestricted flow of steam. In the very respect that Webb's compounds were hopelessly hamstrung, his earlier simple-expansion were unusually excellent for their day. Seeing their leading dimensions in cold print, the 'Precedents' would not appear to be very formidable engines, especially as they carried a boiler pressure of no more than 140 lb per sq in; but the boilers steamed so well and the valves enabled the steam to be used so effectively that they were vastly stronger and faster engines than mere looks and dimensions might lead one to suppose. Up to the year 1884, however, they had received little scope to show what they could do.

There was another feature of the North Western economy drive that concerned the rolling stock, and was closely linked up with the slow-scheduled speeds of the day – that was the form of brakes in use. The Clark and Webb sectional chain brake, which was in use until 1884–5, might have been designed by Heath Robinson instead of by responsible engineers of the world's busiest railway. The details of this crude mechanical contrivance would be laughable if they had not been the cause of many accidents and loss of life. Yet Richard Moon persisted in telling the shareholders that it was the most perfect brake it was possible to devise, and in 1880 his company went so far as to write a letter to the Board of Trade stating that 'out of 501 passenger engines, 464 are fitted with reversing screws, so as to enable the driver to bring the whole steam pressure to bear on the reverse sides of the piston while running at speed'. It is to be inferred that this 'last ditch' measure was approved of on those occasions when the chain brake did not work – and they were many! Of course the chain brake was a cheap device, but one feels that eventually it was the amount the company had to pay in compensation for injuries, and deaths, that hastened the decision to change, though it was merely a change to the simple non-automatic vacuum. No driver is going to run hard in any confidence if the reliability of the brakes is questionable, and that was actually the case with the brakes in use on the London & North Western Railway. The fight put up against the adoption of any automatic form of continuous brake was extraordinary. One can only assume it arose from a fanatical desire to go on alone, independent of, and in defiance of, the strong recommendations made by the Board of Trade.

The North Western's Scottish partner, the Caledonian, had, at an earlier date, adopted the Westinghouse continuous automatic air brake. The pundits of Euston and Crewe strongly disapproved, and disapproved to the extent of insisting that the through Anglo-

Scottish expresses on the West Coast route should be equipped with the sectional chain brake! Thus while the Caledonian had a quick-acting, powerful and reliable brake on its own passenger trains, it was forced to submit to the absurdity of working the London expresses with the chain brake – until 1883, when there was a serious accident to the 'Limited Mail' at Lockerbie, and a further one at Perth, both due to the chain brake failing to work. After that the Caledonian insisted that the Westinghouse brake was fitted to the West Coast Joint Stock; safety would thus be assured in Scotland, whatever the London & North Western chose to do south of Carlisle. As for the simple non-automatic vacuum brake which the North Western next used, apart from the great dangers inherent in it when a train might be parted, its uselessness was shown in the hair-raising accident at Carlisle in December 1886. Again the 'Limited Mail' was concerned, and the vacuum brake pipes between engine and tender had become completely frozen up during the long night run from Crewe. In consequence, when the driver applied the brake about $1\frac{1}{2}$ miles south of Carlisle station, while running at about 50 m.p.h., nothing happened. The train ran clean through Carlisle station, collided with a Midland engine 300 yards beyond the platform end, knocked it out of the way, and ran a further 190 yards before coming to rest.

In 1884–5 Caledonian motive power was in a transition stage. Some two years earlier Mr Dugald Drummond, formerly of the North British Railway, had been appointed Locomotive Superintendent, and already he was building a series of fine new 4-4-os to replace the Conner 8 ft 'singles' on the principal expresses. The new Caledonian engines were very similar in size and appearance to the 4-4-os Drummond had designed for the North British in readiness for the newly opened Settle & Carlisle line. His North British 4-4-os had already proved themselves as excellent hill climbers over the long and severe gradients of the Waverley route; but the incessant curvature that exists over so much of that route precluded anything in the way of fast running. In the early 'eighties, however, despite this handicap, the North British was running the night expresses non-stop over the $98\frac{1}{4}$ miles between Waverley and Carlisle in 2 hours 20 minutes. The Caledonian, with the advantage of a much straighter road, was taking the same overall time over its route of $100\frac{3}{4}$ miles, but making two intermediate stops. Until the new Drummond engines appeared on the scene any Caledonian train that was at all heavy was double-headed; the prospects for further acceleration were obscure since the new engines had not been tested in high-speed running conditions.

So far as the route itself is concerned, the going is fairly easy to a point about 235 miles north of London; there were at that time speed restrictions to 40 m.p.h. at Rugby and Stafford and a very severe one to 15 m.p.h. round the curve immediately to the north of Preston station, but the gradients are easy. It is true that there are one or two steep pitches in South Lancashire, but they are too short to present any serious hindrance. North of Carnforth, however, the whole character of the line changes. In the 63 miles remaining to Carlisle the railway is carried to an altitude of 915 ft above sea-level at Shap Summit, and then down to little more than sea-level at Carlisle. The long rise of 31½ miles from Carnforth up to Shap can be very trying to a hard-worked engine and crew, especially when the weather is bad, and storms of wind and rain sweep across the bleak, exposed stretches of line north of Oxenholme. Although the descent from Shap to Carlisle is an exact counterpart, so far as the average gradient is concerned, one cannot fully recover on the descent any time lost on the ascending side; speed must be moderated through Penrith, and with the brake power then available it was advisable to start slowing down well before reaching Carlisle! Owing to the 'small-engine' policy pursued for so many years by the London & North Western Railway a great deal of double-heading was needed over Shap, and in many cases the assistant engines were carried throughout from Preston, or even from Crewe. The line of demarcation between the old Southern and Northern Divisions of the L.N.W.R. still remained very pronounced, and on all the Anglo-Scottish expresses engines were changed at Crewe.

The Caledonian line is still harder. Although there are some favourable stretches in the first 40 miles out of Carlisle the general tendency is markedly adverse out to Beattock, after which there follows the worst incline between Euston and Edinburgh, the 10-mile ascent of Beattock Bank. Here the gradient is mostly 1 in 75, but nearing the summit there are some short lengths even steeper than this. The summit is reached at a point 1,015 ft above sea-level, and a long descent of 23 miles through Upper Clydesdale gives some respite to the engine and crew of an Edinburgh express; but while trains for Glasgow have only a short and easy climb to surmount after passing through Carstairs Junction, Edinburgh trains have another 10 miles of stiff climbing ahead of them, to cross Cobbinshaw Summit at an altitude of 880 ft above sea-level, before the final descent begins. Furthermore, the climb to Cobbinshaw is commenced at very low speed, because of the exceptionally sharp curve between Strawfrank and Dolphinton junctions on the outskirts of

Carstairs. Altogether the Caledonian had a very hard route from Carlisle to Edinburgh, and the overall speed scheduled in the early 'eighties, 43¼ m.p.h., inclusive of two stops, was extremely good.

Turning now to the East Coast route, the Great Northern was unquestionably the fastest line in the world. Despite the preferential treatment given to the 'Flying Scotsman', it was not the fastest train. The East Coast companies held such an easy supremacy over their rivals on the London–Edinburgh service that extreme speed was unnecessary – as yet! But with Leeds it was another matter, and in competition with the Midland four very fast trains were put on in the summer of 1880, covering the 185½ miles between Kings Cross and Leeds in 3¾ hours, inclusive of three stops – an overall speed of 49¼ m.p.h., and including such a brilliant run as that of 77 minutes for the 70 miles from Wakefield to Grantham (54 m.p.h.). The 'Flying Scotsman' ran the 105½ miles from Kings Cross to Grantham at an average speed of 49 m.p.h., but again much faster running over this same stretch was made by the highly competitive Manchester expresses, including one run at an average of 54 m.p.h.

In contrast to the West Coast lines, where a variety of locomotives was in regular service on the best trains, on the Great Northern one class overshadowed all others, the ever-famous 8 ft bogie 'singles' of Patrick Stirling's design. So distinctive in outward appearance with their domeless boilers, their outside cylinders, and the elegant sweep of the running plates over the driving-wheel bosses, they captured the imagination of the travelling public to a greater extent, perhaps, than any British locomotive of the day. Moreover, their drivers were practised hands at high-speed running. There was no need to flog a Stirling 8-footer to attain 60 m.p.h.; with one of them at the head of a train one could always expect a spin of 70 to 75 m.p.h. somewhere in the journey, and those high speeds were reached with relative ease. The 'eight-footers' were as beautifully designed mechanically as they were beautiful in outward appearance, and they maintained a very high standard of reliability, in all conditions of working, rather than putting up an occasional performance of sensational merit amongst many of mediocre or nondescript character. From 1885 onwards this famous stud was reinforced by Stirling's new 2-2-2 'singles' with 7 ft 6 in driving wheels, and inside cylinders. These also were excellent engines, and for many years they worked turn-and-turn-about on similar duties with the 8 ft bogie engines.

The year 1884 found the North Eastern Railway in the midst of a domestic crisis. Edward Fletcher, who for thirty years had ruled over the locomotive department in a benevolent autocracy, had been succeeded by that zealous reformer from Ireland, Alexander McDonnell; and his reforms were so flagrantly and tactlessly applied that before many months were out the whole locomotive department was seething with unrest. Fletcher, a genial soul no less than a fine mechanical engineer, had earned the lasting respect and affection of the men. The locomotives he designed were appreciated and prized, to the detriment of all others which came within the ken of the North Eastern men, at York, Leeds, Newcastle, Carlisle and Edinburgh. It is, therefore, not difficult to imagine the consternation, alarm and anger with which these men saw some of the most cherished of the Fletcher 'gadgets' removed, and new engines put on the road which did not come up to Fletcher standards either for power or efficiency. Protests were lodged, indignation meetings were held, and eventually the situation worked up to such a pitch that McDonnell just had to resign. The management of the North Eastern Railway was caught very much 'on the wrong foot'. New express engines were urgently needed; a gesture was urgently needed to restore the confidence, morale, and loyalty of the men, and so, pending the appointment of a new Locomotive Superintendent, the General Manager, Henry Tennant, formed a locomotive committee to carry on the general business of the department.

It was during this intervening period that a fine new express-engine design was worked out, a 2-4-0 based generally on Fletcher's practice but of greater power, and including several improved features. Thanks to the circumstances of their design and construction, these engines were always known as the 'Tennants', though actually, of course, the General Manager was not responsible for any of the technical details. One can appreciate, however, that he insisted to the committee that the engines should please the men; they were designed by practical engineers who knew the requirements of the train services, and as a result they proved instantly welcome and popular, and completely master of the work. These engines were built in 1885, and went straight into the heaviest express duties between York, Newcastle and Edinburgh, though at that time the scheduled speeds were not high. In his classic work of 1889, *Express Trains British and Foreign*, Professor Foxwell wrote scathingly:

'The North Eastern metals traverse a district ever memorable in railway history, and its main track is comparatively level; but neither easy gradients nor proud memories can prevail against an unexcitable executive and consciousness of a safe monopoly. The company know that they can always rely on that willing horse, the Great Northern, to do wonders south of York, so they have for years shirked their share of speed in the Scotch traffic, and the public accordingly speak of the East Coast route as "the Great Northern route", oblivious of the fact that the longer half of the journey is run by North Eastern engines . . .'

The East Coast route as a whole was much the easier. The total distance from Kings Cross to Edinburgh was then slightly longer than the usual route today, as trains entered Newcastle by the High Level Bridge and had to reverse direction after the stop in the Central station; but even so the distance was 393·2 miles, as against 399·7 miles from Euston to Edinburgh, Princes Street station. Although there is some climbing north of the Border there is nothing to compare for difficulty with Shap, Beattock and Cobbinshaw, and the speed restrictions at Peterborough, Selby, Durham and Berwick were no more hampering in the aggregate than Rugby, Stafford, Preston and Strawfrank Junction.

So far as locomotives and gradients were concerned, if one takes the year 1885 as a time for a survey the prospects might perhaps be summed up as follows. The West Coast had the longer and considerably the harder route. Against this the Great Northern locomotives and men, practised though they were in fast running, had some formidable rivals in the North Western 'Precedents'. It did not need much study of the drawings of the valves and valve chests for an experienced engineer to realize the potentialities of those Crewe engines. Farther north one could be sure that the new Drummond 4-4-0s on the Caledonian would climb well, but as to high speed they were still more or less an unknown quantity. The Great Northern single-wheelers had already proved themselves up to the hilt, and there were signs that the new 'Tennant' 2-4-0s on the North Eastern were fast engines. Theoretically they were more powerful than the North Western 'Precedents'. At that time, therefore, the advantage would appear to lie with the East Coast.

The quality of the tools certainly have an important bearing upon the ultimate execution of any job; but the tools are not the sole criterion. Managerial policy, the leadership of divisional and district officers, and above all the personalities and inclinations of individual men, can play a vital part. Before closing this brief survey of rival prospects we can well take a look at some of the leading men who seemed likely to play principal parts in any speed contest that might brew up. On the West Coast side Richard Moon tended to dominate everything; but under him there were some first-class railwaymen. Francis W. Webb, the Chief Mechanical Engineer, had made Crewe Works pre-eminent the world over as a locomotive-building establishment, and in any question of comparison he was prepared to go to any length to prove the superiority of his own products. He had a very able assistant in charge of the running in the person of George Whale: a dour unsmiling little man, devoted to the L.N.W.R., and understanding to the last degree the men who had to drive and fire the locomotives. The triumvirate was completed by G. P. Neele, Superintendent of the Line, another very able and experienced officer. He had grown up in the steady, solid, punctual atmosphere of the old North Western, and one gathers that he had little time for the spectacular; the North Western earned princely dividends for its shareholders by sterling all-round service, and Neele seemed ready enough to carry out the policy of Richard Moon and to look askance at the dashing exploits of his counterpart at Kings Cross.

The Great Northern had in its Superintendent of the Line an outstanding figure in Francis P. Cockshott. In his reminiscences Neele has recorded the many times Cockshott warned the Midland Railway how useless it was to compete for the Leeds traffic. 'Whatever time you leave', he emphasized, 'the Great Northern will leave after you, and be in Kings Cross before you are in St Pancras.' It was through Cockshott's energy and drive that the Great Northern and the Manchester, Sheffield & Lincolnshire in partnership were actually able to equal the North Western's best time from London to Manchester, despite a route 14 miles longer, and the climb over Woodhead, 1,015 ft above sea-level. The astonishing thing is that for a time the North Western did not rise to this audacious challenge. Cockshott reflected the enthusiasm of his General Manager, Henry Oakley – a man who had been in the service of the Great Northern since his boyhood, and who was intensely proud of the prestige and success his company had attained. He would be the last man to see it equalled, let alone eclipsed. And then there was Patrick Stirling. Although his locomotives were among the best known in the whole country, although he was the hero of many a schoolboy enthusiast, he was actually a man of the most retiring nature. It was not for him to go to the Institution of Civil Engineers and tell in strident phrases of the engines he had built at Doncaster; he rarely joined in gatherings of his fellow railwaymen, and yet by his justness, his uprightness of character, and the success of his locomotives he was greatly respected by all his men. It was not the pleasant *bonhomie* enjoyed by Edward Fletcher on the North Eastern, nor yet the boisterous slap-on-the-back kind of *camaraderie* established by Charles Sacré on the Manchester, Sheffield & Lincolnshire. Stirling's popularity was that of a discreet, rather distant reverence.

On the North Eastern, following the McDonnell episode and the interregnum presided over by the General Manager, locomotive affairs settled down again under the new chief, Thomas W. Worsdell, elder brother of the man who had managed to keep things going during the stormy months that followed Fletcher's retirement. Wilson Worsdell might, in fact, have expected to succeed at once to the chieftainship; but his time was yet to come, and he served loyally enough under his brother, who had come from the Great Eastern Railway. The second power behind the throne in the 'eighties and 'nineties was the redoubtable Walter Mackersie Smith, Chief Draughtsman in the locomotive works at Gateshead. Smith was a most forceful and resolute character; a designer never slow to speak his mind, to argue with, and even to criticize his chief. If he had ever succeeded to the supreme command he might have become as autocratic and unapproachable as F. W. Webb on the London & North Western; but Smith served both the Worsdells as Chief Draughtsman, though a mighty power in the land for all that.

I have left the Caledonian men until last because they were perhaps the most picturesque characters of all. There was Dugald Drummond, the Locomotive Superintendent – dour, tough Clyde-sider, but a man that others would follow to the ends of the earth. He ruled with a rod of iron, but without any harshness, injustice or favouritism, and in later years when he went to the London & South Western Railway many of the Scottish enginemen who had known him on the Caledonian and on the North British went south too. The accents of Clydeside, Stirling, and Perth became familiar sounds on many a southern English footplate. Drummond had no standard less than the very best, and if the call came to run fast one might be fairly certain that he would strain every nerve to beat all comers. Finally there was Irving Kempt, Superintendent of the Line, a 'character' if ever there was one. He dressed like a buck of the Regency days, with gills to his shirt and a ribbon from which dangled gold seals. That, however, was not all. The greatest sight was to see him on an inspection. He would enter the saloon at Glasgow in a tall hat, the very picture of dignity and elegance; but once away from headquarters the 'topper' was discarded and he would emerge at some country station in a Balmoral bonnet worn at a rakish angle. So bedecked, the years seemed to fall away from him, and he regained all the energy and exuberance of youth.

Such, then, were the men responsible for running the trains between London and Edinburgh. In 1885 it was Cockshott, and Cockshott alone who was forcing the pace, but in working the

The West Coast racer of 1888 climbing Beattock, hauled by the Caledonian 4-2-2 No. 123.

[From a painting by Jack Hill

L. & N.W.R. 2-2-2 SINGLES

Above: No. 610 *Princess Royal*, with original boiler and smokebox, as used in 1888 race.

Below: No. 1430 *Pandora*, as finally rebuilt by Mr Webb, and used as pilots in the 1895 race.

[*Locomotive Publishing Co*

NORTH EASTERN RAILWAY   *Above:* Tennant class 2-4-0 No. 1506

Below: 'J' Class 4-2-2, rebuilt as a simple, with piston
valves, and used in the 1895 race.

[*Locomotive Publishing Co*

John Lambie, Caledonian Railway.
[Courtesy: "The Engineer"

Patrick Stirling, G.N.R.
[Courtesy: "The Engineer"

FOUR FAMOUS LOCOMOTIVE ENGINEERS

Matthew Holmes, N.B.R.
[Courtesy: "The Railway Magazine"

F. W. Webb, L. & N.W.R.
[Courtesy: "The Railway Magazine"

principal Scotch expresses the Great Northern had established such a comfortable supremacy, to which the West Coast were making no signs of reply, that rivalry was for a time unusually subdued. The Midland and North British together made a brave attempt to break in upon this very choice and exclusive traffic and ran the morning express from St Pancras to Edinburgh in 10 hours 7 minutes, carrying first- and third-class passengers. The services offered to the public at that time may therefore be summarized thus:

Route:	E. Coast	E. Coast	M. & N.B.	W. Coast
Class of passenger:	1st & 2nd	1st, 2nd & 3rd	1st & 3rd	1st, 2nd & 3rd
London　.　.　. dep.	10 a.m.	10.10 a.m.	10.35 a.m.	10 a.m.
Edinburgh　.　.　. arr.	7 p.m.	8.10 p.m.	8.42 p.m.	8 p.m.

At that time there were no runs on the Scotch services booked at more than 50 m.p.h. start to stop; the fastest was the Great Northern run from Grantham to York – 82·7 miles in 100 minutes, or 49·6 m.p.h. These times remained unchanged until the summer of 1888, except for one brief period of acceleration in 1887. Then strangely enough it was the West Coast that mildly took the initiative. It was in that Golden Jubilee year of Queen Victoria's reign that Richard Moon, the Chairman of the L.N.W.R., received the honour of a baronetcy; whether or not the quickening of the 'Day Scotch Express', as the 10 a.m. from Euston was then advertised, had anything to do with this it is not possible to say, but for the period of the summer service the arrival time in both Edinburgh and Glasgow was 7.45 p.m. The North Western share of the acceleration was 10 minutes, made up of 4 minutes saved between Rugby and Crewe, 1 minute between Crewe and Preston, 3 minutes between Preston and Carlisle, and 2 minutes off the stopping time at Rugby. Even so, the new 95-minute allowance between Rugby and Crewe gave an average speed of no more than 47·7 m.p.h. In the winter of 1887–8 the arrival at Carlisle was 5 minutes later, but the Caledonian, for some reason, held the Edinburgh portion for no less than 25 minutes at Carlisle, and the booked arrival in Edinburgh reverted to the traditional 8 p.m. So, in the late autumn of 1887 the *status quo* was largely restored, and in any prospects for further developments the Midland and North British seemed to have as good a chance as the West Coast, on their current form.

c

The 'Eighty-Eight'

Just as in eighteenth-century Scottish history one refers to the two Jacobite rebellions as the 'Fifteen' and the 'Forty-five', from the years of their occurrences, so also may the disturbances in Anglo-Scottish railway relations be thus distinguished. In the meantime the hidden fires, fed upon the historic and sustained antagonism towards the Great Northern, began to crackle more noisily. The Midland bombshell of 1879, abolishing the second class, had so far had little effect upon the speed of the Scotch expresses. The West Coast route, despite an overwhelming advantage in the physical nature of its route, had remained content with a 10-hour schedule for its 'Day Scotch Express', while the Midland and North British, with the added attraction of Pullman parlour cars on their 10.35 a.m. train, took only 7 minutes longer. Then, in November 1887, came the stroke that fairly 'set the heather alight'. The East Coast companies announced that their 'Special Scotch Express', as the 10 a.m. from Kings Cross was billed, would convey: '3rd class passengers from London (Victoria, L.C. & D., Moorgate Street, Kings Cross and Finsbury Park) to Edinbro'; also from Broad Street (N.L.) to Edinbro'.'

The above announcement is taken from the relevant pages of *Bradshaw*, and includes the curious and incorrect abbreviation for Edinburgh that infuriated all good Scots. Apparently, third-class passengers were not conveyed to places south of Edinburgh, and it is interesting to see that the connections from the southern stations were also included. There was an advertised connection with the L.C. & D. R. train leaving Victoria at 8.52 a.m. and due at Kings Cross at 9.53 a.m. The inclusion of Broad Street, too, was a piece of defiance, for the North London Railway was very much in league with the L.N.W.R. One fears, however, that very few passengers would avail themselves of such a facility, as it would mean travelling first to Finsbury Park, then into Kings Cross, and finally by the 'Scotsman' itself. Only in the case of the evening Leeds express did the Great Northern have a stop at Finsbury Park to connect directly with North London trains from the City. As a result of this change of tactics, the East Coast service from London to Edinburgh was now superior on all counts to those of the Midland and the North Western, and there were some heart-searchings at both Euston and Buchanan Street.

One can sense the undercurrents that were flowing during the winter of 1887–8 from some feelings expressed by G. P. Neele many years later in his reminiscences. Following some references to the establishment of the joint West to North express service via the Severn Tunnel he writes: 'If however the arrangements between the North Western and the Great Western were assuming a friendly aspect, those between the North Western and the Great Northern did not run quite so smoothly.' Apart from any direct negotiations between the two companies, Neele had many opportunities of seeing his great rival, F. P. Cockshott, in action. He was awed, if not over-awed, by the summary way in which Midland opposition in the London–Leeds traffic had been swept aside, and he wrote of Cockshott: 'I am satisfied his mind was quite as determined that we should not run on equality to Edinburgh.' But then the West Coast allies were still labouring under the false precepts of Sir Richard Moon, who not only stood firm to the standard of the 40 m.p.h. express train, but who openly ridiculed the idea of speed prestige being any advantage. In the face of such an attitude by the Dictator of Euston Square, what could the traffic and locomotive officers do?

Events were not long in forcing the hand of Sir Richard Moon. Already the East Coast had a very strong hold on the Anglo-Scottish traffic, and the admission of third-class passengers to the 'Flying Scotsman' began to drain away from both West Coast and Midland the cream of the third-class business as well. At various meetings during that winter the Great Northern people picked up some very broad hints that the North Western was far from satisfied with the position, whatever its Chairman might decree, and the summer of 1888 promised to be livelier than for many a long day on the main lines to Scotland. When battle was joined in earnest it was, sur-prisingly, the West Coast that seized the initiative, and in such a way as to put their rivals at a distinct disadvantage. Delaying their announcements to the very last minute, the North Western suddenly told the world that from June 2nd the 'Day Scotch Express' would be accelerated by a full hour, to both Edinburgh and Glasgow. Although some adjustment had been expected at Kings Cross, the magnitude of the cut and the suddenness of the announcement caught the East Coast companies unawares, and a full month went by with both sides making the same overall time between London and Edinburgh.

So far as speed was concerned, the North Western improvement was a very substantial one. The old and new times, with the average speeds involved, were:

WEST COAST DOWN 'DAY SCOTCH EXPRESS'

		January, 1888		June, 1888	
		Time	Av. speed m.p.h.	Time	Av. speed m.p.h.
Euston . . . dep.		10.00 a.m.		10.00 a.m.	
Willesden Junc.	⌠ arr.	10.10		10.09	
	⎩ dep.	10.12		10.11	
Rugby . .	⌠ arr.	11.50	47·3	11.42	50·9
	⎩ dep.	11.55		11.47	
Crewe . .	⌠ arr.	1.33 p.m.	46·3	1.15 p.m.	51·5
	⎩ dep.	1.40		1.22	
Preston .	⌠ arr.	2.45*	47·1	2.22*	51·0
	⎩ dep.	3.10		2.47	
Carlisle . . arr.		5.17	42·6	4.40	47·7

* Lunch interval: 25 min.

It was certainly an unprecedented state of affairs that the aloof, leisurely L.N.W.R. should have start-to-stop averages not merely equal, but superior to those of its Great Northern rival. In Scotland it had hitherto been the practice to run separate trains to Edinburgh and Glasgow throughout from Carlisle. The Edinburgh train, indeed, was not booked away until 5.42 p.m. Over the Caledonian line the acceleration of June 2nd involved practically nothing in the way of increased speed; instead of the protracted station stop, and the remarshalling to make up separate trains, the express waited only 7 minutes at Carlisle, and continued as a combined train to Carstairs. Compared with the previous 2 hours 18 minutes taken by the Edinburgh portion to run from Carlisle to Princess Street, the new time was 2 hours 13 minutes. In June 1888 the honours were with the North Western.

Both the West Coast partners had no hesitation in double-heading the trains, and in this respect the East Coast reply could not be made quite so quickly as one might have been led to expect. On the Great Northern Patrick Stirling did not merely *dislike* double-heading; he forbade it, and, to make doubly sure, there were no brake connections on the front buffer beams of his express engines. The East Coast was dealing with the rush of traffic resulting from their provision of third-class accommodation on the 'Special Scotch Express'; loads were heavier than ever before, and since the Great Northern loco-motive department had denied itself the easy way out in cases of exceptional traffic the consequences of acceleration had to be carefully weighed. The expected reply came from the East Coast in mid-June, announcing that from July 1st the time from Kings Cross to Edinburgh would be 8½ hours. Of this cut the Great Northern and the North Eastern each contributed 10 minutes, while the remaining 10 minutes was cut out of the luncheon interval at York. The East Coast times of June and July 1888 were thus:

EAST COAST: 'SPECIAL SCOTCH EXPRESS'

		June, 1888		July, 1888	
		Time	*Av. speed m.p.h.*	*Time*	*Av. speed m.p.h.*
Kings Cross .	. dep.	10.00 a.m.		10.00 a.m.	
	⌠arr.	12.09 p.m.	49·0	12.04 p.m.	51·0
Grantham .	{				
	⌊dep.	12.15		12.09	
	⌠arr.	1.55*	49·6	1.45*	51·6
York . .	{				
	⌊dep.	2.25		2.05	
	⌠arr.	4.07	47·3	3.42	49·8
Newcastle .	{				
	⌊dep.	4.12		3.47	
	⌠arr.	5.38	46·6	5.08	49·5
Berwick .	{				
	⌊dep.	5.43		5.13	
Edinburgh .	. arr.	7.00	44·7	6.30	44·7

* Lunch interval.

Although it must have been expected at both Euston and Buchanan Street, this East Coast acceleration came as a big disappointment. It would certainly seem that it had not been expected quite so soon, and while the West Coast timing of June had been planned with great deliberation and care during the winter and spring, the East Coast promptitude in going one better was disconcerting, especially as the North Western and Caledonian were then approaching their busiest time for the Scottish tourist traffic. The idea of a further disturbance of their traditional timetable was abhorrent to all concerned. Yet once having achieved equality of speed many of the leading personalities in both England and Scotland felt that they must never again be content with second place. The honour of the Royal Mail route was at stake. Moreover, did they not have the privilege every year of conveying Her Majesty the Queen on her autumn holiday visit to Balmoral? Events were beginning to move too fast for Sir Richard Moon. Most of his senior officers were relishing the prospect of a real 'crack' at the Great Northern, and when intense pressure for retaliation came from the Caledonian too the North Western Board set up a Special Committee of Directors to deal with the whole matter. This august body agreed with the Caledonian that from August 1st the 10 a.m. from Euston should run to Edinburgh in 8½ hours.

Having cut their own time between London and Carlisle by 37 minutes in the June acceleration, the North Western authorities evidently felt that it was now up to the Caledonian, and in the new schedule planned for August the arrival time at Preston remained unchanged. Then, so far as Edinburgh passengers were concerned the East Coast precedent was followed, in a cut in the luncheon interval from 25 to 20 minutes at Preston; there the train was divided, and the Edinburgh portion departed at 2.42 a.m., leaving the Glasgow portion to follow at the previous time of 2.47 p.m. With the load thus lightened, a notable acceleration was possible between Preston and Carlisle, from 113 down to 105 minutes for the 90 miles. The start-to-stop averages on the North Western were now very uniform, namely 50·9, 51·5, 51·0 and 51·3 m.p.h. – Shap apparently making no difference at all. So far, however, only 13 minutes had been gained, and 5 of these at the expense of the passengers' digestions. Furthermore, although another 90 miles of train mileage had been added, the 'Day Scotch Express' had hitherto been so frequently piloted over Shap that in actual fact the additional expense was probably very small indeed. In practice, there was one engine on each portion of the divided train instead of two engines on the combined train. In Scotland, up to this time, the cities of Edinburgh and Glasgow had received equal treatment from the West Coast companies; but now all attention was focused upon Edinburgh. The North Western brought the train into Carlisle at 4.27 p.m., and the Caledonian were away at 4.32 – 15 minutes ahead of the Glasgow portion, and non-stop to Edinburgh. Again the average speed of this train fell around the 'magic' West Coast standard of 51 m.p.h. – 50·8 to be exact. Nevertheless, the train was planned to be of light formation, not exceeding 100 tons if possible, so that even over the gradients of Beattock and Cobbinshaw the effort demanded from the locomotives was not likely to be excessive.

Remembering how quickly the East Coast had replied to the June acceleration, elaborate precautions were taken to keep the next West Coast move secret until the very last minute. There was an air of suppressed excitement at both Euston and Kings Cross, though as yet the general public had not become aware of what was going on. The Great Northern had its scouts out, and more than one apparently ordinary member of the public studying time bills and frequenting the platforms and buffets at Euston was a clerk from the Superintendent of the Line office at Kings Cross, doing what he could in the way of eavesdropping. Railway enthusiasts as we know them today did not exist, but there was a handful of men, for the most part unknown to each other, who took a keen interest in various aspects of railway working, and to them we are indebted for much of the data on which it has been possible to reconstruct something of the spirit of those great days. Of these men Professor Foxwell drops out of the picture at an early stage, and appears to have played no part in the establishment of the railway enthusiast hobby. But he has left with us a classic, in collaboration with T. C. Farrer, in his statistical account of all the express trains in the world, dated 1889. He may have been a statistician, but as a journalist he had a racy style, and a gift of vivid description far above the usual ponderous prose of the day. Some comments of his on the London & North Western aptly set the stage:

'The North-Western has a perfect permanent way with very easy gradients (except between Preston and Carlisle), and Mr Webb's superb "compound" engines have lately been pouring out in quantities regardless of cost; the rolling stock is probably the best in the kingdom; the company holds the preference share of our richest traffic, and its revenue is indeed princely. We merely remark that its average speed is not quite up to the level of all this splendour and prestige. Except in this one item, there is no doubt that the North-Western is "the leading line". And in the vital matter of *punctuality* this company easily carries off the prize; its arrivals are a lesson to the Midland or smaller delinquents north of the Thames. (As for the Southern companies, they have a futile yearning after punctuality, but it is an aspiration towards an ideal which they do not hope to see realized in this world.) Hence business people are strongly prejudiced in favour of the North-Western as against alternative routes; and in consequence its carriages are, on the average, more crowded than those of any other trunk line. North-Western porters and guards do their work with military precision, but with a finished nonchalance which is very appropriate to the oldest and most punctual of our great companies.'

In view of the foregoing one can perhaps understand a little more readily the reluctance of the L.N.W.R. to indulge in wholesale acceleration, lest they should be unable to run the trains punctually, and would sacrifice something of the comfort of travel for higher speed.

Foxwell's famous book was not published until a year later, and in 1888 the three men who did more than anyone else to arouse the interest and enthusiasm of newspaper editors, and so to bring the affair prominently before the public, were W. M. Acworth, Norman D. Macdonald and the Rev. W. J. Scott. For some little time prior to 1888 all three in their several spheres had, through their cultured interest and literary work, cultivated the acquaintance and friendship of senior railway officers. Scott was an advanced Anglo-Catholic, and something of a stylist; he had already broken down the barriers at Kings Cross, and was well known to F. P. Cockshott and his assistant, J. Alexander. Although his writings are carefully phrased to appear impartial, one can sense that his sympathies were very much with the East Coast. On the other hand, Acworth, a regular correspondent to *The Times*, was equally well known at Euston, while Macdonald, son of a famous Scots advocate and an advocate himself, had the means of entry to the inner circles of both Caledonian and North British Railways. The events of July 1888 kept all three men agog, and when the North Western suddenly announced, on July 27th, that from August 1st the 10 a.m. from Euston would run to Edinburgh in $8\frac{1}{2}$ hours the excitement really began to mount up. It was not that the trio of free-lance railway *littérateurs* themselves wrote sensationally of what was to come. The daily newspapers, becalmed in the 'silly season', sent their staff reporters after copy.

Publicity for this speed contest was the last thing the leading railways wanted; for against the sensationally written-up glamour of acceleration there was inevitably a good deal of scaremongering among the fainthearts. The editors' post-bags contained letter after letter protesting against the danger involved, and at that time it must not be forgotten that the London & North Western, despite its splendour and prestige, had a bad accident record, and was still inadequately equipped with brakes on many of its faster trains. But the offices of the respective Superintendents of the Line at Kings Cross and Euston had no time to brood over possible dangers; as Foxwell wrote:

'It requires a railway training to contemplate with a cool head the urgent introduction of "accelerations" like these, involving special "shunts" and signalbox instructions all along the route – these to be rapidly arranged in the very busiest week in the railway year. Hence people who would themselves have been driven wild by such responsibility rushed to the papers with forcible feeble remonstrances against the "danger" incurred.'

When the North Western finally announced their $8\frac{1}{2}$-hour service to Edinburgh, on July 27th, there must have been many in both senior and junior positions at Euston who sat back with a sigh and hoped that would see the end of it, for the year 1888 at any rate. After all, the Bank Holiday was close at hand, on August 6th that year, and following that both East and West Coast companies would be so involved with the flood of Scotch traffic leading up to 'The Twelfth' that any further thoughts of acceleration would be out of the question – or so they thought! Moreover, the average speed of the West Coast would make a new record for long-distance travel; although the overall time from London to Edinburgh was to be the same as that of the East Coast, on account of the greater distance from Euston the speed on the West Coast route was higher.

Whether Kings Cross got wind of the West Coast intentions or not I cannot say, but Cockshott acted like lightning, and on that very memorable August 1st, when the North Western and Caledonian first ran to Edinburgh in $8\frac{1}{2}$ hours, the East Coast train was there in the level 8 hours! One can well imagine the feelings of dismay and rage among all concerned at Euston when their carefully planned record was broken before they had made it – as an Irishman might say it. To write that the great dignified establishment was in a furore is perhaps an exaggeration; certainly everyone was roused to a fever of partisanship. The day was a Wednesday, and telegrams were despatched right, left and centre. George Whale, the Locomotive Running Superintendent, was summoned to Euston; the Directors' Special Committee was called for the following day and by the afternoon of August 2nd Euston and Buchanan Street had agreed that they too would run to Edinburgh in 8 hours. The new schedule was to be put into operation on the following Monday – August Bank Holiday of all days! G. P. Neele and George Whale were instructed to arrange details with the Caledonian, and they travelled to Glasgow by the 'Limited Mail' that very night. That train then left Euston at 8.50 p.m. and reached Glasgow Central at 7 a.m. All preliminaries had been fixed by telegram, and soon after arrival they met Messrs Eddy and Kempt, of the Caledonian; the details were quickly fitted in, and the North Western men left again by the 10 a.m. up Scotch express for Euston. The Caledonian share was to effect an acceleration from 118 to 112 minutes over the 100·6 miles from Carlisle to Edinburgh, and it might be thought that the northward dash of Neele and George Whale was hardly necessary to settle so straightforward a point; but the two North Western men used the return journey to see, personally, the district officers concerned at Carlisle, Preston, Crewe, and Rugby. The locomotive and traffic men had all been summoned by telegram to meet the up

'Day Scotch Express' so that Neele and Whale could impress upon all the importance of the changes to come on the following Monday.

On the North Western two of the changes were unprecedented; the train was run in two portions throughout from Euston, and the first, or racing, portion was run non-stop from Euston to Crewe. This latter was the longest non-stop run that had ever been attempted in this country, and it was made possible by the existence of water troughs, which none of the East Coast companies then used. The schedule laid down for August 6th was:

			Time	Av. speed m.p.h.
Euston.	.	. dep.	10.00 a.m.	—
Crewe.	.	. arr.	1.00 p.m.	52·7
		dep.	1.05	—
Preston	.	. arr.	2.03	52·8
		dep.	2.23	—
Carlisle	.	. arr.	4.03	54·0
		dep.	4.08	—
Edinburgh	.	. arr.	6.00	53·8

It is curious to see that the booked speed over the two mountain sections was higher than that over the very easy course from Euston to Crewe; there may have been two reasons why the latter stretch was easily timed – to give something in hand against a possible further acceleration, and the difficulty of getting a better path over what was then undoubtedly the busiest main line anywhere in the world. On Bank Holiday it was small wonder that crowds gathered at Euston to see the new flyer go off. Enginemen and officials were besieged by reporters; the affair had now reached the stage of a popular sporting contest, and wagers were freely made among the betting fraternity.

Excitement, however, turned to astonishment and even apprehension when the engine for this historic trip came backing down; for it was quickly seen to be *not* one of Webb's 'superb' compounds, nor yet a 'Precedent', but a 25-year-old 2-2-2 of the 'Lady of the Lake' class. Surely not! Had the booked engine failed? But no; it was deliberate enough – No. 806 *Waverley*, as if to cast the name of their destination into the teeth of the East Coast. And what a picture the little engine looked; her black paint shone so that it looked more like a midnight blue, her nameplate shone like burnished gold. Despite her splendid appearance and despite the lightness of the load, there were some on that platform who doubted the wisdom of putting such a veteran on to make the longest non-stop run ever yet attempted anywhere in the world. Alongside her rival, the tall Stirling 'eight-footer', which at that moment would be standing at the head of the East Coast 'Special Scotch Express' in Kings Cross, she would have looked a tiny little thing. Sharp at 10 o'clock she went off, amid cheers from the crowd of onlookers; many were on the platform, some had gathered at the end of the arrival platform No. 1 from which they could get a broadside view as she went out, and others were swarming on to the parapet of the road bridge crossing all the tracks at the entrance to the station yard. It was not long before telegraphic advice of her running began to come and the authorities at Euston were soon assured that all was going well. She was through Rugby, 82·6 miles in 94 minutes; and Stafford, 133·6 miles in 148½ minutes, having averaged 54 m.p.h. from the start, so that the driver had to ease down in order not to be too early at Crewe.

Engines were changed, and a 'Precedent' came on for the run to Carlisle. No point in hurrying on to Preston, for there was that wretched luncheon interval to be endured; then on to Carlisle, and with only four coaches totalling 80 tons at the most, the *Vulcan* made short work of Shap. At Carlisle the Caledonian had a star of the first magnitude waiting to take on, the new 4-2-2 'single', No. 123. This beautiful engine, the only one of her kind, looked as stately and modern as the little North Western *Waverley* had looked quaint. But again, when the Caledonian had a stud of fine 6 ft 6 in 4-4-0s that had already proved very speedy, why had a single-wheeler been chosen for a run that included the Beattock and Cobbinshaw summits? Surely a coupled engine would have been more suitable. But on the very first day No. 123 scored a resounding triumph; instead of the 112 minutes scheduled, she ran the 100·6 miles from Carlisle to Edinburgh in 104 minutes, and stopped in Princes Station at 5.52 p.m. – 8 minutes early. To this engine fell the task of securing the early arrivals of the West Coast train; for with an advertised departure time of 4.8 p.m. at Carlisle the train could not be started earlier. Throughout the month of August No. 123 did wonderfully consistent work; her average time was 107¾ minutes, for a remarkable average speed of 56 m.p.h.

The swiftness of the West Coast response to the 8-hour run of August 1st seems to have taken even Cockshott by surprise, and for a further week the two trains ran on equality. Both sides ran ahead of time, and as Scott afterwards wrote, Norman D. Macdonald nearly bisected himself lengthwise trying to be at both ends of Princes Street at the same time! He would wait for the Kings Cross train to come into Waverley, and then leap into a hansom cab and drive like Jehu to Princes Street station to see if the 'Caley' was in. An exciting time was had by all, but it is amusing to recollect that Neele, Cockshott and the other highest officers would have to wait for news of those arrivals until it came in by telegram the following morning. Telegraphic advice of the running was sent to many places all over the world. On the evening of August 6th a full account of the inaugural West Coast 8-hour run was cabled to the *New York Herald* and included the news of an arrival 8 minutes early.

One day during the first week Sir Edward Watkin was a passenger, and on arrival in Edinburgh he gave some most interesting comments on the run:

'I have travelled all over the world and I have never had a pleasanter journey. There was steadiness, noiselessness, continuity of speed; no rushing up and down, no block, except just once at Atherstone; always before time. It was capital in every way. And then the refreshment part – the lunch at Preston – soup, choice of meat, sweets, cheese, and a cup of coffee, and all for three shillings . . .'

And, I may interpose, all eaten in 20 minutes! Sir Edward continued:

'It is a *train de luxe*. The highest speed travelled was not more than 65 m.p.h. The great secret in getting a steady train is to have the vehicles the same length, the same weight, and all coupled well together. That was the case today, and I never experienced easier running.'

The 'block' at Atherstone to which Sir Edward refers was not due to signals in the ordinary way or to a temporary speed restriction on account of relaying or other engineering work, but due to a block at a level-crossing with the Holyhead Road (now A5). Delays here were a frequent bone of contention between the L.N.W.R. and the local authorities, and eventually an injunction was obtained *against* the railway company, which for a time was compelled to slow all trains down to 4 m.p.h. over the crossing.

On Friday, August 10th, came news of a further acceleration: the East Coast train was to make the run in $7\frac{3}{4}$ hours, as from August 13th. Throughout the month of August the East Coast carried the heavier load; normally the train consisted of seven six-wheeled coaches, with a tare weight of $100\frac{1}{2}$ tons. Both before and after the acceleration of August 10th the booked times between Kings Cross and Newcastle were the same; the cut in time was achieved in omitting the 5-minute stop at Berwick, and making an excellent non-stop run of 137 minutes over the 124·4 miles from Newcastle to Edinburgh. The Great Northern used both the 8 ft bogie 'singles', and the new 7 ft 6 in 2-2-2 engines of Patrick Stirling's design. Between London and Grantham the running was characterized not by any extreme speed, but by the uniformity of the work, although ten different engines were used. There were twenty-seven runs made to the fastest timing; the average of all twenty-seven trips gave a speed of 55·7 m.p.h. start to stop, and the slowest of all was made at 54·5 m.p.h. The fastest run of the whole month was made by a 2-2-2 engine, No. 233, when Grantham was reached in 105 minutes from Kings Cross. The same uniformity was shown between Grantham and York, though on this stretch only four different engines were used during the month. The Great Northern men were clearly working strictly to schedule. In any case there was nothing to be gained by racing ahead of time, except perhaps to give passengers a little longer at York.

North Eastern performance on schedules of unprecedented rapidity was watched with great curiosity. The company had previously shown not the slightest inclination or desire to run fast, and the new compound 4-4-0 locomotives, working on the Worsdell-von Borries system, were largely an unknown quantity. These new engines were used turn-and-turn-about with the 'Tennant' 2-4-0s, and both classes did well. Between York and Newcastle the 80·6 miles were booked to be covered in 93 minutes; but very often the luncheon interval at York was exceeded and that gave the 'Tennants' their chance. The actual average running time between York and Newcastle for the twenty-seven runs made to the fastest booking was 83½ minutes – a daily gain of nearly 10 minutes on schedule, and an average speed of 58 m.p.h. Here, indeed, was one of the surprises of the race. Whereas real fireworks might have been expected from the Great Northern men, who were the most experienced of all the contestants in the art of fast running, it was the hitherto comfortable, leisurely, unexcitable North Eastern that stole the show. North of Newcastle the running was at times even faster; it was here that one of the footplate 'discoveries' of the century was made in the person of Driver R. Nicholson, a terrific 'speed merchant', who on one occasion made the Newcastle–Edinburgh run at an average speed of 59·3 m.p.h. with one of the new two-cylinder compounds. It is extraordinary to realize that less than a month earlier the best North Eastern speeds had been 49·5 m.p.h. from Newcastle to Berwick and 44·9 m.p.h. from Berwick to Edinburgh.

However things might have been taken on the Great Northern,

there is no doubt that racing fever had taken complete hold upon the West Coast companies. In countering the final East Coast acceleration of August 14th they threw the ordinary conventions of passenger train operating to the winds, and without the flicker of an eyelid ran their train as far ahead of time as their engines could take it. No more than a week of really fast running had given them supreme confidence; leaving intermediate stations as soon as they were ready, without waiting for booked time, they made a remarkable run, and not for the last time in Anglo-Scottish railway history broke a proudly advertised East Coast 'record' before it had been made. Many enthusiasts will recall the amusing episode of the inaugural London–Edinburgh non-stop run of 1928 with the 'Flying Scotsman', when the L.N.E.R. were to commence the widely advertised world's longest non-stop run, 392·7 miles, on May 1st, and how the L.M.S.R., by dividing the 'Royal Scot' and running non-stop one portion to Glasgow and the other to Edinburgh, respectively 401·4 and 399·7 miles, eclipsed the L.N.E.R. project in advance. In 1888 time-gaining began from the very start; the little Ramsbottom 2-2-2 *Waverley* ran from Euston to Crewe in the excellent time of 166 minutes, making in this start-to-stop average speed of 57 m.p.h. what was probably the fastest run ever put up by one of this class. But although getting away from Crewe 14 minutes early the 'Precedent' that had taken over, made what was a relatively poor run; in the first week a time of 50 minutes from Crewe to Preston had been made on one occasion, and was succeeded by one of 90 minutes from Preston to Carlisle – a gain of 18 minutes to engine. On August 13th, however, the times were 56 and 99 minutes, and with one minute lost over lunch the arrival at Carlisle was no more than 16 minutes early. On the form shown on August 7th this might have been 31 minutes. But even as it was, with a splendid concluding run by No. 123, the Caledonian brought the train into Edinburgh at 5.38 p.m.

As if to emphasize the triumph of the West Coast on that day the East Coast failed to keep their new schedule, and registered one of the very few late arrivals during the whole racing period. Next day, however, to make sure of things, the North Eastern double-headed the train and reached Waverley at 5.32 p.m. 13 minutes early. But August 13th really marked the end of the 'race'. On the 14th a conference was held in London; the two sides agreed that there should be no further acceleration, and that the overall times of 7¾ hours by the East Coast, and 8 hours by the West Coast should remain in force for the rest of August. G. P. Neele comments:

'The advent of the holidays had a very tranquillizing effect on the racing spirit, the affair was at an end, and in September our Time-Table reverted to the table in force for July, showing 6.30 p.m. as the time for the London and North Western Express to be due in Edinburgh, the East Coast showing 6.15 p.m. as their arrival, and thus the sharp race to Edinburgh eventuated till a further disturbance arose in 1895.'

So far as overall running time was concerned, the East Coast had the last word in 1888. On August 31st, in the hearts of some who joined the 'Flying Scotsman' at Kings Cross that morning there were high hopes of a record, since on this final day it was understood that the train would be got away as soon as possible from intermediate stations. The Great Northern were 7 minutes early into Grantham, and would have gained handsomely to York had it not been for two checks: one was a moderate signal check approaching Doncaster, but the second was a most infuriating delay, due to a hay barge having been given priority at Selby swing bridge. Even so, the 'Scotsman' was into York at $1 \cdot 22\frac{1}{2}$ p.m. – $7\frac{1}{2}$ minutes early. But then, instead of carrying on the good work, the luncheon interval was prolonged. It seemed evident that the North Eastern authorities were going to maintain schedule times, no more. The passengers who had partaken of lunch were all back in the train and ready for a start at 1.41 or 1.42 at the latest, but no engine had so far put in an appearance. At 1.45 p.m. she backed down – not a Worsdell-von Borries compound 4-4-0, but a 'Tennant' 2-4-0 No. 1475 – and the general air of leisured ease in coupling on and making ready for departure gave no hint of any intention to hurry. The train was eventually despatched from York at 1.49 p.m. and to everyone's surprise and delight made a most brilliant run. There were a dead stand for signals at Ferryhill, lasting $1\frac{3}{4}$ minutes, and checks approaching Chester-le-Street, yet the $80\frac{1}{2}$ miles from York to Newcastle were covered in $83\frac{1}{4}$ minutes. Arriving at and leaving Newcastle 10 minutes early, it was finally the turn of Driver R. Nicholson, with the new compound 4-4-0 No. 117; he ran the 124·4 miles on to Edinburgh in 130 minutes and reached Edinburgh at 5.27 p.m.

This proved to be the 'fastest yet' at the end of the 1888 race, and gave an overall average speed between London and Edinburgh of 52·7 m.p.h. – lunch intervals, hay barges and all. By comparison, the West Coast fastest, on August 13th, over a slightly longer route gave an overall average of 52·3 m.p.h. One can, indeed, say that the honours were even. On the other hand, on the day that the West Coast made its fastest run, the locomotive work between Crewe and

Carlisle was below standard. The running averages on these two superb 400-mile trips are most interesting to compare:

WEST COAST: AUGUST 13th

Section	Miles	Min.	Av. speed m.p.h.
Euston–Crewe . . .	158·1	166	57·1
Crewe–Preston . . .	51·0	56	54·6
Preston–Carlisle . . .	90·0	99	54·5
Carlisle–Edinburgh . .	100·6	105	57·4

Overall running average 56·2 m.p.h.

EAST COAST: AUGUST 31st

Section	Miles	Min.	Av. speed m.p.h.
Kings Cross–Grantham .	105·5	110	57·5
Grantham–York . . .	82·7	86½*	57·3
York–Newcastle . . .	80·6	81½*	59·4
Newcastle–Edinburgh . .	124·4	130	57·5

Overall running average 57·7 m.p.h.
* *Deducting time spent waiting signals.*

On the West Coast, although August 13th witnessed the fastest overall time, on August 7th, there was some much faster running between Crewe and Carlisle, with average speeds of 61·2 m.p.h. from Crewe to Preston and 60 m.p.h. from Preston to Carlisle. Again on August 9th, when the North Western engine failed at Shap and the train left Carlisle 45 minutes late in consequence, the 'Caledonian' No. 123 went on to Edinburgh in the remarkable time of 102½ minutes. The fastest aggregate running time on the West Coast occurred on August 7th, when the time was 423 minutes, but on that occasion the train waited for time at Crewe, Preston and Carlisle. Both sides had shown that they possessed splendid engines, and drivers who were prepared to run hard; and although, by common consent, the very fast times scheduled at the height of the race were not maintained after the end of August, the travelling public had every reason to be satisfied with the eventual result:

OVERALL TIME: LONDON TO EDINBURGH

	Winter 1887/8	Winter 1888/9
East Coast . . .	9 hours	8¼ hours
West Coast . . .	10 hours	8½ hours

A family group of the Racing Days.
Driver Tom Robinson of the Caledonian engine
No. 78 (in cap, centre of back row) with his
family and friends.

[*Courtesy: E. Perry*

L. & N.W.R. EXPRESSES
AT SPEED

Above: A 'Jumbo' breasting Shap Summit with a five-coach train of stock similar to that used in 1888.

[*R. J. Purves*

Below: Jeanie Deans picking up water at Bushey troughs.

[*Locomotive Publishing Co*

GREAT NORTHERN RAILWAY   *Above:* Up stopping train, hauled by 2-2-2 No. 879, near Hadley Wood.

[*C. Laundy*

Below: The 'Flying Scotsman' passing Sandy, hauled by 2-2-2 No. 230.

[*Courtesy: K. H. Leech*

Two of the cele-
brated L. & N.W.R.
'Teutonic' Class
compounds, Nos.
1304 *Jeanie Deans*
and 1312 *Gaelic.*
[*Locomotive
Publishing Co*

V
Locomotive Performance - 1888

BEFORE continuing this story of the mounting rivalry for the Anglo-Scottish traffic it is interesting to pause for a while and analyse the locomotive performance. While one cannot entirely agree with a remark made afterwards by Mr John A. Barker at a meeting of the Cleveland Institute of Engineers, the running of individual loco-motives provides, as always, a fascinating study. Barker said: 'The all-important factor in the race was the locomotives, all else being as nearly perfect as anything human could make it.' He went on to say that he had been asked what good had come of it; many people expressed their disapproval from every point of view. 'Was it worth all the fuss to save $1\frac{1}{2}$ hours on a 9-hour journey?' But Barker had no doubts himself, for he continued: 'It had been a grand awakening to locomotive engineers; their branch of engineering had been for the past twenty-five years at a standstill, and the fact that Mr Rams-bottom's *Waverley* and *Marmion* engines, twenty-five years old, ran so well clearly proved it.'

Unfortunately there is no log of the run on August 13th, when *Waverley* ran to Crewe in 166 minutes, but later that same week a correspondent of *The Engineer* travelled by the train from Euston to Edinburgh, and a study of the details of this journey shows how easily the locomotive was being run for much of the distance. The times were taken to the nearest half-minute, and in the accompany-ing log I have worked out the average speeds against the mileages now used in logs over this route. I mention this because the results cannot be regarded as other than approximate.

From the foregoing it is clear that the crew were taking things quite easily from Tring down to Bletchley, and again very much so after Rugeley. Had the downhill running from Tring been as brisk as that from Nuneaton, and had the uphill work from Stafford been as vigorous as that from Willesden to Pinner many minutes could have been saved on the journey. On this occasion the engine from Crewe to Carlisle was a new 'Precedent', No. 1219 *Lightning*, built in 1888 in replacement of the Ramsbottom 'Newton' class 2-4-0 of the same number and name. The run was characteristic of the train during the racing period, but not to be compared with the grand run of August 7th, when No. 275 *Vulcan* made the trip in even time. Skeleton details of the two runs are tabulated herewith:

L.N.W.R.: 10 a.m. EUSTON–CREWE

Load: 4 bogie coaches, 80 tons
Engine: 2-2-2 No. 806 *Waverley*

Miles		Min.	Av. speed m.p.h.
0·0	EUSTON . . .	0	
5·4	WILLESDEN JUNC. .	10	32·4
11·4	Harrow	16½	55·3
13·3	Pinner	18½	57·0
16·0	Bushey	21½	54·0
21·0	Kings Langley . . .	27	54·5
—		p.w. slack	—
24·5	Boxmoor . . .	32	42·0
30·0	*Milepost 30* . . .	38	55·0
31·7	Tring	39½	
40·0	*Milepost 40* . . .	48	60·0
46·7	BLETCHLEY . . .	54½	61·8
50·0	*Milepost 50* . . .	58	63·4
59·9	ROADE	68	59·3
62·8	BLISWORTH . . .	71½	49·7
69·7	Weedon . . .	78	63·7
80·0	*Milepost 80* . . .	90	51·6
—		sig. check	—
82·6	RUGBY	94	39·0
97·1	NUNEATON . . .	110	54·8
102·4	Atherstone . . .	115	63·5
110·0	TAMWORTH . . .	121½	70·1
116·3	Lichfield . . .	128½	54·0
124·3	RUGELEY . . .	136½	60·0
127·2	Colwich	140	49·7
133·6	STAFFORD . . .	148½	45·2
146·0	*Milepost 146* . . .	163¼	50·3
150·1	Madeley	168	51·8
158·1	CREWE	178	48·0

L.N.W.R.: 2.23 p.m. PRESTON–CARLISLE

Load: 4 bogie coaches, 80 tons

Miles	Engine No.: Engine name:	1219 Lightning		275 Vulcan	
		Min.	Av. speed m.p.h.	Min.	Av. speed m.p.h.
0·0	PRESTON . .	0	—	0	—
21·0	LANCASTER . .	23	54·8	21	60·0
27·3	CARNFORTH . .	29	63·0	26½	68·8
34·6	Milnthorpe . .	35½	67·4	33	67·4
40·1	Oxenholme . .	42½	47·2	39	55·0
47·2	Grayrigg . .	52	44·8	48	47·3
53·2	Tebay . .	58	60·0	53½	65·5
60·7	Shap* . .	69½	39·0	63½	45·0
72·2	PENRITH . .	80	65·7	73	72·0
79·3	Calthwaite . .	88	53·3	80	61·0
85·2	Wreay . .	93½	64·3	85	70·8
90·1	CARLISLE . .	98½	—	90	—

* Shap station.

No passing times were taken at Shap Summit on either run, but with *Lightning* the minimum speed was 32 m.p.h.; this would indicate a time of about 2¾ minutes from Summit to Shap station, and suggests a time at Summit of about 66¾ minutes from Preston. The climb from Carnforth, 31·4 miles in all, thus took approximately 38 minutes, an average speed of almost 50 m.p.h. On the companion run, *Vulcan* took this same climb in less than 35 minutes – a remarkable uphill average, for that period, of 54 m.p.h. There is always a tendency to dismiss these runs, and no less those of 1895, owing to the lightness of the loads hauled; but if one compares the 1888 'racer' with the 'Caledonian' of today the difference is remarkably small:

	Load tons tare	Engine tons	Tender tons	Load behind engine tons	Load total: engine weight
1888 'Racer' . .	80	33	27	107	3·24
'Caledonian' . .	264	105¼	56½	320½	3·05

In fact, in relation to its own weight, the 'Precedent' of 1888 had the heavier load! On the same basis of reckoning, the 'Lady of the Lake' class engines were hauling nearly four times their own weight, but the fastest run from Euston to Crewe, at an average speed of 57 m.p.h. over an easy road, hardly compares with the brilliant 54 m.p.h. of *Vulcan* from Carnforth to Shap Summit. The awakening of the North Western had indeed been to some purpose.

The work of the North Eastern 'Tennant' 2-4-0s may be taken next, as there is some similarity in their proportions to those of the 'Precedents'. Unkind things were said about the North Eastern in the preliminary stages of the race, of which this comment in a leading article in *Engineering* is typical. In relation to the East Coast prospects that journal wrote: 'Unfortunately, for the Great Northern and North British Companies, they have a somewhat laggard partner in the North Eastern, and have to do a great deal to make up for its comparatively leisurely running. . . .' As things turned out, as I briefly mentioned in the preceding chapter, the performance over the North Eastern was one of the surprises of the 1888 race. As with *Waverley*'s star performance it is unfortunate that no details are available of the occasion on which the run of 80·6 miles from York to Newcastle was made in 78 minutes, but there were several observers on board on the last day of the race, when No. 1475 ran through in

83¾ minutes, inclusive of a dead stand for signals at Ferryhill lasting
1¾ minutes. From various sources I have built up the following
skeleton log of the trip:

N.E.R.: 1.50 p.m. YORK–NEWCASTLE
Load: 7 six-wheelers, 105 tons
Engine: 'Tennant' type 2-4-0 No. 1475

Miles		Min.	Av. speed m.p.h.
0·0	YORK	0	—
11·2	Alne	13½	49·8
22·2	Thirsk	24½	60·0
30·0	Northallerton . . .	32	62·4
44·1	DARLINGTON . .	44¾	66·4
—		sig. stop	—
57·0	Ferryhill	59½	52·5
66·1	Durham	69	57·5
71·9	Chester-le-Street . .	75½	53·5
77·6	Low Fell	80	76·0
80·0	Gateshead . . .	82½	57·6
80·6	NEWCASTLE* . . .	83¾	—

* Via High Level Bridge. Net time about 80 min.

This was a grand run. As usual with 'Tennants', the start was a
little on the leisurely side, and her time of 22¾ minutes for the first
21 miles out of York was slower than *Vulcan*'s first 21 miles out of
Preston; but after this stop outside Ferryhill she must have been taken
along in terrific style to average 60 m.p.h. from Ferryhill station to
Gateshead. She would not have been doing more than 20 or 25
m.p.h. at the station in getting away from the signal stop, and there
was the slack over the Durham viaduct to be reckoned with, too.
Some really fast running was made down the bank from Chester-le-
Street, and Foxwell reports that four consecutive miles there were
run at 75·7, 76·2, 76·5 and 76·5 m.p.h. In all probability the
'Tennants' were making some of the fastest daily speeds in the whole
race. The intermediate times would have to be closely similar to
those of the log on this page, to permit of the overall times of 80
minutes made on August 25th, 81 minutes on the 29th, and 82 on the
30th. On the Northern Division there is a good deal of conflicting
evidence on the locomotive performance. It was, for example,
claimed that a Worsdell Class 'F' compound 4-4-0 had run the
124·4 miles from Newcastle to Edinburgh in 125 minutes, but the
merit of this run was somewhat reduced by a later revelation that the
train had been double-headed. Again, the times for the final run on
August 31st vary from 126 to 130 minutes. In view of this there is not
a great deal to be said.

No such doubts exist where the Great Northern Railway is concerned, for Patrick Stirling himself contributed to *The Engineer* a full summary of the running throughout the month of August. From this document I have prepared the tables on pages 54 and 55. Between Kings Cross and Grantham perhaps the most extraordinary feature of the working was the number of different engines employed; bogie eight-footer, or 7 ft 6 in 2-2-2 – it did not seem to matter which was put on, for each did the job with magnificent regularity. The fastest run of the whole month was made on August 25th with a 7 ft 6 in engine, No. 233, in 105 minutes, to Grantham; no detailed record is available, but the Rev. W. J. Scott was a passenger on the last day of all, and from his notes the following log has been prepared:

G.N.R.: 10 a.m. KINGS CROSS–GRANTHAM
Load: 7 six-wheelers, 105 tons
Engine: Stirling 8 ft 4-2-2 No. 98

Miles		Min. Sec.	Av. speed m.p.h.
0·0	KINGS CROSS . .	0 00	—
2·6	Finsbury Park . .	5 15	29·7
12·7	Potters Bar . . .	17 25	49·9
17·7	Hatfield . . .	22 10	63·1
31·9	HITCHIN . . .	35 25	64·3
58·9	Huntingdon . .	60 05	65·7
76·4	PETERBOROUGH . .	77 27	60·7
88·6	Essendine . .	91 10	53·4
100·1	*Stoke Box* . . .	104 42	51·1
105·5	GRANTHAM . .	110 02	—

There was some splendid work on this run, such as the average speed of almost 50 m.p.h. from Finsbury Park to Potters Bar; but at the same time, such a time as 24 minutes 40 seconds from Hitchin to Huntingdon hardly suggests racing. On the long climb to Stoke speed was sustained above 50 m.p.h. to as high up the ascent as Corby, but then the pace fell off somewhat, and the minimum at Stoke Box was a little under 45 m.p.h. The continuation run to York behind another 8-footer, No. 95, was hindered by checks, and is not tabulated in any detail:

GREAT NORTHERN RAILWAY

RUNNING OF 10 a.m. SCOTCH EXPRESS: AUGUST 1888

I. Kings Cross and Grantham

Date	Engine No.	Load Coaches/Tons	Time Kings X to Grantham min.	Net time min.	Net av. speed m.p.h.
1st	671	8/120	119	119	53·2
2nd	233*	9/135	118	118	53·6
3rd	776	9/135	116	116	54·5
4th	233*	9/135	118	118	53·6
6th	98	8/120	120‡	113	56·0
7th	69	9/135	116	116	54·5
8th	48	8/120	117	117	54·1
9th	776	9/135	117	117	54·1
10th	234*	10/150	117	117	54·1
11th	776	8/120	115	115	55·0
13th	237*	8/120	115	115	55·0
14th	7	8/120	115	115	55·0
15th	98	8/120	115†	113	56·0
16th	22	9/135	111	111	57·0
17th	22	8/120	115†	113	56·0
18th	7	8/120	116	116	54·5
20th	233*	7/105	110	110	57·5
21st	237*	7/105	109	109	58·1
22nd	98	7/105	113	113	56·0
23rd	233*	7/105	108	108	58·6
24th	98	7/105	113	113	56·0
25th	233*	7/105	105	105	60·3
27th	22	7/105	111	111	57·0
28th	98	7/105	112	112	56·5
29th	22	7/105	109	109	58·1
30th	69	8/120	114	114	55·5
31st	98	7/105	110	110	57·5

* *7 ft 6 in 2-2-2 type. All other engines are 4-2-2.*
† *Delays of 7 min.*   ‡ *Delay of 2 min.*

Between Grantham and York there was more system in the working in that the eight-footers had the train for a week at a time. Only No. 775 was on for more than one week, and she ran the 'Scotsman' continuously for a fortnight. The regularity in running was even more pronounced than between Kings Cross and Grantham. Inclusive of all incidental checks, the time over the 82·7 miles between Grantham and York varied between the narrow limits of 88 and 92 minutes. The net times must be treated with something of reserve. The estimates of time lost are taken directly from Stirling's report, but on the last day of all, when the Rev. W. J. Scott was a passenger and

GREAT NORTHERN RAILWAY

RUNNING OF 10 a.m. SCOTCH EXPRESS: AUGUST 1888

2. Grantham and York

Date	Engine No.	Load Coaches/Tons	Time Grantham to York min.	Delays min.	Net time min.	Net av. speed m.p.h.
1st	3	8/120	91	—	91	54·4
2nd	3	9/135	91	—	91	54·4
3rd	3	9/135	91	—	91	54·4
4th	3	9/135	93	3	90	55·1
6th	777	8/120	92	2	90	55·1
7th	777	9/135	92	2	90	55·1
8th	777	8/120	92	—	92	53·8
9th	777	9/135	90	—	90	55·1
10th	777	9/135	90	—	90	55·1
11th	777	8/120	91	6	85	58·3
13th	775	8/120	90	2	88	56·3
14th	775	8/120	90	—	90	55·1
15th	775	8/120	89	—	89	55·7
16th	775	8/120	88	—	88	56·3
17th	775	8/120	89	—	89	55·7
18th	775	8/120	90	—	90	55·1
20th	775	7/105	90	—	90	55·1
21st	775	7/105	89	—	89	55·7
22nd	775	7/105	90	—	90	55·1
23rd	775	7/105	89	—	89	55·7
24th	775	7/105	88	—	88	56·3
25th	775	7/105	89	9	81	61·2
27th	95	7/105	92	3	89	55·7
28th	95	7/105	91	2	89	55·7
29th	95	7/105	90	4	86	57·7
30th	95	8/120	89	—	89	55·7
31st	95	7/105	89	4*	85	58·3

* Not mentioned in P. Stirling's summary.

witnessed the check at Balby Junction (Doncaster) and the swing bridge check at Selby, the official report shows no time lost by checks. Though there may be detail inaccuracies, Stirling's report gives an overall picture of deep significance; herein were to be found no 'all-out' dashes, none of what G. P. Neele once called 'slap-dash' running downhill, but a steady, solid reliability of which Stirling and his men might well be very proud. In the working of the Scotch express speeds of 70 m.p.h. were rarely exceeded, and even on the day that Grantham was reached at 11.45 a.m. it was by the excellence of the uphill work that the cut in time was achieved.

Finally I come to the Caledonian, and here we are concerned not merely with one locomotive class, but with one locomotive. In 1891 W. M. Acworth wrote:

'The most famous Caledonian engine – some people might say the most famous engine at present running in Great Britain – the wonderful No. 123, which, week in, week out for nearly two years has taken the Carlisle-Edinburgh express up the Beattock Bank with its gradient of 1 in 75 to 80 for ten miles, at a speed which most lines would term express along a level line . . .'

It is easy to imagine that Acworth had rather lost himself in his enthusiasm; and one might question whether, if the little 'Jumbo', *Vulcan*, had averaged 60 m.p.h. from Preston to Carlisle, there was anything very wonderful in a larger engine averaging 59 m.p.h. from Carlisle to Edinburgh with the same train. Fortunately, however, of that amazing run on August 9th the most complete details are available. Mr Dugald Drummond afterwards allowed to be published in *The Engineer* a diagram showing the speed over every mile, and from this document I have prepared the log on page 59. Before dealing with the record Caledonian trip of the whole race it will be as well to note the performance of No. 123 during the twenty-three days of the accelerated service. Commencing on Monday, August 6th, her results were:

C.R.: ENGINE 123: OVERALL TIMES, CARLISLE TO EDINBURGH 100·6 MILES: SCHEDULE 112 MINUTES

Week ending:	August 11th	August 18th	August 25th	August 31st
Monday . . .	104	105	109	109
Tuesday . . .	104	110	109	109
Wednesday . .	105	110	108	108
Thursday . .	102½	108	108	108
Friday . . .	110	110	109	109
Saturday . . .	108	107	108	*

* Train decelerated after August 31st.

The fastest run was made on the one day in the whole month that the L.N.W.R. handed over the train late at Carlisle. The engine had failed at Shap, and the arrival was 45 minutes late. No. 123 and her crew rose to the occasion nobly, and won back nearly 10 minutes. Apart from this, the train never reached Edinburgh later than 5.58 p.m. – 2 minutes early.

And now for the run of August 9th. It can have been little better than the runs on the three preceding days, but as so much detail is available for the fourth run of the accelerated period it is on this that we must concentrate. On studying the detailed log of the journey the first thing that immediately strikes one is the passing time at Beattock Summit – 53 minutes 4 seconds from Carlisle. *Fifty-three minutes four seconds* – in 1888! And then there is the average speed from Gretna Junction – 56·9 m.p.h. over the 41·1 miles to Summit. Well can one appreciate W. M. Acworth's eulogy. The average gradient between Gretna and Beattock Summit is 1 in 207, and here, indeed, No. 123 was making an average speed that would have contented many other railways on level track. It is true that on the very fastest North Western run *Vulcan* maintained an average speed of 54 m.p.h. between Carnforth and Shap Summit, where the average gradient is 1 in 185; but this was very much an isolated effort, whereas the Caledonian engine produced closely similar times on at least three other occasions, and could have done it regularly if required. Moreover, No. 123 is a single-wheeler, with no more than 16 tons of adhesion. If one compares adhesion weight, a modern 'Duchess' class 4-6-2 would need to be hauling 425 tons behind her tender to be working in similar conditions to those of No. 123 in the race of 1888.

No. 123 got away with tremendous rapidity from Carlisle, touching 72 m.p.h. at the Solway Firth; then the two stages of the climb to Castlemilk siding were cleared at minimum speeds of 54·5 and 57 m.p.h. Onwards through Lockerbie and Wamphray, where modern expresses often make very high speed, No. 123 did not greatly exceed 70 m.p.h. and then there came the extraordinary ascent of Beattock Bank. Passing Beattock station at exactly 60 m.p.h. the engine climbed the 10 miles of 1 in 75–80 in 13 minutes 51 seconds at an average of 43·3 m.p.h. This famous run of 1888 was brought very much to my mind recently when I enjoyed a remarkable trip on the footplate of the 'Duchess' class engine working the down 'Mid-day Scot', and we passed Beattock Summit in 3 minutes less than the racing time of No. 123. The two engines practically dead-heated to Gretna, but there the Pacific was doing 77 m.p.h., and with impetus from this and very fast running from Lockerbie to Wamphray, she had gained 4 minutes on No. 123 by the time Beattock was passed. Up the great bank, however, the honours were with the single-wheeler; for although passing Beattock station at 72 m.p.h. as against 60, the Pacific took 14 minutes 48 seconds up to Summit, and fell at one point to 31 m.p.h. The load was 390 tons behind the tender, or less in relation to the adhesion weight of the locomotive than the load conveyed by No. 123. I would not stress the comparison, except that it underlines the magnificent work of No. 123, and the fact that maximum speeds in 1888 did not much exceed 70 m.p.h.

On the run of August 9th, 1888, the descent of the Clyde valley was taken very gently. Speed just reached 70 m.p.h. at the crossing of the river by Elvanfoot, again near Abington, and in that usual place for a spurt, approaching the viaduct at Lamington. From the original speed chart it appears that there were several slight touches of the brake on this descent, though the engine was given her head on the dip past Thankerton, and in the approach to Strawfrank Junction. The original reports states that speed was reduced to 35 m.p.h. over the curve between Strawfrank and Dolphinton Junctions; but the actual minimum must have been considerably less as the average speed between mileposts 74 and 75 was only 36 m.p.h. A reduction to 20 m.p.h. fits in more appropriately with the passing times and the subsequent accelerations. The ascent to Cobbinshaw was taken in great style, with speed worked up to 64 m.p.h. after Carnwath, and the last three miles of steep ascent cleared at a minimum speed of $54\frac{1}{2}$ m.p.h. Then again, after a brief maximum of 74 m.p.h. below Harburn the steep descent into Edinburgh was taken at quite moderate speed, until the very end, when the final run in and stop were in the style of a London tube train! For some little time the Caledonian had been using the Westinghouse brake, and with the West Coast Joint Stock dual-fitted they were able to run with immense confidence. On this run, indeed, the average speed between mileposts 99 and 100 was 65 m.p.h., and the efficacy of the brake then in use goes most of the way towards explaining the rather startling 1 minute 5 seconds for the last 0·6 miles into Princes Street.

To those not used to it, the regular Caledonian practice of running hard into stations and then throwing out the anchors, as it were, could be hair-raising; but it was done on the fast runs between Perth and Forfar, and most thrilling of all, on the Oban line. So far as fast running generally was concerned in the 1888 race, the 'ceiling' then appeared to be 75 or 76 m.p.h. This was the common experience of enthusiasts who took detailed records of locomotive performance at that time, not only in the race, but on other occasions such as with the Manchester expresses of the Great Northern, with the faster of the Midland expresses, and also on the London & South Western Railway. Yet within twenty years from the race to Edinburgh a British express train was to top 100 m.p.h., and many other instances were to be noted by Charles Rous-Marten and others of speeds over 90 m.p.h. E. L. Ahrons puts the change down, not so much to improvements in locomotive design, as to the use of higher quality steel for both wheels and locomotive tyres, in which there

AUGUST 9th, 1888

CALEDONIAN RAILWAY: 4.8 p.m. CARLISLE–EDINBURGH

Load: 4 bogie coaches, 80 tons
Engine: Drummond 4-2-2 No. 123

Miles		Time min. sec.	Speed m.p.h.
0·0	CARLISLE . . .	0 00	—
4·1	Rockcliffe . . .	5 35	62
8·6	Gretna Junc. . . .	9 38	72
13·1	Kirkpatrick . . .	14 07	57
—	*Brackenhill* . . .	—	54½
16·7	Kirtlebridge . . .	17 46	65½
20·1	Ecclefechan . . .	21 04	57
—	*Castlemilk* . . .	—	57
25·8	LOCKERBIE . . .	26 46	64½
28·7	Nethercleugh . . .	29 22	70
31·7	Dinwoodie . . .	31 54	72
34·5	Wamphray . . .	34 26	65/72
39·7	BEATTOCK . . .	39 13	60
42·0	*Milepost 42* . . .	41 44	52
44·0	,, 44 . . .	44 20	43
46·0	,, 46 . . .	47 17	39
48·0	,, 48 . . .	50 23	38½
49·0	,, 49 . . .	51 58	37½
49·7	*Beattock Summit* . . .	53 04	36½
52·6	Elvanfoot . . .	56 05	70
55·3	Crawford . . .	56 42	64
57·8	Abington . . .	59 52	70/64
63·2	Lamington . . .	65 35	71½
66·9	SYMINGTON . . .	69 04	62
68·5	Thankerton . . .	70 29	73
70·0	*Leggatfoot* . . .	71 45	65
72·0	*Milepost 72* . . .	73 28	72
73·2	*Strawfrank Junc.* . . .	74 44	slack
74·8	Carnwath . . .	77 16	—
78·0	*Milepost 78* . . .	80 51	64
79·1	Auchengray . . .	81 55	61
80·0	*Milepost 80* . . .	82 51	58½
81·0	,, 81 . . .	83 54	56½
82·2	Cobbinshaw . . .	85 13	54½
85·3	Harburn . . .	88 16	74
89·3	*Midcalder Junc.* . . .	91 45	60
95·1	Currie Hill . . .	96 58	70
98·4	Slateford . . .	99 58	60
99·4	Merchiston . . .	100 55	64
100·0	*Milepost 100* . . .	101 28	66
100·6	PRINCES STREET . . .	102 33	—

was a notable improvement in the period 1890–5. That locomotive design was not directly involved was shown by the astonishing speeds run at a later date by the North Western 'Precedents', and the speeds of over 80 m.p.h. run by the Stirling 'singles'. This is not to 'write down' in any way the achievements of 'the Eighty-Eight', for the metamorphosis in Anglo-Scottish running wrought in the months of

July and August 1888 had been little short of phenomenal. The Great Northern had, to use a modern colloquialism, 'started something'.

While traffic officers on both sides heaved a sigh of relief when August came to an end, and the morning Scotch expresses on both routes were decelerated, there were others who took a longer view. *Engineering*, in a leading article, wrote:

'The 2nd of June, the 1st of July, the 1st of August, and the 6th of August 1888 will long be remembered in the railway world as red-letter days. They mark the stages in a struggle for the Scotch traffic which is only just beginning, and which will grow fiercer as the Forth Bridge nears completion. For years the London & North Western Company has been calmly sleeping like the enchanted princess in the fairy tale, secure in its comfortable surroundings which defended it against the intrusion of strangers. But now the period of the magic spell is ending, not with the kiss of the enamoured prince, but with a challenge from another princess, which purposes seizing some of the territory held so easily . . .'

How the 'sleeping princess' awoke, and not merely met the challenge, but seized the initiative to such an extent as to force her rival to fight it out on West Coast terms is a later story.

Before leaving the 'Eighty-Eight', however, I must refer briefly to the campaign waged by certain faint-hearted persons stressing the dangers of such high speeds, and the 'fearful strain' imposed upon the enginemen concerned. There have been 'faint-hearts' in every generation, and *The Engineer*, in a leading article in August 1888, disposed of such sentiments in characteristic style:

'The sympathy extended by a section of the public to the drivers and firemen is about as well placed as it would be were it expended on the jockeys who ride the Derby. To drive one of the flying expresses is the highest pinnacle of honour to which a driver can attain, and not the least enjoyable moment of a man's life is that when he draws up to the platform with three minutes' time to spare, and finds himself and his engine the centre of attraction for an admiring crowd.'

VI

Uneasy Truce

EARLY in September 1888 the *Pall Mall Gazette* published a summary of the race, quoting all the now familiar statistics; but in winding up it included an interesting comment on the development of Anglo-Scottish services generally, referring not only to the racing rivals, but also to the Midland:

'In August 1888 the three companies together had twenty-nine trains (counting both ways, but not including the short-lived "grouse-trains") between London and Scotland which were really "express", *i.e.*, which satisfied the exacting standard of "forty miles an hour, stops included". In the summer of 1885 there were sixteen. Besides these are six more real expresses between Lancashire and Scotland, and a dozen others between London and Scotland which miss the proud title only by stopping oftener. Not only is there this increase of fifty per cent in the number of Scotch expresses since 1883, but their average speed has risen too. The twenty-nine "express" journeys of this summer average a quarter of an hour less than the nineteen of 1885, and half an hour less than the sixteen of 1883. We are here not counting the new expresses from Bristol via Severn Tunnel, which we come to later. Such is five years progress, as persistent as the "depression of trade" during which it has occurred.

'A foreigner taken on to the midnight platform at Shap in the earlier nights of August would have been surprised to see *five* expresses roaring through within two hours, one laden with "Horses and Carriages only", another full of beds and lucky people whose rest the North Western will not allow to be broken by the entry of a single passenger between Euston and Perth, all five steaming without a stop the ninety miles from Preston to Carlisle, except one (from Liverpool and Manchester) which takes the 105 from Wigan in a breath. Down the adjacent Eden valley he might almost have heard the *three* Midland night expresses, sweeping two without a stop from Skipton to Carlisle, one in a longer burst of ninety-six miles from Keighley. Away on the East coast *five* Great Northern trains would be doing similar deeds, two from York to Newcastle (80 miles) without a stop, all five from Newcastle to Berwick (66 miles), and two of them without a pause from Newcastle to Edinburgh, 124 miles. Still more incredulous would our visitor have been when told that these were not *luxe* or "limited" trains with extra fancy fares, but that all alike conveyed the common third-class traveller.

'In dilating on the speeds of these new Scotch expresses we wish to give a wide berth to that odious habit of trying to set one favourite company on a peerless pinnacle of its own by means of dishonest depreciation of its rivals. The three great lines that start from London for the North are too first-rate in every way for such vulgar and petty comparisons. Any other country would be proud to possess any one of them; all three are ours. Besides, for an honest comparison of rival trains many considerations have to be carefully combined. Speed is not everything, and even speed must be judged according to the toughness of the obstacles over which it triumphs. To begin with, the weight of what is dragged at this whirlwind pace. At extreme speeds such as we have chronicled every extra ton (much more every extra carriage) is an important factor in the result. Now the West Coast train throughout the race was unquestionably the lighter of the two; and the Midland was heavier again than the East Coast. But gradients are an equally vital element in the comparison. Here the East Coast have distinctly the easy route, while the West Coast have a decided advantage (especially South of Crewe) over the Midland, whose line is hilly from end to end.'

Earlier, the same newspaper had scented the prospect of a greater and more severe contest between the East and West Coast routes. It spoke of the Great Northern admission of third-class passengers to the 'Flying Scotsman' as 'a provoking incident', and of the 1888 affair as a series of 'trial heats' in which the combatants were nerving themselves for the *real* fight. But what was the fight to be about? Had not the East and West companies agreed upon a minimum journey time from London to Edinburgh? The *Pall Mall Gazette* put the case dramatically:

'The main cause confronts us when we see those three stupendous towers of steel which loom above the horizon of Edinburgh. When the Forth Bridge is finished the North Western and Caledonian will have to struggle hard if they wish to retain much of the traffic to Dundee or Aberdeen, and may possibly be robbed of some of that to Inverness.'

From the map on page 15 it will be seen that the completion of the Forth Bridge altered the whole balance of railway operating in eastern Scotland. Such a gigantic project could not have been under-taken by a single railway company; it was an Anglo-Scottish enter-prise, in which not only the three East Coast partners, but the Midland also had shares. While it must have been obvious that the East Coast would continue to take the lion's share of the through traffic from London, the days of Midland expansionist activities were not yet at an end, and Derby had visions of through expresses from both St Pancras and Bristol to the Highlands, building up a profit-able business from intermediate places such as Leicester, Nottingham,

Sheffield, Gloucester and Birmingham. To such a challenge it was thought that the East and West Coast companies would find it difficult to make a really adequate reply. So the Midland became an equal partner with each of the three East Coast companies in the Forth Bridge. Travelling by the new route the distance from Kings Cross to Perth became 440·9 miles, against 449·9 from Euston, and the distance from Kings Cross to Aberdeen 523·2 miles, against 539·7 from Euston. These reduced distances were in themselves a challenge.

Judging by the general flow of traffic in the early spring of 1890, just prior to the completion of the Forth Bridge, it seemed likely that Perth might become the principal Scottish focal point of East Coast and West Coast rivalries. The palatial new Station Hotel was opened ready for the summer traffic in that same year, but no actual move towards acceleration of the train services came until October, when the 10.30 a.m. express from Euston was altered to reach Perth at 8.27 p.m. instead of 8.45, and Dundee at 9.15 p.m. instead of 9.35. Certain interested parties were all ready to proclaim another 'race', but the East Coast had then scarcely settled into their stride. Seeing what had been done for Edinburgh by the contest of 1888 it was not surprising that the claims of Perth, Inverness and the northern Highlands were now being pressed. A race to Perth would be infinitely more exciting than that of 1888, as the two routes converged at Hilton Junction immediately to the south of the Moncrieff Tunnel. The West Coast evidently had their eyes on Dundee, too. Hitherto they had enjoyed an easy supremacy; but as with Perth and Aberdeen, the East Coast route was now shorter, by 19 miles in the case of Dundee – 451·9 miles against 471·0. The new routes to both Perth and Aberdeen certainly looked attractive on paper, but in practice they included a number of severe operational handicaps.

The North British routes from Edinburgh to both Perth and Dundee suffered from being built up piecemeal. Neither was planned as a through express route; they consisted of a series of 'bits and pieces' constructed to serve local needs in Fife, and in consequence there were numerous curves, difficult junctions, and severe gradients to be negotiated. The constituents of the Caledonian, although originating as a series of independent companies, were laid out by Joseph Locke as component parts of one great project, largely sponsored by the Grand Junction Railway, and designed to make up a crack main line. The East Coast main line south of Edinburgh was built with the same object in view, but the North British lines in Fife not only include all the inherent disadvantages of alignment and grading, but

possessed one or two local peculiarities of their own, such as the
reverse curve in the middle of Kinghorn Tunnel. So, in the 59¼ miles
from Edinburgh to Dundee there were imposed six severe speed
restrictions for junctions, in addition to the 40 m.p.h. limit laid down
over the length of the Forth Bridge, and lesser slacks imposed at
points like Ladybank Junction, Cupar, and Leuchars Junction.
One has only to glance at the accompanying gradient profile to
realize that most of the severe restrictions could not be sited in more
awkward places. Inverkeithing, Burntisland, and Thornton Junction
lie at the foot of steep inclines in both directions, while Ladybank,
Cupar, and Leuchars, coming one after the other, spoil what might
otherwise be a fast finish from Lochmuir summit into Dundee. The
actual gradients are really severe. A bank including 2 miles at 1 in
94 can be charged easily if an express train strikes it at 65 or 70
m.p.h.; but if, as at Inverkeithing, it comes immediately after a slack
to 25 m.p.h. it is a very different matter. Nowhere in the run from
Edinburgh to Dundee can one settle down to a spell of continuous
hard work. After blasting up one steep bank, and coasting down the
next decline, there must be a heavy brake application for the
inevitable junction at the foot before the cycle is repeated again.

The Perth road, which swings away to the north at Inverkeithing,
is rather more straightforward, but even more severe where gradients
are concerned. There is a continuous 8-mile climb from Inverkeithing to Cowdenbeath, and a very steep descent of 6 miles from
Glenfarg into Strathearn; between these two summit points there is
a high, sharply undulating road for some 15 miles, again much
handicapped by the intermediate curvature. When the Forth
Bridge route was first opened the timings of the principal expresses
were:

Kings Cross	.	.	. *dep.*	10.00 a.m.	8.00 p.m.
Edinburgh	.	.	. *dep.*	6.55 p.m.	5.30 a.m.
Dundee	.	.	. { *arr.*	8.25 p.m.	6.55 a.m.
			{ *dep.*	8.30 p.m.	7.00 a.m.
Aberdeen .	.	.	. *arr.*	10.20 p.m.	8.55 a.m.

Prior to the opening of the Forth Bridge the arrival times in Aberdeen by these two services had been 11.20 p.m. and 9.55 a.m.
respectively. To Perth, the summer night service of 1890 was:

Kings Cross .	.	*dep.*	7.45 p.m.	8.00 p.m.	—
St Pancras	.	*dep.*	—	—	7.50 p.m.
Edinburgh	.	*dep.*	4.35 a.m.	4.55 a.m.	5.23 a.m.
Perth .	.	*arr.*	5.50 a.m.	6.15 a.m.	6.45 a.m.

Above: Engine No. 123 'racing from Carlisle to Edinburgh in 1888'.

CALEDONIAN
POSTCARDS
COMMEMORAT-
ING THE RACE

Right: Engine No. 17, with driver Soutar, at the conclusion of the final run of 1895.
[*Courtesy: E. Prance*

Great Northern Railway Stirling 8-foot 4-2-2 No. 1003 on a down express near Hadley Wood.

K. Nunn

The East Coast record-breaker of 1895 leaving the Forth Bridge, hauled by N.B.R. 4-4-0 No. 293.

[From a painting by *Jack Hill*

The Marquis of Tweeddale,
Chairman, N.B.R.

The Hon. W. L. Jackson (afterwards
Lord Allerton), Chairman, G.N.R.

EAST COAST PERSONALITIES

Sir George S. Gibb,
General Manager, N.E.R.

Sir Henry Oakley,
General Manager, G.N.R.

[Courtesy: "The Railway Magazine"

The possibility of a competition for Aberdeen traffic was certainly not ruled out by the commentators of 1890, and here again the North British was handicapped by the physical character of its route. The joint line with the Caledonian extending to St Vigean's Junction, just beyond Arbroath, was certainly a straight and level course, well suited to fast running; but from St Vigean's Junction to Kinnaber, where the East and West Coast routes to Aberdeen converged, the North British line could scarcely be more difficult. The gradients are steep enough in themselves, as brief study of the gradient profile shows, but this line was then single-tracked throughout, and slacks had to be made for hand exchange of tablets at St Vigean's Junction, Letham Grange, Inverkeilor, Lunan Bay and Montrose, not to mention the final slack at Kinnaber Junction itself. With such hindrances, and those encountered on the run from Edinburgh to Dundee, it will be apparent that the advantage of 16 miles less journey by the East Coast route might be whittled down to a very little, by the disheartening succession of permanent speed restrictions to be observed north of Edinburgh. Between Arbroath and Montrose one could not expect the most expert of firemen to catch the tablets at much over 35 m.p.h.

While the North British Railway was feeling its way with the new services in Fife, and observers were for ever looking for signs of fresh railway rivalry, some big changes were taking place in the high command at Euston. Foremost among these was the retirement, in February 1891, of the Chairman, Sir Richard Moon. In him the North Western lost a great man; although he was an unrelenting autocrat, and one who had fixed, not to say bigoted, ideas on many aspects of railway management and operation, many of the officers who served under him testified to his inspiring, if sometimes terrifying leadership. When an officer was appointed Sir Richard interviewed him personally, and always with the same admonition: 'Remember, first, that you are a gentleman; remember, next, that you are a North Western officer, and whatever you promise you must perform – therefore, be careful what you promise, but having promised it, take care that you can perform it.' His reluctance to agree to drastic acceleration of train services most likely arose from his own doubts as to whether they could be satisfactorily maintained. Sir Richard Moon was succeeded by Lord Stalbridge.

Three years earlier another link with previous days had been severed by the death of Stephen Reay, who had been Secretary of the Company for twenty-two years. This cold, austere, unsympathetic

E

man had been the confidential friend of Sir Richard Moon throughout this period. In his time the Secretary wielded great power,
dealing with much of the general business that in later years fell to
the General Manager. The partnership between Moon and Reay
was indeed a formidable one, and Reay's authority and influence
were perhaps greater than they might otherwise have been, by reason
of the genial and contrasting personality of the General Manager,
George Findlay, who had held the office since 1880. Findlay was
above all a traffic man, and he exercised a general supervision over all
matters concerning the running of the trains with great success; but
although he was only just over sixty years of age he was not in good
health, and in the year 1892 he was often prevented by illness from
attending Board and other important meetings. In March 1893 he
died, a much loved and greatly respected railwayman. He was succeeded by Frederick Harrison, a man of great energy and strength of
character, who before long had gathered the entire reins of management into his own hands. Far more so than any of his predecessors
Harrison was very definitely the 'commander-in-chief', and other
companies were not long in feeling the effects of the enterprise and
drive he put into the whole direction of affairs at Euston.

Already there were signs of interest in the night Aberdeen service.
The Forth Bridge had not been open long before the East Coast
companies accelerated the 8 p.m. from Kings Cross to reach Aberdeen at 8.15 a.m. Following this the West Coast, which had been
taking 12 hours 50 minutes for the run of the 8 p.m. from Euston,
accelerated that train to an arrival at 8.5 a.m. In actual practice,
the superiority of the West Coast was far better than the timetable
showed, for their train kept good time, whereas North British trains
were subjected to such chaotic delays in the old Waverley station at
Edinburgh that the actual running was in reality very poor. In 1891
the East Coast made their arrival 7.45 a.m., and in 1893 a further
cut of ten minutes was made. The East Coast train had, on paper,
connected with the Deeside express of the Great North of Scotland,
which left Aberdeen for Ballater at 7.50 a.m. In June 1893, however,
the West Coast companies persuaded the Great North to alter their
departure to 8 a.m., and by further accelerating the 8 p.m. from
Euston to an arrival at 7.50 a.m. in Aberdeen they were able to
make connection. The East Coast companies were running from
Kings Cross to Aberdeen in 11 hours 35 minutes that summer, a
gain of 15 minutes over the West Coast, roughly equal to the difference in mileage. But the East Coast train was still suffering from
unpunctuality, and in his reminiscences G. P. Neele writes:

'The change entailed very close running with the East Coast train, and the signalman at Kinnaber Junction had daily anxiety as to the priority of passage of the two rival trains. Telegrams at Euston of the morning arrivals at Aberdeen were among the first tidings of the day's work.'

Those with an eye for such activities saw in this working the germs of another race; but relations between the rival groups were outwardly most friendly, and the preservation of 15 minutes difference between the booked running times from London was in the spirit of the truce agreed upon in August 1888.

In Scotland, however, there was a new factor in the situation. With Edinburgh as the goal of the 1888 race the North British Railway had been forced to play no more than a passive part; the East Coast train had run over their metals north of Berwick, but the motive power had been provided by the North Eastern Railway. Furthermore, the race each day ended in uncertainty for the competitors, as they came into different stations in Edinburgh and the one could not be certain of the other's time of arrival. In the early 'nineties things were very different. The convergence of the two routes at Kinnaber Junction, the close running between the rival trains, the hereditary enmity between the North British and Caledonian companies served to fan the fires. All North British men had been brought up to regard the Caledonian as the arch-enemy, just as the men of the Glasgow & South Western did farther south; no subterfuge could be too tricky, no action too mean for a Caley man! And when the North British were running late and a Caley signalman at Kinnaber held them up for the West Coast express to pass, the situation began to get strained, however polite contemporary relations might be between Kings Cross and Euston.

The situation in the North was not improved by a series of incidents arising from a West Coast acceleration of the 'Day Scotch Express' hitherto booked into Aberdeen at 10.55 p.m. From January 1st, 1893, this train was re-timed to arrive in Aberdeen at 10.25 p.m., or just 5 minutes after the corresponding East Coast train, which it was booked to follow closely from Kinnaber Junction. Now, any practical railwayman would have realized at once that the day-to-day variations of train running would result on occasions in both trains being offered to Kinnaber Junction at once, or equally the Caledonian train before the North British. The 'daily anxiety' of the signalman, referred to by G. P. Neele, was certainly foreseen by the Caledonian timetable people, and they devised a distinctly original way of solving his problems. In the working timetable for January 1893 they showed a pass-to-pass time of 6 minutes for the 1·2 miles between Dubton and Kinnaber. At first sight this might appear innocent enough, providing some 4 minutes recovery time, after the style of so many modern schedules today; but the method of working, in actual fact, was most ingenious. Whether the Euston train was approaching or not, Dubton offered the train to Kinnaber at the time it was booked to pass by the timetable, whereas the North British train was not offered until it was actually passing Montrose.

This delightfully simple ruse succeeded in blocking the East Coast train three nights out of four. It was some little time before the North British realized what was happening; the circumstances were related in a memorandum prepared by the General Manager's office in Edinburgh, and sent to other East Coast companies:

'This method of timing enabled the Caledonian Company's signalman at Kinnaber Junction to accept the Caledonian train some time before it actually reached Dubton, even although the North British train was then close to Kinnaber Junction, but this was not observed by the North British officials until February 16th, 1893, when, on the North British train approaching Kinnaber Junction *three* minutes late, which Junction it would have passed, if its journey had not been interrupted, *four* minutes before the Caledonian train was due there; the North British train was stopped by signal while the Caledonian was allowed to come forward to the Junction and proceed in front, whereby a further delay of *thirteen* minutes was caused to the North British train before it reached Aberdeen. On the following day the North British train approached Kinnaber Junction on time, or *seven* minutes before the Caledonian train was due to pass, but it was again stopped by signal while the Caledonian was allowed to come forward to the Junction and again precede the North British train, which consequently lost *sixteen* minutes on the remainder of its journey to Aberdeen.'

This was obstruction in the style of railway pioneer days, and amply confirmed the popular North British view that the Caledonian were a gang of buccaneers, and no better! No time was wasted in remonstrance at this stage. The departures from Edinburgh of the Aberdeen and Perth sections of the London train were transposed, sending the former away at 6.40 p.m. instead of 6.55, and the Perth section at 6.50 instead of 6.40 p.m. That settled the troubles at Kinnaber Junction, for a time at any rate; Perth, six months later, was the scene of another Caledonian attempt to 'pull a fast one' over the North British. Prior to June 1st of that year the 8 p.m. expresses from London had reached Perth at 5.55 a.m. by West Coast and 5.45 a.m. by East Coast. The Caledonian train went forward at 6 a.m., providing a useful connection for East Coast passengers to

Forfar, Brechin, and so on. During May the North British authorities at Perth learned, by unofficial means, that the West Coast train was to be accelerated, and would leave Perth at 5.45 a.m., thus severing the important connection with the North British train arriving at the same time. Thus forewarned, the North British quickly made arrangements to bring their train into Perth at 5.40 a.m. as from June 1st. The Caledonian left their announcement of the change to the very last minute, to embarrass their rivals; but when at last notification did come the North British was able to acknowledge by advising the Caledonian of their own acceleration. Although not a major item, the incident is enough to show how strongly the tide of suspicion, distrust and rivalry was flowing between the Caledonian and North British railways.

In the meantime there are some important locomotive developments to be reported. The Caledonian presented perhaps the least change of all since 1888. The Drummond 4-4-0s still reigned supreme, and although they had been reinforced by the building of the Lambie variation of the design, these latter engines had closely similar dimensions and running characteristics; in them, however, the picturesque safety valve on the dome disappeared, never to appear again on the Caledonian. In the Lambie engines the boiler pressure was increased from 150 to 160 lb per sq in. On the North Western Webb's compound locomotive development was still in full swing, and following his 'Experiment' and 'Dreadnought' classes, he had produced, in 1889, a three-cylinder compound that could run really fast – the famous *Teutonic*. This engine and her nine 'sisters', built in 1889–90, had 7 ft driving wheels, and while uncoupled, like the 'Experiments' and 'Dreadnoughts', they had a much better design of valves and steam ports that permitted, at last in the Webb compounds, a free flow of steam. They had larger boilers too, and were generally more powerful locomotives than their predecessors. While the 'Experiments' had to be flogged to reach as much as 60 m.p.h., and while the 'Dreadnoughts' rarely touched 70, the 'Teutonics' needed little encouragement to work into the '80s'. It is true that they were no faster than those wonderful little engines the 'Precedents', but with their larger boilers and greater cylinder capacity they could take heavier loads. Their weakness lay in the uncertainty of their starting, due to the driving wheels being uncoupled and giving rise sometimes to a lack of synchronization between the high-pressure and low-pressure cylinders. In the 'Teutonics', however, Webb came nearer to complete success than with any other of his compound designs; but he built no more than ten of them, and then went on to the eight-wheeled 'Greater Britain' class, which were not anything like so successful.

No new express locomotive design had been prepared on the Great Northern since 1888, but on the North Eastern there had been some notable developments. In 1890 Wilson Worsdell had succeeded his brother as head of the Locomotive Department, and in the following year the retirement of Henry Tennant from the position of General Manager was followed by the appointment of George Stegmann Gibb. It was not long before every department on the railway had begun to feel the effects of Gibb's dynamic, invigorating leadership, and Wilson Worsdell soon found himself in a very fortunate position. As he was a first-rate mechanical engineer, with two brilliant assistants in Walter M. Smith and Vincent Raven, and the whole-hearted backing of one of the most energetic and progressive of general managers, the way was clear for big things. Moreover, Worsdell's own sport-loving nature relished the prospect of another contest with the West Coast: the whole change in the North Eastern attitude towards speed shown in the later stages of the race to Edinburgh owed much to his own influence, and he had not been long in the chair at Gateshead before the drawing office was busy on some striking new projects. While Worsdell himself laid down the broad outlines of the development, its ultimate success was due in no small measure to the genius for detail displayed by Walter Smith.

It was characteristic of the new order of things at Gateshead that the first new passenger locomotive to be turned out should be the largest and heaviest express engine yet to be seen in Great Britain. This was the celebrated 1620, the first of the 'M' class 4-4-0s, completed in 1892. At the time, however, considerable surprise and not a little criticism was aroused in the engineering world by the fact that she was not a compound. To many men it seemed a retrograde step, particularly in view of the success that had apparently attended the working of T. W. Worsdell's two-cylinder 'F' class 4-4-0 locomotives. This line of comment gathered strength in 1893 when the fourth engine of this new series was built as a two-cylinder compound on the Worsdell-von Borries system. As originally built, the simples had the valve chests outside the frames; although this was rather an exposed position, the arrangement was fairly common on the Continent of Europe at the time, if not in this country. Apart from details of construction, however, the basic dimensions of the 'M' class 4-4-0s were certainly impressive, with cylinders 19 in by 26 in stroke, a total heating surface of 1,341 sq ft, a grate area of 19½ sq ft, and a boiler pressure of 180 lb per sq in. With their massive appearance and great canopied cab they earned the nickname of the 'rail-crushers'.

At that time, too, Smith was experimenting with segmental ring piston valves. They were tried first on one of the 'M' class engines, No. 1639, built in 1894; but something approaching finality in piston-valve design on the North Eastern was reached some months later, and applied to the 'J' class, 7 ft 7 in 4-2-2 singles of T. W. Worsdell's design, when these engines were converted from compound to simple working in the early months of 1895. The free-running of these rebuilt engines and their economy in fuel consumption immediately made them great favourites with the men, and despite the great size and undoubted success of the 'M' class, the 'singles' seem to have been regarded as the pride of the line. In view of subsequent events it is interesting to compare their basic dimensions with those of the Stirling eight-footers:

EAST COAST 4-2-2 LOCOMOTIVES: 1895

Railway: Class:	G.N.R. '771'	N.E.R. 'J'
Driving wheels dia. .	8 ft 0 in	7 ft 7 in
Cylinders dia. (in) .	18	19
stroke (in) .	28	24
Boiler pressure (lb/sq in) .	160	175
Boiler: heating surface		
tubes (sq ft) .	936	1,016
firebox (sq ft)	109	123
total (sq ft) .	1,045	1,139
Grate area (sq ft) .	17·75	20·7
Adhesion weight (tons) .	17·0	19·0
Total weight of engine (tons) .	45·1	47·0
Nominal tractive effort at 85% B.P.U.	12,820	14,130

In the above comparison I have chosen the 1884 batch of Stirling eight-footers rather than the final batch of 1894–5, which had $19\frac{1}{2}$ in cylinders and an adhesion weight of $19\frac{1}{2}$ tons. The reason for ignoring this final development of the eight-footers will be apparent later.

Finally among these locomotive comparisons there was the North British Railway. By the year 1894 there were four classes of 4-4-0 express passenger engines on this line, the earliest being of Drummond design, and the rest from Matthew Holmes.

On paper the '633' class brought the North British level with the Caledonian, so far as the nominal tractive effort of the rival 4-4-0s was concerned, since the basic dimensions were in all cases identical to those of the Drummond 4-4-0s of the '66' class. In 1894, however,

NORTH BRITISH 4-4-0 LOCOMOTIVES

Year First built: Class:	1876 '476'	1884 '574'	1886 '592'	1891 '633'
Cylinders dia. (in) . .	18	17	18	18
stroke (in) . .	26	26	26	26
Coupled wheels dia. . .	6 ft 6 in	6 ft 6 in	7 ft 0 in	6 ft 6 in
Boiler pressure (lb/sq in) .	140	140	140	150
Total heating surface (sq ft) .	1,099·3	1,059	1,136	1,266
Grate area (sq ft) . . .	21	17½	21	21

when John Lambie produced his variation, the boiler pressure was increased to 160 lb per sq in, and this put the Caledonian ahead once more; but there was a good deal more to it than mere dimensions or design details of locomotives.

As with the traffic working, so in the functioning of the motive power department it was the North British Railway and its men that provided the unknown factor in the gathering storm. True, there was plenty of incentive. 'Beat the Caledonian' was the watchword at Waverley and Dundee, as much as it was at St Enoch, Ardrossan, Currock Road, and other strongholds of the 'Sou'West'; but mere enmity and combative ardour is no substitute for hard experience. The question asked by many onlookers was: how would the North British fare over a newly consolidated and very tortuous main-line against such practised runners as the Caledonian over a route practically free from any restrictions? More than this, traffic delays on the North British were enough to discourage any keen engine-man. Of the locomotives of Matthew Holmes all that could be said so far was that they were built on the solid basis of the Drummond design of 1876; that they were good-looking, and good steamers. The '633' class, specifically built for the new trains running to Aberdeen over the Forth Bridge, had all the grace of the original design, with a skilful and individual touch in the use of the Stirling type of cut-away cab.

The year 1894 drew to a close. All was still calm and outwardly peaceful, though the enmity between the North British and Caledonian was at times ill-concealed, and the hidden fires were fanned by letters from rival partisans published in various organs of the Scottish press. The night expresses leaving Kings Cross and Euston at 8 p.m. were still due at Aberdeen at 7.35 and 7.50 a.m. respectively. As the period of the summer tourist traffic drew nearer, however, the West Coast felt that their 7.50 a.m. arrival did not give sufficient margin for connection with the Deeside train leaving Aberdeen at 8.5 a.m. The North Western night trains did not show the same standards of punctuality that distinguished the business expresses from Euston to Birmingham, Manchester and Liverpool, and so from June 1st, 1895, they cut 10 minutes off the overall time of the 8 p.m. from Euston, bringing it into Aberdeen only 5 minutes behind the East Coast and sowing the seeds of further trouble at Kinnaber. What happened during the month of June it is not possible to say, except that the West Coast action put the East Coast very much on the alert, and from July 1st the 8 p.m. was booked into Aberdeen at 7.20 a.m., the earliest yet. Up to this time there had been a reluctance on the part of Kings Cross and York to acceleration south of Edinburgh, in view of the agreement of 1888 with the West Coast not to book any time less than $8\frac{1}{2}$ hours between Kings Cross and Waverley.

Now, under the stress of another competition, it was argued that as there was no question of rivalry with the West Coast for Edinburgh traffic the agreement of 1888 was not binding, and in re-timing the 8 p.m. from Kings Cross to reach Aberdeen at 7.20 a.m., a time of 8 hours 13 minutes from London to Edinburgh was fixed upon. So during the first fortnight in July 1895 the West Coast accepted an inferiority of 20 minutes – on paper. In actual fact the disparity was much worse, as during that fortnight the running of the 8 p.m. from Euston was very bad. Twice only was the train on time at Aberdeen; the other arrivals were 8.0, 8.5, 7.55, 8.0, 8.7, 7.50, 7.45, 8.7, 8.6 and 8.15 a.m. – not a distinguished record. Full details of this period of the competition from the West Coast angle are given in the Appendix. The train was then stopping at Bletchley, Rugby, Crewe, Wigan, Carlisle, Stirling and Forfar; the load was never less than 'equal to 15' from Euston, and trains up to '17' were taken unassisted by Webb compounds of the 'Dreadnought' and 'Teutonic' classes. Although traffic and other incidental delays caused late arrivals at Carlisle up to a maximum of 28 minutes, in no case was there any time whatever to be booked against the locomotives.

The time had now come for the West Coast companies really to assert themselves, and without giving their opponents a day's warning they struck. On Monday, July 15th, came advertisements in all the newspapers, and by the hugest blue posters on the portals of Euston, that on the very next morning the 8 p.m. express would reach Aberdeen at 7 a.m. This time there was to be no mistake about it; every effort was made to secure punctual running, and on the morning of July 16th the train actually arrived in Aberdeen at 6.47 a.m.

VII

1895 - Building Up

THE hunt was now on in earnest. News of the West Coast acceleration announced on July 15th was not long in reaching Kings Cross, and early that morning Sir Henry Oakley wired Conacher, the General Manager of the North British:

'See North Western notice of further acceleration of night trains. What can you do in response? Gibb is in London and will be here this morning. Wire reply.

OAKLEY.'

As yet attention was not focused, as in 1888, upon one particular train. The East Coast companies continued to regard the night service to Scotland as a whole. In railway communication the telephone was not yet in use, and in all cases where a letter was not quick enough a wire had to be sent. The response of the East Coast to every move of their rivals was of the swiftest. Again, as in 1888, the West Coast had seized the initiative, but the East Coast high command, at Kings Cross, York, and Waverley alike, needed no prompting into making a full-blooded reply. Later that same morning Sir Henry wired again:

'Scotch train service. Have seen Gibb, and arranged for Superintendents to meet tonight at York. Please instruct Deuchars to attend.

OAKLEY.'

The first reply from the North British was non-commital. Sir Henry Oakley's second telegram looked suspiciously like a command, and at 2.45 p.m. in the afternoon Conacher sent his first wire back:

'Your telegram. Deuchars is to go to York by train leaving here 2.50 p.m. As he requires to be back here tomorrow morning, I trust you have made arrangements for meeting of Superintendents taking place tonight.

CONACHER.'

And so the three men – Cockshott of the Great Northern, Welburn of the North Eastern, and Deuchars of the North British – foregathered at York, and behind them loomed the great personality of Sir Henry Oakley, who had become the greatest driving force in the East Coast alliance. At 4.55 p.m. Conacher wired again:

'Your three telegrams of today. If you can take fifteen minutes less by the 8.0 p.m. to Edinburgh we can save another fifteen here and on the way to Aberdeen, arriving 6.50. The 10.0 p.m. train cannot be accelerated to get to Aberdeen before 10.40 without running a new train throughout from Edinburgh, and I do not think the traffic will justify our increasing the expense. If, however, as a matter of policy it is necessary to show West Coast that persistence in their present moves will not secure the advantage in time to them I shall be willing to join in accelerating this train also for present season if you and Gibb will secure us against absolute loss. In that case we should reach Aberdeen at 9.25. Deuchars has gone to York with instructions to this effect.

CONACHER.'

That very night, while the East Coast Superintendents were still in conclave at York, the 8 p.m. Tourist express from Euston set out for the first time to run the 540 miles to Aberdeen in 11 hours. Next morning, at Kings Cross, York, and Waverley the baldest details of that inaugural journey may well have been read in letters of fire! No ancient single-wheelers took the train out of Euston this time. Two Rugby 'Precedents', both in the pink of condition, were allocated specially to the job, Nos. 749 *Mercury* and 394 *Eamont*; with four exceptions these two engines had the Tourist express to themselves for the first month. Each engine had its regular crew, and no other:

> *Mercury:* Driver E. Holt and Fireman A. T. Hewins
> *Eamont:* Driver J. Daynes and Fireman J. Stinson

The timing to Crewe was at first the same as that of the racing 10 a.m. of 1888, namely 3 hours; but this was cut down, by stages, to 2 hours 53 minutes. I must not, however, anticipate the tale of that astonishing 'first night'. *Mercury*, hauling a load of about 130 tons, had a placid trip to Crewe and arrived dead on time; but then engines were changed, and in place there backed on another 'Precedent', none other than No. 790 *Hardwicke*, with Driver Ben Robinson and Fireman W. Wolstencroft, of Crewe shed. There were no scheduled stops for refreshments with this train; the 141·1 miles from Crewe to Carlisle were taken non-stop, and on that very first night Robinson got through in 163 minutes, arriving in Carlisle 12 minutes early.

Next came the event which, if it had become widely known, would have shaken the East Coast companies to their very foundations. In the dim light of Citadel station, *Hardwicke* uncoupled and drew quickly clear, while one of Drummond's 'flyers', 4-4-0 No. 90, came backing down; and at 1.54 a.m., *eleven minutes before time*, she was given the right-away. When the train eventually sailed into Aberdeen at 6.47 a.m., 13 minutes early, the East Coast were not to know that all the time had not been gained since the last passenger stop, at Forfar. But the Caledonian had 'got away with it' in the 'wee sma' hours', and although their rivals came to have growingly stronger suspicions, several weeks were to pass before their convictions became certainties. That first night showed the shape of things to come in more ways than one; it showed how considerable a factor was the personality and temperament of individual drivers. *Hardwicke*'s crew, for example, was a resolute, fearless, stop-at-nothing pair; Robinson – 'Big Ben', as he was known – was a tall, bearded man, contrasting absolutely with his dapper, slight young fireman. But *Hardwicke* did not have the sheltered, carefully nurtured existence of most other nineteenth-century locomotives. Like many North Western express engines on top link duty, she was double-manned, and for the first ten days of the accelerated schedule she made the Crewe – Carlisle run every night manned alternately by Robinson and Wolstencroft one night, and Driver P. Howman and Fireman J. Harrison the next.

On the Caledonian, the drivers taking the train forward from Carlisle were Kingmoor men, and except for two days – July 17th and 21st – there were only two men concerned from July 15th to the third week in August, Archibald Crooks with engine No. 90, and Thomas Robinson with engine No. 78. One could hardly imagine a greater contrast than between these two men. They were next-door neighbours and lived in Caledonian Cottages, a row of railway workmen's dwellings in the Carlisle suburb of Etterby, near to the Kingmoor sheds. Both were first-class enginemen, but while 'Baldie' Crooks was reserved and cautious, Tom Robinson was a veritable aristocrat of the footplate. Crooks, careful and economical runner that he was, hardly rose to a supreme occasion, whereas Robinson revelled in it. Always ready to share the thrills and fascination of his craft with those who were interested, Robinson became well known to the railway enthusiasts of the day. The Rev. W. J. Scott was an occasional visitor at his home, so was Mr A. C. W. Lowe. But so far as locomotives were concerned, Tom Robinson scarcely acknowledged the existence of any other than those of the Caledonian. When engines were changed at Carlisle one might have imagined there would be waves, greetings and an occasional jest as the North

Western men came off; but not with Tom Robinson! The Crewe engines were just beneath his notice. Apart from this highly professional attitude, he was a great-hearted soul, much loved by his family and a wide circle of friends. As to his running with the Drummond engine No. 78, well, more of that in a moment.

At the northern end of the Caledonian line John Soutar, the driver from Perth to Aberdeen, was one of a link of six, each of whom had the 'flyer' at different times. The other five had Drummond engines of the same type as those driven by Baldie Crooks and Tom Robinson; but John Soutar had one of the very latest Caledonian 4-4-0s, No. 17 of the Lambie series. These were similar in general design and capacity to the Drummonds, but were readily distinguishable in having safety valves over the firebox instead of on the dome. John Soutar was to earn special fame before the following month was out. He was a stocky, immaculate little man, boots polished brightly, and his white beard as spotless at the end of a run as when starting. He was one of that race of enginemen who took such pride in their machines as to give the cleaners a shilling from their own pockets to shine the buffers! Such, then, were some of the men who were entrusted with the running of this extraordinary West Coast train.

It came as no surprise to the East Coast authorities to learn that their rival was 13 minutes early on the first day; but then, look what happened on the night of July 16th–17th: Driver Howman, with *Hardwicke*, came into Carlisle just a quarter of an hour early; in 5 minutes engines were changed, and Tom Robinson was away, on No. 78. He reached Perth *twenty-eight minutes early*, having run the 150 miles from Carlisle in 167 minutes inclusive of a stop at Stirling. One might have thought that by this time the West Coast men would feel that honour was satisfied, and that on the final stage it would be enough to keep the point-to-point time schedule. Not a bit of it! Robinson and No. 78 were relieved by William Kerr and No. 70, and over the remaining 90 miles from Perth to Aberdeen, booked in 110 minutes, the train took no more than 98 minutes inclusive of a stop at Forfar, and so came into Aberdeen at 6.21 a.m. – 39 minutes early. There was consternation and bewilderment in East Coast circles. Euston and Buchanan Street had published no intermediate times, and they had succeeded in fogging their rivals completely. The official arrival time remained as 7 a.m. Then from Monday night, July 22nd, the East Coast advertised their train as due in Aberdeen at 6.45 a.m., instead of the previous 7.20; it was a modest reply, by way of a start, and the West Coast were more than ready for it. A week of superb running, in which the arrivals at Aberdeen were 13, 39, 5, 9, 10 and 21 minutes early, had shown what could be done, and so without any previous advertisement they applied the Cockshott technique. On the first day the East Coast were due in Aberdeen at 6.45 a.m., the West were there at 6.39. Whatever pretences might still be kept up in England, there were no doubts in Scotland. It was another race, and with the two routes converging at Kinnaber Junction, a race of the most exciting kind. Aberdeen was agog. The running of the North British and Caledonian trains was a topic of daily conversation in all walks of life, and partisan feelings began to run high.

Actually, the working time of the West Coast train had been made 6.35 a.m. from July 22nd, but this was not revealed to the public, who were still told 7 a.m. The East Coast soon got wind of this, and there was then exchanged one of the most dramatic series of telegrams in the history of the East and West Coast companies. The Caledonian arrival on July 23rd might have been a piece of *joie de vivre* on the part of the driver, but on the morning of July 24th, when Sir Henry Oakley was advised that the Caledonian were in at 6.30 a.m., while still advertising 7 a.m., he wired Conacher. Things were getting serious. It seemed as if the West Coast people were set upon asserting their superiority at all costs. When he replied, however, later that day, the North British General Manager was evidently thinking of improvements to the night service as a whole rather than countering the West Coast activities on the 8 p.m. Tourist express. He wired Oakley:

'Your telegram. We could reach Aberdeen at 6.25. Should not like to attempt earlier arrival meanwhile. Now that West Coast have advertised their arrival 6.35 I think we had better accelerate 10 o'clock also and get both trains into Bradshaw and other guides for August. What can you do in improving 10 o'clock train. We can take twenty minutes off time Edinburgh to Aberdeen. With corresponding acceleration south of Edinburgh we could make connection with the express to Ballater and 9.30 express to Elgin and Inverness.

CONACHER.'

The West Coast did *not* advertise the 6.35 a.m. arrival. It was, however, so well known in Scottish railway circles that it was evidently as good as advertised!

And now Sir Henry Oakley hesitated before calling upon his allies for a further acceleration. After consultation with the Great Northern Chairman, the Hon. W. L. Jackson, he wired Conacher again, on July 25th:

'My Chairman would like opinion of your Board as to desirability or otherwise of his communicating with Lord Stalbridge re acceleration of Scotch trains. Reply.

OAKLEY.'

One can almost read between the lines of this telegram the sentiment: 'It's no use trying to argue directly with Harrison. Let's try working on him from above'! Conacher was ready enough to negotiate, and as the North British Chairman, the Marquis of Tweeddale, was in London at the time he wired off at once:

'Oakley wires me to know opinion of my Board as to desirability of his Chairman writing Lord Stalbridge on subject of accelerating Scotch trains. West Coast have shortened Aberdeen journey by another ten minutes this week and we are ready to beat them, but I think seeing West Coast began it would be good policy that Jackson should write Stalbridge as suggested. Please wire me instructions.

CONACHER.'

The noble Lord's reply was very much to the point:

'My opinion is our best policy is to beat them at any cost and having done it proceed remonstrate. Stalbridge has always complained of the speed being too great and has suggested more moderate speed, but the present is deliberate and well-considered attempt to show what they can do, and we should strive to win.

TWEEDDALE.'

At any cost! The italics are mine. There was no room for compromise, or doubts after such a directive. The substance of this remarkable telegram was duly conveyed to Sir Henry Oakley by wire next morning, and from that moment the gloves were off in deadly earnest. On July 29th the East Coast put into operation the 10 hour 25 minute schedule suggested by Conacher, with the following intermediate times:

Section	Miles	Time min.	Av. speed m.p.h.
Kings Cross–Grantham . .	105·5	116	54·5
Grantham–York . . .	82·7	88	56·3
York–Newcastle . . .	80·6	92	52·6
Newcastle–Edinburgh . .	124·4	140	53·3
Edinburgh–Dundee . . .	59·2	73	48·7
Dundee–Arbroath . . .	17·0	22	46·3
Arbroath–Aberdeen . . . (Ticket platform)	54·2	69	47·1

The Aberdeen ticket platform was due to be reached about 3 minutes before arrival in the general station. In passing, when com-

paring the above with present-day standards the very fast speed
scheduled between Edinburgh and Dundee will at once be noted.
Today the fastest train between the two places takes 97 minutes. On
the very first day of the accelerated schedule the North British made
the run in 71½ minutes with a load of 'equal to 9½' – about 150 tons.
Aberdeen was reached at 6.23 a.m., but on arrival it was found that
despite their continuing advertisement of '7 a.m.' the 8 p.m. from
Euston had arrived 17 minutes earlier, having sailed in at 6.6 a.m.!

The East Coast running was patchy that night. From Kings Cross
the load was 'equal to 11½', about 180 tons, and the Great Northern
engines managed it comfortably. A new 7 ft 6 in 2-2-2 single, No.
874, was used to Grantham, relieved there by an 'eight-footer', No.
1002; the times achieved were 112 minutes 50 seconds to Grantham,
and 86 minutes 25 seconds on to York – averages of 56·2 and 57·3
m.p.h. respectively. At York a saloon conveying a private party was
attached, bringing the load up to '12½', 195 tons; the engine was a
'J' class 7 ft 7 in 4-2-2, No. 1522, recently converted to a two-
cylinder simple. She was not equal to the task, and lost 6 minutes
between York and Darlington alone – 44 miles in 54½ minutes; but
with one slight check she practically held her own on to Newcastle,
arriving 7 minutes late. Northwards to Edinburgh the train was
double-headed, and with No. 1621 (Class 'M') and another single,
No. 1525, the lateness was practically wiped out; the two engines
ran the 124·4 miles in 136 minutes 10 seconds. The North British
did magnificently, using the new 6 ft 6 in 4-4-0 locomotives built by
Matthew Holmes in 1894/5. The train left Waverley 1½ minutes
late, but was early at Dundee, and thereafter ran well ahead of
intermediate booked times, with average speeds of 50 m.p.h. from
Dundee to Arbroath, and exactly the same from there to Aberdeen
ticket platform, despite all the hindrances of single-line working to
Montrose. The locomotive work is analysed in some detail in a later
chapter. On this same night the West Coast running was as follows:

Section	Engine	Load	Time min.	Av. speed m.p.h.
Euston–Crewe . .	Mercury*	'10½'	171	55·5
Crewe–Carlisle . .	Tennyson*	'10½'	160	52·9
Carlisle–Perth . .	No. 90†	'10½'	163‡	55·2
Perth–Aberdeen . .	No. 76	'10½'	98§	55·0

* 'Precedent' class.
† Double-headed to Stirling, and banked to Kinbuck.
‡ Inclusive of stop at Stirling.
§ Inclusive of stop at Forfar.

The 8 p.m. from Euston climbing Shap at midnight, while heavy loads were still being conveyed. 2-2-2 No. 610 *Princess Royal* pilots 'Jumbo' No. 790 *Hardwicke*.

[*From a painting by Jack Hill*

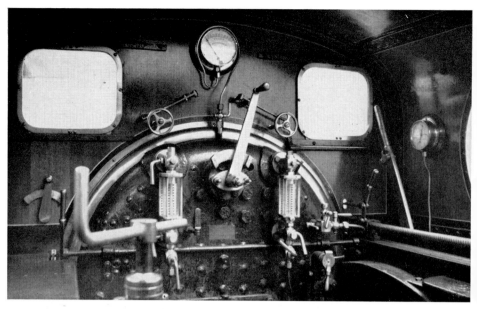

FOOTPLATES OF THE
RACING PERIOD

Above: North Eastern 'Fletcher' 2-4-c.

[*O. S. Nock*

Below: Stirling 8-foot 4-2-2 No. 1.
[*British Railway*

Below: The Caledonian 4-2-2 No. 123.

[*Ivo Peters*

L. & N.W.R. COMPOUNDS
OF THE RACING DAYS

Above: No. 1104 *Sunbeam*, one of the 'Experiment' Class, occasionally used for piloting.

Below: No. 1312 *Gaelic*, of the 'Teutonic' Class.

[*Locomotive Publishing Co*

Sir Frederick Harrison,
General Manager, L. & N.W.R.

G. P. Neele, Superintendent of
the Line, L. & N.W.R.

WEST COAST PERSONALITIES

Sir James Thompson, General
Manager, Caledonian Railway.

Irvine Kempt, General Superintendent, Caledonian Railway.

[*All Courtesy: "The Railway Magazine"*]

No further acceleration by either side took place during the ensuing month. One could scarcely expect it during the period leading up to the 'Twelfth', when Anglo-Scottish passenger traffic is the heaviest of the whole year. The East Coast ran to an advertised arrival time of 6.25 a.m., while the West Coast still showed 7 a.m. on posters, bills, and every L.N.W.R. horse-drawn cart in London, and elsewhere. The working time of arrival was 6.20 a.m. It must be conceded that between July 29th and August 18th the West Coast made by far the better showing. Right through the holiday season they were late on only one occasion, while the East Coast were only punctual six times out of twenty-four. The actual record of arrivals is as follows:

8 p.m. EXPRESSES LONDON TO ABERDEEN
Times of arrival

Date	West Coast	East Coast	
	Time	Time	Min. late
	a.m.	a.m.	
July 29	6.05	6.23	2 early
,, 30	5.59	6.40	15
,, 31	6.16	6.50	25
August 1	6.16	6.54	29
,, 2	6.15	6.33	8
,, 4	6.09	7.05	40
,, 5	6.08	6.25	0
,, 6	6.18	6.42	17
,, 7	6.15	6.28	3
,, 8	6.17	6.50	25
,, 9	6.09	6.45	20
,, 11	6.11	6.30	10
,, 12	6.12	6.20	5 early
,, 13	6.15	6.28	3
,, 14	6.13	6.22	3 early
,, 15	6.18	6.25	0
,, 16	6.10	6.27	2
,, 18	6.23	6.17	8 early

In the meanwhile the enthusiasts were working overtime. Acworth, Macdonald and Scott were frequently together on the same train, clocking the speeds throughout the night. Since the days of the 1888 affair their little band had been reinforced by the redoubtable personality of Charles Rous-Marten, Editor of the *New Zealand Times*, who had undertaken a survey of the British railways on behalf of the Government of New Zealand, and eventually took up permanent residence in this country. Rous-Marten had all the flair of a professional journalist for vivid description, and for feats of

F

endurance when first-class copy was to be had. He never varied his picturesque attire – black frock coat and tall hat – and it was shown to splendid advantage one memorable morning when he had travelled to Aberdeen by the 8 p.m. from Kings Cross. In order to pursue his ordinary duties he was anxious to get back to London as soon as possible; the 'flyer' was coasting into the station just as the up express for Edinburgh was starting, and racing across the platform with coat tails flying he just managed it. He was assisted in by an astonished guard, who remarked: 'Ye'll no' be makin' a long stay in Aberdeen the mor-r-n.'

By the first week in August the London newspapers were beginning to talk about the Race to the North, and young and old began to flock to Kings Cross and Euston to see the rivals start away. W. J. Reynolds was taken by his father, and had vivid recollections of the crowd round the engine at Kings Cross. C. J. Alcock saw the West Coast train every night the race was on, either from Euston itself, or from the old L.N.W.R. station at Chalk Farm. At that time the principal expresses used to leave from Platform 6, but by a curious twist of older history the 8 p.m. 'racer' always went from No. 9, the platform known to this day as 'the York', from its original use for traffic by the Hudson route to the North. It is always understood that No. 9 was used for the racing train because it afforded the least curving start of any out of the terminus, and in consequence engines were less likely to slip. Interest and enthusiasm came from all grades of the railway service. Mr W. H. Brown, of Newark-on-Trent, now eighty-one years of age, has told me how, as a lad-porter at the Great Northern station, he used to return long after his working hours were over in order to see the Aberdeen express dash under the footbridge, while Mr Cecil W. Longley, then nine and a half years old, was allowed to stay up long after bedtime in order to see the North Western train come streaking into Carlisle. He tells how he used to stay with his parents at St Stephen's Vicarage, Carlisle; the house and garden stand on a red sandstone eminence in the V made by the North Western and Maryport & Carlisle lines about half a mile south of the Citadel station. It is indeed a testimony to the hold the race had taken on the public that children of nine and a half years of age – and Victorian children at that! – were allowed to stay up until after 1 a.m. to see the train go by. Longley confesses, however, that his mother was a railway enthusiast herself.

Farther north some good yarns began to circulate about the 'close finishes' that sometimes occurred at Kinnaber Junction. One of the newspapers printed this item:

'The following story is told by the Caledonian Railway officials in connection with the railway race: Both trains they declare, reached Kinnaber junction where the two routes meet, at precisely the same time. On Thursday morning, 22nd, ult., the trains from Arbroath, on the East Coast route and Forfar, on the Western line, were sighted by the signal-man in the Kinnaber box at an identical moment. The signalman is a Caledonian man belonging, of course, to the West Coast route, and one would naturally expect that he would have let his own train through first. By a rare act of chivalry, however, he gave priority to the East Coast train, which consequently arrived in Aberdeen first. This story is right enough, no doubt, but we should like to hear it from the lips of other than Caledonian officials.'

So would I! On the other hand, a story to the opposite effect is said to have been told by one of the Caledonian firemen, how one day they were signalled through Kinnaber, only to find the East Coast train held by signal and waiting for them to go ahead. A rather more imaginative version of this same story tells how when the East Coast train did eventually arrive in Aberdeen the two engine crews had a free fight on the platform.

The prophets of dire disaster were loud on every hand. There was an alarmist rumour that persisted for some time among the dons of St Andrews University, of all places, that on one occasion the North British train had reached a speed of 200 m.p.h. in descending from the Forth Bridge to Inverkeithing. There is no denying that it was a hectic time for all concerned, particularly for the civil engineers. Trains were running faster than ever before, and if the superelevation on curves was adequate to give safe travel, much of the ballasting was insufficiently strong to maintain alignment. At Cupar, Fife, it is said that the permanent-way gang were called out nightly to correct the curve after the 'flyer' had passed; the average amount of distortion was about 3 inches. In passing on these stories, which have come to me from persons who were living at the time of the race, I do not necessarily expect them to be taken for gospel; they are recalled here in order to try and convey something of the atmosphere of excitement that prevailed during that hectic month of August. There is no doubt that the speeds run scared many people, particularly those who were not frequent travellers, and who unwittingly found themselves on the racing trains when their previous experience of rail travel had been far otherwise. Mr T. C. L. Swaine, who now lives in Sussex, travelled with his mother from Euston to Aberdeen when the arrival was supposed to have been 7 a.m.; riding in a six-wheeled non-corridor coach, which had little upholstery and not much padding in the seats, they had a very rough night, and were not altogether surprised to find their arrival in Aberdeen was 50 minutes early!

Mr D. A. Guild, of Elgin, has some boyhood reminiscences of the Caledonian that help to fill in some more detail in a fascinating picture. He tells how each year he went for the summer holidays to a farm in Angus.

'Those were the years' [he writes] 'when I saw and marvelled at the great Drummond 4-4-0 engines. I was always fascinated by the safety valve mounted on the top of the dome, with the lever shaped like a magnificent moustachio. . . .'

Coming to the race itself, he continues:

'I remember the stern comments of some of the grave and revered seniors, who were appalled that such dangerous goings-on should be allowed. I remember one pleasing tale of an old gentleman we knew who was going north by Perth. The driver must have been feeling his oats. Anyhow, coming down from Crieff Junction (now, of course, Gleneagles) the train started to shift a bit. This got on the old boy's nerves. After a while he could stand it no longer, and in the face of threatened penalties he decided to pull the communication cord. However at that time the communication cord only functioned on the right hand side of the compartment facing in the direction of travel. There might be a cord on the left hand side, and often was, but it was not connected up. In his agitation the old boy got hold of the wrong cord. He pulled and pulled until he got to the end of the rope, and then gave it up in despair. He arrived at the north end of the tunnel in a state of tremendous agitation with his compartment festooned with communication cord. He confided his woes to the ticket collector at Perth, and all the consolation he got was to be told that he was adjectively lucky it had happened that way or else he would have been fined £5.'

Between the scaremongering, and those who revelled in the speed and were for ever crying 'Faster, faster', there were many men who began to question whether there was any real advantage in these successive accelerations. A Caledonian pointsman had expressed his doubts, in a letter to *The Railway Herald*; by way of reply, some extracts from a letter written by Mr W. D. J. Edwards, of Chelsea, on August 15th, 1895, put the opposite view admirably:

'To state the case briefly' [he writes] 'it would be difficult to measure accurately the advantage to the shareholders of the Company. Certainly at first sight it does not seem consistent with economy to have, as was the case in the famous race in August 1888, five separate expresses on the West Coast to different parts of Scotland within two hours, where two or three trains as far as Carstairs Junction would have been sufficient, with three Midland trains, and five Great Northern expresses on different routes, but with the same objective points, when one or two respectively might have sufficed also for the greater part of the journey. But each Company has its prestige to maintain, otherwise public support is withdrawn and if it be suggested that amalgamation might result in more economy to the shareholder, the reply is that the British public have a most steady inclination in favour of competitive railways. Moreover, progress requires competition.

'Again, permanent acceleration follows upon such contests and thus railway travelling is encouraged. When the journey to Glasgow or Edinburgh took, as was the case twenty years ago, 11 hours, even in the fastest train, and in third-class trains several hours more, a journey demanded almost heroism; whereas now, when $8\frac{1}{2}$ hours suffices, even for third-class passengers too, there is no hesitancy, the journey is less serious, and the number of passengers has increased enormously. At the same time, economy in working becomes, with keener competition, a necessity, so that ingenuity towards this end is stimulated. Thus there is a measure of permanent good even to the shareholders, which cannot be accurately estimated.

'That there is advantage to the general public there is no doubt. The 1888 race gave ample proof of this.

'Then again, the advantages to the profession are almost self-evident. In the first place it has been found absolutely necessary to have the best of permanent way, and strong, well-built bogie carriages. As to the permanent way, the London & North Western have recently introduced 60-ft rails, and although some consider the length unwieldly, the reduction in the number of joints may prove of advantage. The fact that the great speed attained is scarcely appreciable in the carriages at once attests their smooth-running qualities. The comfort and convenience in most cases introduced by the introduction of the corridor arrangement, are luxurious as compared with the old carriages.

'The racing trains, it is true, are comparatively light. Those on the Aberdeen service just now consist of from 6 to 11 eight-wheel bogie carriages, the train weight being from 130 to 175 tons, but the speeds got with the heaviest trains show that even to Aberdeen the speed now recorded is not abnormally great. The $8\frac{1}{2}$-hours run to Edinburgh was made with similar light trains, but now the mid-day dining train, leaving Euston at 2 p.m. and Kings Cross at 2.20 p.m. covers the distance to Edinburgh in $8\frac{1}{2}$ hours easily. These trains of themselves weigh 360 tons on the West Coast route, and on the East Coast route 300 tons – very much more than the racing trains of 1888. It is true that on some occasions, when the traffic is heavy, two engines are used, but as a rule one engine takes the load, the coal consumption being from 30 lb to 31 lb for compound, and 33 lb to 34 lb for non-compound locomotives – much having been gleaned from these performances in reference to locomotive running.'

Throughout the early weeks of August loads continued heavy on both sides. Trains up to '12½' were taken unassisted from Euston to Crewe by the Webb 'Precedents'. Some particularly fine runs may be mentioned.

L.N.W.R.: 8 p.m. EUSTON TO CREWE

Date	Engine		Load		Time min.	Av. speed m.p.h.
	No.	Name	Coaches	Tons		
July 30	394	Eamont	10½	165	171	55·5
August 2	749	Mercury	12½	195	170	55·7
,, 8	749	Mercury	12	188	169	56·1
,, 15	394	Eamont	11½	180	169	56·1

Only on one occasion during the period of the 10 hour 20 minute schedule was a pilot taken south of Crewe; this was on August 9th, when *Eamont* tried a load of 'equal to 13'. Driver Daynes found he was losing time, and stopped at Rugby for assistance. A second 'Jumbo' was attached, and the two pairs of enginemen did well to reach Crewe only 3 minutes late. The next down journey, curiously enough, was one of the very few on which neither *Eamont* nor *Mercury* was used; instead the engine was No. 790 *Hardwicke*, with Driver Ben Robinson and Fireman Wolstencroft. The load, however, was only 'equal to 7' and they went through easily in 168 minutes.

North of Crewe the train was double-headed throughout when the load exceeded '11½'. Two 'Lady of the Lake' class 2-2-2s were specially set aside for piloting the 'racer' when required, 610 *Princess Royal* and 622 *Prince Alfred*, and some splendid runs were made. The following table summarizes a few of the best, during the period from July 29th to August 18th.

L.N.W.R. 10.58 p.m. CREWE–CARLISLE
Unpiloted

Date	Engine		Load		Time min.	Av. speed m.p.h.
	No.	Name	Coaches	Tons		
July 31	1213	The Queen	11	165	159	53·2
August 4	2192	Caradoc	7½	115	157	53·9
,, 13	790	Hardwicke	11	165	160	52·9
,, 14	1213	The Queen	11½	175	155	54·5

Piloted

Date	Engine		Load		Time min.	Av. speed m.p.h.
	No.	Name	Coaches	Tons		
August 2	622	Prince Alfred	12½	190	156	54·3
	1213	The Queen				
,, 8	622	Prince Alfred	12	180	156	54·3
	790	Hardwicke				
,, 9	622	Prince Alfred	13	195	152	55·7
	1213	The Queen				

The Great Northern was the only one of the five railways involved that ran no double-headed trains at all during any period of the race. The Stirling 'singles', both 2-2-2 and 4-2-2, handled trains up to 180 or 190 tons most competently, and the late arrivals in Aberdeen were incurred by incidents occurring north of York.

With the easing of the pressure of northbound traffic after August 12th, one felt that the East Coast companies must press for a settlement in some way or other. So far they had had very much the worst of it, and on actual performance there seemed every sign that summer would slip into autumn with the West Coast triumphant on all counts. All this was so unlike the normal character of the Great Northern as to make the West Coast companies more than ever on the alert for any surprise that might be sprung suddenly. There was a great deal of 'snooping' on both sides, especially at Kings Cross and Euston. Mr F. G. Cockman, of Bedford, writes:

'My father-in-law, Mr. A. E. B. Mason, commenced his railway career in the booking office at Little Bytham, in 1889, and duly proceeded to the Passenger Manager's office at Kings Cross. In 1895, during the competitive running, he was instructed to go to Euston daily as a 'spy' and to keep his eyes and ears open for any information on what 'the enemy' proposed to do next day. No doubt many G.N. officials were detailed for this duty, but it goes to show how very keen the competition was. He had particularly to find out what the schedule was being cut to, until schedule times were abandoned, and I believe he was able to assist the G.N.R. by ascertaining the L.N.W. plans.'

So, to outside observers the third week in August quietly drew to a close, with the East Coast noticeably improving their running, and on the 18th actually getting into Aberdeen first. The curtain was about to rise on the final and most thrilling act of all.

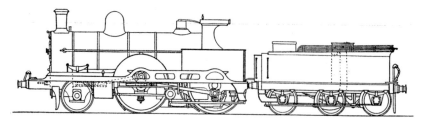

L.N.W.R. 'Teutonic' class compound

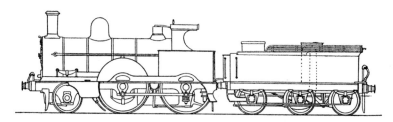

L.N.W.R. 'Precedent' class

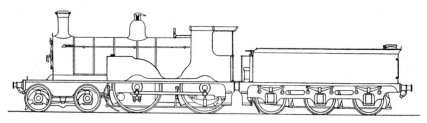

Caledonian Railway 'Drummond' 4-4-0

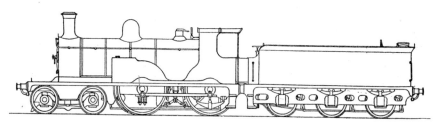

Caledonian Railway 'Lambie' 4-4-0

THE RIVALS

WEST COAST

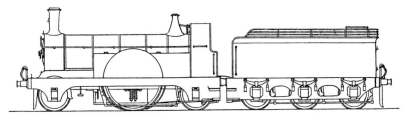

G.N.R 'Stirling' 2-2-2

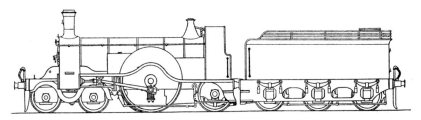

G.N.R. 'Stirling' 8ft. 4-2-2

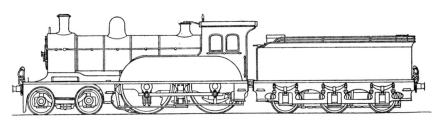

N.E.R. 'MI' class 4-4-0

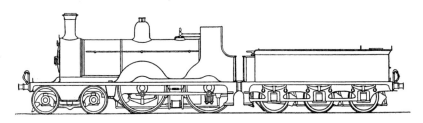

N.B.R. 'Holmes' 4-4-0

COMPARED

EAST COAST

VIII

Nearing the Climax

ON Tuesday, August 13th, there was a meeting of East Coast officers at York. The flood of traffic preceding the 'Twelfth' was over, and with Mr Welburn of the North Eastern presiding, a startling acceleration of the 8 p.m. from Kings Cross was planned. The Great Northern was represented by Mr Alexander; Matthew Holmes and David Deuchars were there for the North British, and there was a galaxy of North Eastern officers, including Vincent Raven, then Locomotive Running Superintendent. Up till then the earliest Caledonian arrival in Aberdeen had been 6.6 a.m., and with the intention of settling the matter once and for all, to quote the actual minutes of the meeting:

'It was agreed that from the 19th to the 23rd instant the following be the accelerated times of the 8 p.m. train from Kings Cross:

Kings Cross	.	.	.	*dep.*	8.00 p.m.
York	.	.	.	*arr.*	11.18
				dep.	11.23
Newcastle	.	.	.	*arr.*	12.43 a.m.
				dep.	12.46
Berwick	.	.	.	*pass*	1.55
Edinburgh	.	.	.	*arr.*	2.55
				dep.	2.58
Dundee	.	.	.	*arr.*	4.08
				dep.	4.10
Arbroath	.	.	.	*arr.*	4.30
				dep.	4.32
Kinnaber Junct.	.	.	*pass*	4.56
Aberdeen	.	.	.	*arr.*	5.40

'The foregoing times are subject to alteration if the Great Northern Company can to-morrow see their way to further acceleration.

'That the train be made up of the following vehicles:

Aberdeen brake van	Composite carriage (corridor)
Third-class carriage (corridor)	Third-class carriage (corridor)
Sleeping carriage	North British brake van

'The train not to exceed eight vehicles under any circumstances whilst it is running at the accelerated times.'

The North Eastern contribution was a massive one. Here was the laggard among the East Coast companies now booking the fastest start-to-stop average speed of the entire journey – 80·6 miles from York to Newcastle in 80 minutes. The Great Northern share was to run from Kings Cross to Grantham in 109 minutes, and Grantham to York in 86 minutes, average speeds of 58·1 and 57·7 m.p.h. Every attempt was made to keep these intentions from the West Coast, and the minutes of that momentous meeting included this note: 'It was the feeling of the meeting that the accelerated times of the train should not be advertised.'

The point-to-point average speeds scheduled over the Great Northern and North Eastern lines were:

GREAT NORTHERN:

Miles						Minutes	Average speed m.p.h.
0·0	Kings Cross	.	.	.	.	0	—
17·7	Hatfield	.	.	.	.	19	55·9
31·9	Hitchin	.	.	.	.	34	56·8
58·9	Huntingdon	.	.	.	.	61	60·0
76·4	Peterborough	.	.	.	.	79	58·3
105·5	Grantham .	.	.	.	.	109	58·2
0·0						0	—
14·6	Newark	.	.	.	.	15	58·4
33·1	Retford	.	.	.	.	34	58·4
50·5	Doncaster .	.	.	.	.	52	58·0
68·9	Selby .	.	.	.	.	71	58·1
82·7	York .	.	.	.	.	86	58·2

NORTH EASTERN:

Miles						Minutes	Average speed m.p.h.
0·0	York .	.	.	.	.	0	—
11·2	Alne .	.	.	.	.	11	61·1
22·2	Thirsk	.	.	.	.	21	60·0
30·0	Northallerton	.	.	.	.	28	62·8
38·9	Dalton*	.	.	.	.	37	59·3
44·1	Darlington .	.	.	.	.	42	60·8
57·0	Ferryhill	.	.	.	.	55	59·5
66·1	Durham	.	.	.	.	65	54·5
71·9	Chester-le-Street .	.	.	.	71	58·0
80·6	Newcastle .	.	.	.	.	80	57·9
0·0						0	—
16·6	Morpeth	.	.	.	.	19	52·5

* Now Eryholme

Miles		Minutes	Average Speed m.p.h.
34·8	Alnmouth	37	60·7
51·6	Belford	53	63·0
66·9	Berwick	69	57·4
124·4	Edinburgh	129	57·5

It is interesting to see that on paper, at any rate, it was proposed to keep the accelerated times by making very rapid starts rather than by really fast running out on the open road. The North Eastern 11 minutes from York to Alne was an absolute counsel of perfection. The traffic department circulars issued to the staff by the Great Northern and North Eastern Railways are reproduced in full in the Appendix, but some points from them are worth special mention here. Referring to the 8 p.m. from Kings Cross, Mr Welburn's circular stated:

'It will until further notice convey passengers for Aberdeen and Stations north of Edinburgh via Dundee only, and will not stop to set down passengers at stations at which it is not timed to do so, *neither will it, from August 19th, convey any fish traffic.*'

Then in very heavy type comes this:

'PARTICULAR ATTENTION MUST BE PAID TO THE PROMPT TELEGRAPHING OF THE RUNNING OF THE EXPRESS PASSENGER TRAINS REFERRED TO HEREIN, AND THE MARGINS HITHERTO OBSERVED BETWEEN TRAINS OF LESS IMPORTANCE AND THE 8 P.M. EXPRESS TRAIN FROM KINGS CROSS MUST UNTIL FURTHER NOTICE BE INCREASED TO THE EXTENT OF NOT LESS THAN TEN MINUTES, AND ALL CONCERNED ARE TO UNDERSTAND DISTINCTLY THAT THE LINE MUST BE KEPT ABSOLUTELY CLEAR FOR THESE TRAINS TO RUN.'

On August 14th, the day after the East Coast conference at York, Patrick Stirling wrote his famous letter to his district superintendent at Peterborough:

GREAT NORTHERN RAILWAY

Locomotive Department
Engineers Office
DONCASTER.

Very Important   14th August, 1895

8.0 P.M. DOWN SCOTCH EXPRESS

Dear Sir,

The L. & N.W. Co have expressed their intention to reach Aberdeen before us. This of course we cannot permit and arrangements are being made by this Company and the N.E. and N.B. Railways to accelerate the speed of the above train commencing on Monday next.

We must reach York at 11.15 p.m. The load will not exceed 6 whenever possible to keep it to that number and 7 will be the maximum in every case. The N.E. Company have undertaken to run their share of the distance at high speed, over 60½ miles per hour York to Newcastle and the N.B. also.

Please put your men on their mettle!

Acknowledge receipt of this preliminary notice and oblige

> Yours truly,
>
> P. STIRLING.

F. Rouse, Esq.,
Peterborough.

Evidently, however, there were some misgivings in the Locomotive Department as correspondence that passed in the next few days strongly suggests. It is surprising that the Great Northern, once leading the world in speed, should not have been able to respond to a supreme call so well as the North Eastern did. On the same day that Stirling wrote to Rouse his chief clerk and accountant, J. W. Matthewman, was in London discussing the acceleration with Cockshott's chief assistant, J. Alexander. It seems clear that there were some doubts at Kings Cross, for Sir Henry Oakley wrote to Stirling specially. On August 15th Stirling replied:

THE GREAT NORTHERN RAILWAY

> Locomotive Carriage & Wagon Department
> DONCASTER.
>
> August 15th, 1895

Dear Sir,

I am in receipt of yours of the 14th inst. in reference to the acceleration of the 8.0 p.m. train to Aberdeen and in view of the competitive nature of the traffic and seeing what the L. & N.W. Co are doing I am quite willing to meet the demand made by the Traffic Department, i.e. to engage (wind and weather and other adverse contingencies permitting) to work the 8.0 p.m. train between London and York in 3 hours and 18 minutes.

The load however must be kept down to 6 whenever possible and should never exceed 7 vehicles.* This Mr Matthewman stipulated for in his interview with Mr Alexander yesterday. Under such conditions I have no doubts of its feasibility.

I may tell you that on the 15th inst. with 9 vehicles on we arrived at York at 11.23 p.m. and on the 7th with 10 on we got there at 11.22 p.m.

Yours truly,

Sir Henry Oakley,   (*Signed*) P. STIRLING.
General Manager,
Kings Cross.

    * P.S. (We will not stick at 8 however).

This was rather a 'canny' letter, and after sending it Stirling appears to have gone off to Scarborough for his holiday; but Matthewman followed him, and on the 16th a further letter was sent to Rouse, which is highly revealing:

THE GREAT NORTHERN RAILWAY

Locomotive Carriage & Wagon Department
DONCASTER.

Private   August 16th, 1895
_____

Dear Sir,

RACE TO ABERDEEN

I went down to Scarboro yesterday to consult Mr Stirling in reference to a communication from Sir Henry Oakley upon the subject of the race to Aberdeen, and he desired me to again ask you to impress upon your drivers the absolute need there is that we should get into York at the time booked, viz. 11.18, or a few minutes earlier if possible.

The drivers must not study economy of fuel in the race, but must beat the North Western, whatever they may burn in the way of fuel of the best selected quality.

Tell them please that this will be fully allowed for in the distribution of premiums, and further, Mr Stirling thinks it will be well to give the men some extra pecuniary allowance, such as $\frac{1}{4}$ of a day's pay, whenever they arrive on time, or in any other way by *douceur* or otherwise that may best secure the end in view. What do you recommend please?

He has undertaken to the General Manager to beat everybody else, and he relies on you and all the staff to leave no stone unturned to do this.

There is great anxiety also I may say that the other trains, viz. the 8.30 and 10.0 o'clock as well as the duplicate of the race train should be punctually worked.

Yours truly,

(*Signed*) J. W. MATTHEWMAN.

F. Rouse, Esq.,
Peterborough.

One can do no more than guess at the nature of Rouse's reply. One would imagine he had been defending his men, and the suggestion that they should run hard regardless of coal consumption had caught him rather on the raw. Anyway, Matthewman replied rather brusquely on August 19th:

THE GREAT NORTHERN RAILWAY

Locomotive Department
Engineers Office
DONCASTER.

Private   August 19th, 1895

Dear Sir,

ACCELERATION OF 8.0 P.M. DOWN EXPRESS
Yours of 17th inst.

I am obliged for the above. I may point out however that in the opinion of the Traffic Department the men had *not* been doing well because they had failed to recover the time lost by relayers, station business, signals, etc. and the suggestion that an extra payment should be made as an inducement to the men to do their very best regardless of fuel and premium was put forward in consequence.

Yours truly,

(*Signed*) J. W. MATTHEWMAN.

F. Rouse, Esq.,
Peterborough.

The week ended without a murmur of reply from the West Coast, and all East Coast officers directly concerned, from Kings Cross to Aberdeen, must have waited in almost breathless suspense for the result of all the preparations that had been made for the great effort to be put forth on the night of Monday, August 19th. Well they might, for the 8 p.m. was to run to a schedule far and away faster than anything previously tabled in Britain, or anywhere else in the world; the average speed from start to stop was to be 54 m.p.h. over the entire distance of 523½ miles. Furthermore, by carrying passengers for no stations south of Dundee the train could leave intermediate stations as soon as it was ready, and so get some time in hand to offset any possible delays *en route*. And once clear of Arbroath, there is no doubt that the North British were expected to run their hardest for Kinnaber. By actually scheduling an arrival 26 minutes earlier than the best Caledonian effort up to the time it was fervently hoped, at last, to spring a surprise on the West Coast. The little band of highly privileged enthusiasts was in the secret; Norman D.

Macdonald travelled up to London especially to 'race' down, and with him came W. M. Gilbert, the chief of staff of *The Scotsman*. In London they were joined by the Rev. W. J. Scott, Charles Rous-Marten and W. M. Acworth, all armed with stop watches, and the party was completed by Percy Caldecott, one of the most expert locomotive photographers of the day.

The East Coast authorities appear to have put a sleeper at their disposal, though Scott records that their 'passes' only extended to Kinnaber Junction. They all had to pay full fare for that portion of the route that lay over Caledonian metals! In 1897 Scott wrote:

'Even now, two full years after, it is hard to write about it in cold blood. Beforehand: the reckoning of mileage, and working out of inter-mediate speeds, when the working notices came into one's hands. Then the chat and chaff with the traffic officers, who wavered between drinking delight of battle with their peers and feeling (or making believe to feel) ashamed of the whole thing as not practical "business". This usually ended with a vain effort to keep a certain superintendent away from the engine, that he might not give restraining instructions to the driver – then the whistle, and the train and our chronographs begin moving together.'

That superintendent, strange to say, was Cockshott himself, who was frequently out on the platform at Kings Cross talking to the drivers and urging them to be especially attentive in their work.

'Monday August 19th!
. . . a night of long drawn out excitement' [Scott continued] 'when our hopes were constantly raised by fine running, only to be dashed again by signal stops or "waiting for time", while through good fortune or ill the fifths of seconds ticked off remorselessly, and the friendly conductor stayed us with hot coffee or comforted us with bread and butter.'

Macdonald and his friends were hoping that at last the East Coast was going to play the West Coast at their own game and dis-regard timetables throughout; but there was nothing in the decisions of the East Coast conference of August 13th to justify such an assump-tion. The Great Northern and North Eastern were each going through as fast as possible to offset any chances of exceptional delay, and it was hoped that if the train was on time from Dundee it would be enough to beat the Caledonian.

At Euston the excitement was no less intense than at Kings Cross. On the previous Friday, for the first time since July 21st, the train had been worked by a compound, No. 1307 *Coptic*. Those engines of the 'Teutonic' class were real flyers, but more than this, *Coptic* had been driven by one of the greatest footplate characters on

Euston, about the turn of the century, showing a 'Jumbo'-hauled express about to leave and an interesting selection of rolling stock.

[*Locomotive Publishing Co*

Carlisle Citadel Station about the turn of the century. Up Anglo-Scottish express preparing to leave, hauled by 6ft. "Jumbo" No. 36 *Thalaba* and a "Jubilee" class four-cylinder compound 4-4-0.

[*Locomotive Publishing Co*

North Eastern Railway two-cylinder compound 4-4-0 No. 779 ('F' Class) at Waverley. Engines of this type were used in the 1888 races.

[*Locomotive Publishing Co*

The record-breaker of 1888: Caledonian 4-2-2 No. 123, as restored with two Caledonian coaches for special excursion work in 1958.

[*W. J. V. Anderson*

The down 'Flying Scotsman' near Hadley Wood, taken just after the racing period, and conveying a mixture of six-wheeled and corridor stock. Engines No. 774 (8-footer) leading, and 2-2-2 No. 872.

[*British Railways*

the L.N.W.R., P. Clow of Rugby – 'Peter the Dandy', as he was called. Clow was a 'runner', if ever there was one, and when he was there again, on that fateful Monday, August 19th, with another of the compounds, No. 1309 *Adriatic*, the West Coast fans saw the train away with high hearts. Peter the Dandy! Not for him the peaked cap and blue overalls of the traditional engineman; he wore a black tailed coat, tall hat, and an immaculately white shirt front. In his spare time he kept a public house in Rugby, and ran a highly profitable business as a bookmaker. Yet for all the signs at Euston the public could form no idea of what speed the train would make; the great blue posters still said that 7 a.m. was the arrival time in Aberdeen. So for the moment we also will leave this 'mystery train' to follow the fortunes of our enthusiast friends travelling on the 8 p.m. from Kings Cross.

The load on August 19th was six coaches, as specified in the circulars issued after the meeting of August 13th, behind a Peterborough eight-footer, No. 668. Her driver, J. Falkinder of New England shed, was a taciturn man, silent almost to the point of unfriendliness; a solid, safe man, to be sure, but hardly the one to rise to the heights of so exciting an occasion. There is no doubt that the Great Northern men disliked the race. They had a proud tradition of sound, economical running, and they needed the inducement of extra pay, in order to run as much ahead of time as was needed on those last nights. It was not surprising that the initial booking to Hatfield was not kept, but once over a permanent way slack near Welwyn the engine ran well and averaged $68\frac{1}{2}$ m.p.h. over the 33·9 miles from Knebworth to Huntingdom. At Peterborough they were inside the reputed record of the 1888 race, and a good climb to Stoke brought the train into Grantham 3 minutes early: 105 minutes 55 seconds from Kings Cross. Engines were changed, and with another eight-footer, No. 775 built in 1886, the going onwards to York was rather more enterprising. Sectional time was kept to Newark, and some fine running followed with an average speed of 66 m.p.h. thence to Doncaster. With a smart recovery from the Selby slack the run from Grantham to York was completed in the record time of $79\frac{1}{2}$ minutes, an average from start to stop of 62·3 m.p.h. York was reached at 11.9 p.m. – 9 minutes early, so that Stirling and his men had good reason to be satisfied.

In another 4 minutes engines had been changed, and they were away behind one of Wilson Worsdell's then gigantic 'M' class 4-4-os. But even this engine, No. 1624, was not equal to that extraordinary booking of 21 minutes for the 22·2 miles from York to

G

passing Thirsk; the time was 22 minutes 46 seconds. Then came a stroke of ill luck. A train in front had a tail lamp out, and while this was being put right the flyer had to be stopped at the junction then named Dalton, and now Eryholme. Apparently the time thus lost could not be made up, and eventually Newcastle was reached in 83 minutes 45 seconds, still however 6 minutes ahead of the booked time, 12.43 a.m. So far a distance of 269 miles had been covered in 283 minutes, and one can well imagine how, at intervals, the thoughts of the party in that sleeper must have turned to the West Coast train and speculations as to how she was doing. Had they known it, when the East Coast was crossing the High Level Bridge and running into Newcastle Central their rival was already over Shap and tearing down to Carlisle; she had then averaged nearly 60 m.p.h. from her start, and in the Citadel station was waiting the redoubtable Tom Robinson, ready to carry on the good work with the Drummond 4-4-0 No. 78. But over in Newcastle the North Eastern people had things organized to the last detail. The train ran in over the High Level Bridge with the engine heading as though for Carlisle. In the meantime the fresh engine, backing down from the usual waiting point on the bridge, followed the train in, and so smart was the working that No. 1621 touched buffers only a few seconds after the train had stopped. On another similar occasion the night was hot, and a Scots lawyer left the train in search of a thirst-quencher. The engine change took no more than 2½ minutes, and with the racer away again in record time the tall hat of the hapless passenger went on its journey to Edinburgh leaving its owner still in the buffet at Newcastle. When the gentleman in question was eventually rash enough to tell of his misfortune in a furious letter to *The Scotsman*, all Edinburgh was laughing for days!

The running to Edinburgh was rather uneven. Scarcely any time was gained to Berwick, and for such an occasion the climb to Grantshouse was quite leisurely. I think it was probable that the driver was a little apprehensive about his water supply. The run of 124·4 miles was a long one to be made non-stop, even with the large North Eastern tenders which carried 3,940 gallons of water, and the troughs at Lucker were not installed until March 1898. In any event it seems that the driver was nursing his engine until he was through Berwick and up the long bank to Grantshouse. Then things began to happen. Two years after the event Scott wrote:

'But such a change for the better now befalls us that we spin off the remaining 41¼ miles in just 38 minutes; dropping down by Cockburnspath at 80 m.p.h. easing very little for Dunbar, with a terrific spurt by Portobello, No. 1621 fairly charges up the Calton Tunnel steep and we pull up in Waverley at a trifle before 2.45 a.m., 6 hours 44 minutes 50 seconds for the more than 393 miles from London, or 42 minutes better than the "Race to Edinburgh" best.'

At times Scott was inclined to exaggerate, and the modern reader, knowing the layout at Portobello, might be inclined to dismiss, as a mere form of words, his reference to a 'terrific spurt' at that point. But forty years after the event Macdonald revealed something of what really *did* happen:

'The last week of the "Race" ' [he wrote] 'was nearly the death of a group of famous and infamous folk *i.e.* the Rev. W. J. Scott, Sir William Acworth, C. Rous-Marten, Percy Caldecott, W. M. Gilbert and myself. It fell on this-wise. My East Coast friends (N.E.R., N.B.R., and G.N.R.) always put on a "sleeper" for my party when any new spurt effort came to the birth. Till I got the N.E.R. to build the first transverse-berthed "sleeper" these were made up of cabins of two beds placed longitudinally, entered from a passage across the car.

'At Portobello (Edinburgh) there then was a very bad S-curve with our usual half-hearted British elevation, ending in a high bridge above a wide road.

'At Inveresk Rous-Marten, with his four split watches (one in each hand and one in each trousers pocket) called, "82 m.p.h." I said, "If these two big Worsdells don't slack off we will be thrown through the windows, even if we stay on the rails at the Portobello S." I quickly got the six into the cross passage, where we jammed our legs and arms against the walls, myself at one window and Rous-Marten at the other. Just before the curves he called "81½", and I yelled, "Look out!" as we struck it. The whole of them were thrown on to me, and we collapsed, as does a Rugby maul, and in the next second we were hurled up again and on to the top of C.R-M. In his dry Dutch way he was heard to say, "We would have made bonnie raspberry jam in that Duddington road!" When we emerged into Waverley out of the Calton tunnel (after a mile of 1 in 78 up) we were doing about 64 m.p.h. and Acworth remarked, "Thank goodness we are working Westinghouse and not vacuum, and that Waverley is very long!" '

One would dearly have liked to see the faces and general disarray of that sextet on their somewhat precipitate arrival in Waverley! Still greater must have been the consternation among the ordinary passengers on that train. Macdonald made a slip in referring to the train being worked by *two* big Worsdells. Only one engine was used between Newcastle and Edinburgh that night, namely No. 1621, the engine that is now preserved in the York Railway Museum. But to revert to the events of 1895, they were 10 minutes early, and a truly lightning engine change in 2 minutes raised the highest hopes of the enthusiasts on board; but with the Holmes 4-4-0 No. 293 attached they did not start. A minute went by, and then the awful truth dawned upon them, they were being kept waiting for time. After the excitement of the running in from Grantshouse it must have been the most devastating anti-climax. Some put it down to the mutton-headedness of a local North British official, others to the inefficiency at Waverley, and so on. But looking back to the minutes and circulars of the conference of August 13th I think it was nothing more than the last lingerings of orthodoxy. The acceleration had been planned as a normal railway job; the North British had a schedule to work to, and they above all were anxious to beat the Caledonian. The train was ready to start at about 2.47½ a.m., and while its booked departure time was 2.58, the Waverley officials did actually stretch a point, and send it off at 2.56. But during those 8 minutes that might have been gained the enthusiasts on board fretted and chafed, and Scott reminded them that Tom Robinson, of all drivers, was running for the 'Caley' that night. For them the race seemed as good as lost.

Once away, the driver of No. 293 made what would today be considered as a hair-raisingly fast run to Dundee. In eleven minutes from Waverley they were entering upon the Forth Bridge; the next 11·3 miles on to Burntisland took 12 minutes 35 seconds – at an average speed of 53·8 m.p.h. – and the ensuing 19 miles to Lady-bank Junction were run in only 20 seconds over 'even time'. This made a total of 42 minutes 55 seconds for the 39·1 miles from Waver-ley. One can only guess at the speeds run, both intermediately and round the various sharp curves. I may add, that the 'Aberdonian' at its fastest in L.N.E.R. days was booked to pass Ladybank in 55 minutes from Waverley. From this point onwards, however, the pace was not quite so hot. The 11·8 miles from Ladybank to Leuchars took 12 minutes, whereas I have done it in 13 minutes on an 'A3' Pacific with 510 tons behind the tender, and the last 8·3 miles into Dundee took 9½ minutes. Even so, No. 293 had made what was up to that morning an absolutely record time from Waverley: 59·2 miles in 64 minutes 15 seconds.

Again the enthusiasts chafed as the train 'waited for time', though here it would almost certainly have been necessary to take water, and if the water column at Tay Bridge station was as slow then as it is today the process might easily have taken 4 minutes. Dundee was left at 4.7½ a.m., 2½ minutes early, and now it was a case of 'all out' for the winning post. Whether or not a fresh driver was in charge I cannot say. In all records of the race none of the North British enginemen is mentioned by name. But the work along the straight and level road to Arbroath was disappointing. Nearly as long was taken to cover this excellent 17 miles as for the first 17 out of Edinburgh, and the latter included the slowing over the Forth Bridge, the slack at Inverkeithing and the stiff climb up to Dalgetty. Where he was restricted and slowed this driver seemed to rise to the heights in accelerating his engine and storming up the banks, and against 20 minutes 15 seconds for the straight and level 17 miles from Dundee to Arbroath he took only 19 minutes 45 seconds for the next $16\frac{1}{4}$ miles on to Kinnaber – with heavy gradients, and *six* bad slacks for tablet exchanging! So they came past Kinnaber – all signals clear – $8\frac{1}{2}$ minutes early, having run the $485\frac{1}{2}$ miles from Kings Cross in $527\frac{1}{2}$ minutes. The overall average speed to this point had been 55·2 m.p.h., but deducting the time spent at stations, and at that unfortunate signal stop at Dalton, the running time of $497\frac{1}{2}$ minutes shows a remarkably fine average of 58·6 m.p.h. Kinnaber Junction had been passed in a time 35 minutes faster than the best the West Coast had been known to make, up to then, and as the train sped on towards Aberdeen the enthusiasts hoped against hope. The last 18 miles to the Aberdeen ticket platform were splendidly run in 19 minutes 40 seconds, but there from the Caledonian ticket collector our travellers learned the worst. With justifiable triumph that worthy remarked airily, 'Ay, she's in these sixteen minutes.' Sixteen minutes! All the elaborate preparation, all the secrecy had been of no avail; the West Coast had done it again, with a magnificent overall average speed of 58·4 m.p.h. from start to finish.

No more than a month earlier the running of the West Coast train that night would have read like a fairy tale. The pressure was sustained from start to finish with scarcely a second thrown away anywhere. The load was one of four bogies throughout, about 95 tons behind the tender, and from Euston, with No. 1309 *Adriatic*, Peter Clow ran the 158·1 miles to Crewe in 157 minutes. Engine changing at Crewe can never be so 'slick' as at Newcastle, and the full 4 minutes booked were taken. Then W. J. Phillips came on with the 6 ft 6 in 'Jumbo' No. 1683 *Sisyphus*, and the 141·1 miles from Crewe to Carlisle were reeled off in 140 minutes start to stop. It was next Tom Robinson's turn, and it is a great pity that no intermediate details are now known of what must have been a grand run; for including a stop at Stirling he ran the 150 miles from Carlisle to Perth in 155 minutes. Finally William Kerr came on with another Drummond 4-4-0, No. 70, and ran the remaining 89·8 miles into

Aberdeen in 89 minutes inclusive of the stop at the ticket platform. Thus except for the short stretch from Stirling to Perth every stage of the journey was made at a start-to-stop average of more than 60 m.p.h. The running average for the entire journey was 60·65 m.p.h.

For the indefatigable Norman D. Macdonald the night's entertainment did not cease on arrival in Aberdeen. The tale can again be told most vividly in his own words. He related how on that night:

'I did the feat of having four breakfasts in four divers places. (1) Soon after midnight one of my co-lunatics in our "sleeper" produced a flask and very massive sandwiches. (2) After Berwick-on-Tweed the attendant gave us coffee and biscuits. (3) Not long after 5 a.m. we were hammering the doors of the Imperial Hotel in Aberdeen calling for food. On getting in I said the Cockney pressmen must have real porridge for once, "and mind they have milk, all proper, and no beastly treacle or sugar". The poor waiter said, "There is no milk!" I blazed into Highland fire, which he damped down by saying, "Man! the coos is no' milket yet!" (4) I caught the "Flying Scotsman" portion from Aberdeen and landed in Edinburgh at 9.40 a.m., dashed to my nearby house to find the joyful remains of the family feed still on the table. I had done nearly 200 miles between my second and third breakfasts and about 130 between the third and fourth ones!'

Despite all, it was that hectic 'Rugger-maul' passage through Portobello that was uppermost in all their minds, and fortified by his fourth breakfast Macdonald strode into the North British offices in Princes Street and demanded to see David Deuchars. Ushered into the presence he did not mince his words: 'Look here,' he said, 'I like high speed to save time and develop traffic, but to reverse at Portobello at 81½ is a bit hot!' Deuchars pressed a button on his desk, and in response to a long, loud ring the half-scared chief clerk hurried in to be asked, 'What is the speed limit round Portobello?' 'Ten to fifteen an hour I think, sir.'

Macdonald relates the end of that interview in his own inimitable way: 'Deuchars looked at me with the gentle eyes of a reproving cow, and I felt like a schoolboy caught in his best lie.'

And that was that!

Apart from that 'close-run thing' at Portobello, the race of August 19th–20th left the East Coast authorities and the enthusiasts who travelled in the train with much food for immediate and furious thought. In his famous pamphlet 'Kinnaber', the Rev. W. J. Scott claims a moral victory for the East Coast, asserting that the West Coast owed their triumph 'rather to the stern resolve of the North

British officers not to allow any "before time" departures, than to their own fine running'. But this, on the data he himself published in that pamphlet, was definitely not the case. First of all, the train was despatched 2½ minutes early from Edinburgh, and 2 minutes early from Dundee. Next, the West Coast won by a clear 16 minutes, while the detentions at Waverley and Dundee, after the East Coast train was ready to start, were 9 minutes and 4 minutes respectively. It would have been a very close thing, but there still seems to have been a 3 minute advantage to the West Coast. Rous-Marten seemed to become thoroughly partisan for once, and wrote in *The Engineer*:

'But then 20 minutes had been absolutely wasted in delays at Dalton, Edinburgh and Dundee, in the first case by a blundering signal stop, and in the other by mere idling in the stations long after all was in readiness for the start. These blunders were doubtless due to a misunderstanding, but they were grave blunders nevertheless, and resulted in making a present of an easy victory to the rival route.'

One could hardly call an extinguished tail-lamp a blunder; it is just one of those things that must be taken amidst the luck of the game; and even so Rous-Marten was exaggerating when he claimed that the time lost from the three causes amounted to 20 minutes. The truth is that he, like Scott and the others who travelled on the train, were disappointed with the ultimate result. In the eyes of the world there was no doubt as to who was the winner, and a commentator in London voiced the popular impression: 'The East Coast is thoroughly and hopelessly beaten.'

By the greatest good fortune, however, there was to be a full dress East Coast conference in Edinburgh at 1 p.m. on that very day, Tuesday, August 20th. This had been fixed at the York meeting of the previous week, and the subject was to have been the arrangements for the winter timetables. Be that as it may, that Tuesday of frustration and disappointment found Cockshott and Welburn in Edinburgh, and with Deuchars presiding, one would dearly have liked to see a verbatim report of the proceedings. The Rev. W. J. Scott writes about 'a hasty gathering', that 'untied the red-tape knots', but he also adds that the times agreed upon were unknown to the authorities at Kings Cross. This cannot have been so, seeing that Cockshott was present when the decisions were taken. A minute from that meeting reads:

'*Acceleration of 8.0 p.m. Down Train from London (Kings Cross) to Aberdeen.*
'Agreed, commencing forthwith, in order to admit of showing an earlier departure from Edinburgh than 2.58 a.m., that G.N., N.E. and N.B.

Companies issue instructions to their staff that the line should be kept clear for *10* minutes on G.N. Line, and *15* minutes on N.E. and N.B. Lines, in advance of the present times of the express; also that the train from Edinburgh to Aberdeen be retimed as follows:

Edinburgh .	.	.	.	*leave*	2.43 a.m.
Dundee	.	.	.	*arr.*	3.48
				leave	3.50
Arbroath .	.	.	.	*pass*	4.9
Kinnaber Jct.	.	.	.	*pass*	4.31
Aberdeen .	.	.	.	*arr.*	5.13

the arrangement being that N.B. Company should run as much before these times as possible.

'*Question as to date of discontinuance of present accelerated arrangement as regards 8.0 p.m. Down Express from London (Kings Cross) to Aberdeen.*

'Agreed to continue up to and including 23rd instant, and that, meantime, instructions for the further continuance of the arrangement, or otherwise, be obtained from the respective General Managers.'

The curtain was thus poised ready to rise at 8 o'clock that very night upon the last phase of the great race.

IX

The Amazing Finish

AFTER thirty-one days of sparring, with the East Coast companies striving to maintain orthodox railway working, the time had come for a final 'show-down'. On the evening of August 20th both sides were now intending to go as hard as they could, regardless of time-tables. Even on such an occasion as this, however, it was hardly possible to bring *all* other traffic to a stop to keep the line clear for the racers, and both sides had working times laid down. Between Kings Cross and Edinburgh the schedule of the previous night remained, with the proviso that the line should be kept clear for 10 minutes ahead on the Great Northern, and 15 minutes ahead on the North Eastern. This envisaged the possibility of arrivals at 11.8 p.m. at York, and 2.40 a.m. in Edinburgh. The train was then booked away at 2.43 with a *schedule time* of 65 minutes to Dundee, and 83 minutes for the final 71 miles on to Aberdeen. The West Coast 'schedule' for the night of August 20th–21st was:

		Time	Booked av. speed m.p.h.
Euston	dep.	8.00 p.m.	58·5
	arr.	10.42	
Crewe . . .	dep.	10.46	63·1
	arr.	1.00 a.m.	
Carlisle . . .	dep.	1.18*	57·3
	arr.	3.55	
Perth . . .	dep.	3.58	55·1
Aberdeen . . .	arr.	5.35	

* L.N.W. booked time of arrival was 1.15 a.m. on 19th/20th.

The Caledonian made no changes in their 'working' times after August 19th, whereas the North Western quickened their 'target' times each night during the final week. It is interesting to see that the Crewe–Carlisle booking was considerably faster than that from Euston to Crewe; this persisted throughout the final week, and while it might be attributed to heavy occupation of the line south of Crewe

105

the bookings over the Northern Division were a resounding tribute to the work of the 6 ft 6 in 'Jumbos'.

At Euston and Kings Cross that night the greatest excitement prevailed. The loads were the same as on the 19th, with Falkinder and engine 668 taking the East Coast train. For the West Coast, *Adriatic* was again the engine, but like all the Webb three-cylinder compounds she was regularly double-manned, and so instead of Peter Clow, his partner, R. Walker, was on the job. At first his running was very fine, as the following log shows:

Miles						Min.	Sec.	Average speed
0·0	Euston	.	.	.	.	0	00	—
31·7	Tring	.	.	.	.	32	20	58·8
46·7	Bletchley	.	.	.	.	45	40	67·5
82·6	Rugby	.	.	.	.	78	45	65·1
97·1	Nuneaton	.	.	.	.	92	30	63·3

Then, however, something appears to have gone amiss with the water pick-up apparatus, for a special stop had to be made for water at Stafford. The time to the stop was 127 minutes for the 133·6 miles from Euston; and despite a precious $3\frac{1}{2}$ minutes standing there the 'flyer' still reached Crewe in $156\frac{1}{4}$ minutes – nearly a minute faster than the unchecked time of the previous night, and 6 minutes ahead of the North Western working time. In the meantime Falkinder had run fairly true to form with the 8 p.m. from Kings Cross. In spite of all incentive to run hard he had taken 106 minutes to reach Grantham, with the disappointingly low average speed of 64 m.p.h. over the very favourable 58·7 miles from Hatfield to Peterborough. Again the Great Northern folks did their best work from Grantham to York, and the train arrived at 11.7 p.m. – eleven minutes in advance of the 'schedule' time.

The fast North Eastern booking of 80 minutes from York to Newcastle seemed to be one of the most difficult of those scheduled in the whole race, on either side. When I use the word 'difficult', however, I am referring to the actual accomplishment of the task rather than of the severity of the duty set to the locomotive. Speed for speed, and route for route, one could hardly compare it with a booking of 63 m.p.h. from Crewe to Carlisle, any more than one could compare a little North Western 'Jumbo' with one of Wilson Worsdell's 'rail crushers'! But on the night of August 20th the North Eastern seem to have made one of their best runs from York to Newcastle, doing the 80·6 miles, unchecked, in $77\frac{1}{2}$ minutes, an average speed of 62·3 m.p.h. Newcastle was reached at $12.29\frac{1}{2}$ a.m., nearly 7 minutes ahead of the previous night's run, and showing an overall average speed of almost 60 m.p.h. from London. The running north of Grantham had been so good that there was then very little in it between the two trains:

	Miles	Minutes
East Coast. Kings Cross-Newcastle. . 268·8	268·8	269½
West Coast. Euston-Shap Summit . . 268·7	268·7	266½

At this approximately half-way point on the two journeys the rivals were running neck-and-neck. The West Coast had a route 16½ miles longer, and three stops ahead of them; on the East Coast the big question was how the North British would respond to the call for 'all-out' working, not only on the footplate but at the stations.

That night, while the East Coast changed engines at Newcastle the North Western train was nearing the conclusion of an exceptionally fast run from Crewe to Carlisle. *Hardwicke* was the engine, with Driver Robinson and Fireman Wolstencroft, and with the usual four-coach load they ran thus:

Miles		Min. Sec.	Av. speed m.p.h.
0·0	Crewe	0 00	—
24·0	Warrington . . .	22 40	63·5
35·8	Wigan	33 00	68·5
50·9	Preston . . .	46 30	67·1
91·0	Oxenholme . . .	85 00	62·4
104·1	Tebay	100 00	52·4
109·6	Shap Summit . .	107 30	44·0
141·0	Carlisle . . .	135 45	66·7

On the target schedule of 134 minutes they had actually *lost* time, but there must have been some wonderful running intermediately, with the phenomenal start-to-pass average speed of 65·6 m.p.h. from Crewe to Preston. One can, indeed, turn back through the pages of this book in amazement and note the change that had come over North Western train running in the seven years from 1888. One can assume that the 78·2 miles from Crewe to passing Carnforth would have been covered in about 73 minutes, which, over a road that is roughly level, in the aggregate may be compared with the North Eastern starts out of York, and with the Great Northern runs through Peterborough.

Continuing to follow the West Coast fortunes that night, engine No. 90, with Baldie Crooks, came on to relieve *Hardwicke* at Carlisle.

No intermediate details are available of the subsequent work, but the 117¾ miles to Stirling were run in exactly 2 hours. Such an average speed at 59 m.p.h. over a route including Beattock summit was undoubtedly very good; but the Caledonian Railway, through the agency of that incomparable 4-2-2 No. 123, had set its own standards of performance, and 59 m.p.h. to Stirling, with continuous downhill running nearly all the way from Carstairs, does not seem very exciting in comparison with 58·8 m.p.h. from Carlisle to Edinburgh, Princes Street, seven years earlier. Nevertheless, on reaching Stirling in the early hours of August 21st, a distance of 416·9 miles from Euston had been covered in 417½ minutes, a feat of long-distance running then unparalleled the world over. For Dunblane bank a pusher was provided, and after a stop of only 1½ minutes at Stirling the train went forward to run the 33 miles on to Perth in 34 minutes and make an overall time of 453 minutes from Euston, 449·9 miles. In the meantime the East Coast had been gradually losing the advantage of their shorter distance. The North Eastern, a little chastened perhaps by the remonstrations following the Portobello incident of the previous night, made a relatively poor run from Newcastle to Edinburgh. It took them 68 minutes to pass Berwick (66·9 miles) and another 63½ minutes for 57·5 miles to Waverley, compared with the hectic 57 minutes 10 seconds of the previous night. So the East Coast express did not reach Edinburgh till 2.42 a.m., and only 13 minutes in advance of the schedule times laid down for August 19th. The aggregate time so far was thus 402 minutes for 393 miles.

This time there was no undue delay in Waverley; in fact, the working, for a station with so shocking a reputation, was almost unbelievably smart. The North Eastern engine and the front brake van were off and the North British engine coupled on and away in *two minutes*. With the North British now so obviously on the tips of their toes it was going to be a tremendous race through Scotland. From the times subsequently published I have prepared the accompanying table to show how the fortunes of the rivals fluctuated as they drew nearer to Kinnaber Junction. At 3 a.m. it would have seemed that the East Coast had an excellent chance of pulling it off; they were 5 miles nearer to the winning post than the Caledonian train, and with some astonishing work over the difficult road through Fife they increased their chances substantially in the next 35 minutes. For at 3.35 a.m. the East Coast train was approaching Leuchars Junction, with only 42½ miles left, while the Caledonian, at that very moment pulling out of Perth, had 51·8 miles to go. True the

North British had to stop in Dundee, and there was that awkward succession of single-line sections to come; but that 9-mile lead would

Time a.m.	East Coast		West Coast	
	Location	Miles to Kinnaber	Location	Miles to Kinnaber
3.0	Inverkeithing	79·3	Leaving Stirling	84·3
3.20	Markinch	59·2	Auchterarder	65·5
3.35	Approaching Leuchars	42·6	Leaving Perth	51·8
3.45	Standing in Dundee	33·3	1½ miles north of Stanley	43·1
3.50	Stannergate	30·8	1 mile south of Coupar Angus	37·0
4.5	Arbroath	16·3	Forfar	19·3
4.21	Mile south of Montrose	3·6	Dubton Junc.	1·2

take some pulling down, and when to this was added a truly light-ning stop in Dundee, with the train away in no more than 1½ minutes, it seemed as though the East Coast were turning a good chance into a near-certainty. At 3.50 a.m. they had made their last stop, and passing Stannergate were out in full cry for Kinnaber, with 30·8 miles to go. The Caledonian flyer was then a mile south of Coupar Angus, doing well over 70 m.p.h. on the level, and 37 miles from the junction.

Although at that moment in the race the two trains were 30¾ and 37 miles from Kinnaber, the advantage in distance was still more heavily on the East Coast side. The critical point was not Kinnaber itself, but Montrose on the one route and Dubton Junction on the other. It was from those signal boxes that the 'Train entering section' signal would be sent to Kinnaber, and whichever was first in ringing would get the road. And at 3.50 a.m. the distances of the trains to those critical points were 28·2 and 35·8 miles respectively. In these days of telephones, wireless, and television it is sometimes hard to imagine the slowness of communication and the publishing of news sixty years ago. As those two trains raced towards Kinnaber no one in high authority knew for certain where they were: how one was gaining, the other falling behind, and the only means of convey-ing news quickly was by telegraph. It had been a night of ups and downs for the East Coast. The high promise shown by the run-ning south of Newcastle had faded somewhat with that leisurely run from Newcastle to Edinburgh, 124·4 miles in 131½ minutes. But then hopes had soared again, with that terrific run through Fife, bringing the Edinburgh–Dundee record down to 60½ minutes, and setting the train away on its 'last leg' in such triumphant style.

One of the most marked features of the running of most of the locomotives engaged in the race of 1895 was that the fast level stretches were for the most part covered at no more than moderate speed. And here, along the Angus coast on a superb piece of straight, level road, the North British disappointed their supporters. The going was no faster than that of the previous night, and while the train rolled pleasantly along at little more than 60 m.p.h. John Soutar, with the Lambie 4-4-0 No. 17, was tearing up the equally level and straight miles between Coupar Angus and Forfar at nearer 75 than 70 m.p.h. Before the North British train had even entered upon the single-line sections the gap between it and Caledonian had narrowed ominously, and at 4.5 a.m., while one train was slowing through Arbroath in the same minute as the other was slowing through Forfar, the distance between them was no more than 3 miles. Once through Arbroath the North British driver did some grand work, pounding his engine in terrific uphill accelerations after each tablet slack; and then after Lunan Bay the excitement on board that train reached fever heat. Down the bank they swept, but their energy had come too late! At four in the morning there was enough daylight to see across country, and there, clear enough on the far side of the Montrose basin, was the steam of another train – a train going north, and running very fast indeed.

The Caledonian was first, if by no more than a minute, and passed Kinnaber Junction at 4.22 a.m. The North British, slacking through Montrose, and then pounding up the heavy grade to Hillside, passed through at 4.26 a.m. At the most critical points of all, Dubton on the one hand and Montrose on the other, the passing times were 4.21 and 4.22 a.m. respectively. The West Coast train went on triumphantly to cover the last 37·9 miles to Aberdeen ticket platform in the very fast time of 33¾ minutes, while the final arrival at 4.58 a.m. set up a new London–Aberdeen record. After their disappointment at Kinnaber the East Coast eased down; there was no point in hurrying further and they came into Aberdeen at 5.11 a.m. As regards the race itself, the running between London and Kinnaber is summarized in the accompanying table:

	East Coast	West Coast
Distance from London (miles) .	485·7	501·7
Total time including stops (min.) .	506	502
Average speed (m.p.h.) . .	57·8	59·9
Total running time (min.) . .	493	489
Average running speed (m.p.h.) .	59·2	61·5

It was again an outright win for the West Coast, despite the un-premeditated stop at Stafford; but if the North British driver had shown more energy between Dundee and Arbroath he would have turned the scale.

Later that morning Conacher wired Sir Henry Oakley:

'I again urge your lightening the train from Kings Cross. There is too much room in the train as now made up and if lightened as I suggest we might get to Kinnaber first and so keep ahead. West Coast train to Aberdeen this morning consisted of only two carriages and a fish truck attached to steady it.

'Reply.

CONACHER.'

The West Coast had carried their usual load of four bogies to Perth, and the reduction had taken place there. The official record gives the load as 'equal to $4\frac{1}{2}$' after Perth, but the East Coast load had also been reduced over the Scottish portion of the journey by the detaching of the front brake van at Edinburgh.

Much else transpired that day, no doubt, but at 4.17 p.m. a laconic telegram was sent to Edinburgh:

'To Conacher:

'Traffic by eight o'clock shall be carefully watched and load reduced wherever practicable.

OAKLEY.'

There is no doubt, however, that all concerned on the East Coast braced themselves for a supreme effort on the night of August 21st. They had come so near to a triumph on the previous night that nothing less was to be expected, while on the West Coast route the fact that they had only just scraped home in making their fastest run so far, showed them clearly the calibre of the opposition that they had at last aroused. As the speeds increased night by night, many of the leading newspapers in the country stationed reporters at the engine-changing stations; messages were telegraphed from Crewe, Carlisle, York, and Newcastle, and while as late in the race as August 19th, the Rev. W. J. Scott could write of Newcastle Central as deserted, except for officials, that very week was not far gone before the crowds were gathering in the middle of the night to see the train through.

The *Standard* had an interesting piece on August 22nd:

'There was again a fierce contest on the East and West Coast Routes yesterday morning in the great railway race to the North. Both trains started punctually at eight o'clock on Tuesday night from Euston and Kings Cross, and some splendid running on both routes was accomplished. The West Coast train, however, gained the day, steaming into Aberdeen Station at 4.58 yesterday morning, the journey of 540 miles having been accomplished in 8 hours 58 minutes. Several spurts were run at 64 miles an hour. The East Coast train did not arrive until 5.11 which, however, beats all previous records on this route by 21 minutes. Both trains were well filled with passengers. It will be seen that the West Coast train covered the entire distance at the rate of 60 miles an hour with two minutes to spare.'

After some further details of the trains themselves this newspaper concluded:

'With regard to the complaint that such rapid travelling produces a sensation of nausea, it may be mentioned that the officials at Euston have received from a passenger who travelled by Tuesday night's train a telegram saying that the progress of the train was so smooth and comfortable that the passengers could hardly realize the fact that they were travelling at a higher rate of speed than by ordinary train.'

On August 21st the North Western did not materially improve on their running of the night before. Peter Clow had the *Adriatic*, but he reached Crewe in only a minute less than his partner had taken on the previous night, when the stop for water had to be made at Stafford. Then W. J. Phillips came on with No. 1213, *The Queen*, and ran the 141 miles from Crewe to Carlisle in 135 minutes. *The Yorkshire Post* reported:

'The Express reached Carlisle at 12.53 a.m., or the same time as the morning before. The Caledonian engine No. 78 was hitched on in a big hurry, and the train left Carlisle for Perth at 12.56, amid the cheers of a large crowd who had assembled to have a look at the fast express.'

This was Tom Robinson's greatest night with No. 78. He ran the 117·8 miles to Stirling in the magnificent time of 114 minutes and the overall time from Euston that night, 410 minutes for the 416·9 miles, is without much doubt the fastest start-to-stop journey ever made by train between London and that ancient Scottish burgh. After a stop of 2 minutes the run of 33 miles on to Perth was made in 34 minutes as on the previous night, and Perth was thus reached earlier than ever before, at 3.26 a.m.

In the meantime the East Coast train had also produced its fastest time, so far, between Kings Cross and Newcastle. The Great

Right: No. 1683
Sisyphus.
[Locomotive Publishing Co

FAMOUS
'JUMBOS' OF
THE 1895 RACE

Below: No. 790
Hardwicke photo-
graphed at Crewe,
with Driver Robin-
son and Fireman
Wolstencroft, after
the record run of
August 22nd.
[British Railways

No. 262, which hauled the racing train on the final run from Dundee to Aberdeen.

NORTH BRITISH
4-4-0s

No. 218 of the same class. Note the very poor coal on the tender.

[*Locomotive Publishing Co*

Drummond 4-4-0 No. 90, used from Carlisle to Perth.

CALEDONIAN RAILWAY: ENGINES OF THE WEST COAST RECORD OF 1895

Lambie 4-4-0 No. 17, used from Perth to Aberdeen.

[Locomotive Publishing Co

Francis P. Cockshott,
Superintendent of the Line, G.N.R.

James Conacher,
General Manager, N.B.R.

EAST COAST PERSONALITIES

David Deuchars, Superintendent
of the Line, N.B.R.

Vincent L. Raven, Locomotive
Running Superintendent, N.E.R.

[*Courtesy: "The Railway Magazine"*]

Northern clipped another 6 minutes off the London–York run, with average speeds of 62·7 m.p.h. from Kings Cross to Grantham, and a very fine 65·3 m.p.h. by No. 775 from Grantham to York. Even so the Great Northern did not seem to have reduced the art of engine-changing to such a lightning process as their northern partners had done, and they took the full 4 minutes at Grantham and another 4 minutes to hand over to the North Eastern at York. Nevertheless, to run from London to York in 3 hours 1 minute inclusive of the Grantham stop was no mean achievement. Then the 'M' class 4-4-0 No. 1621 came on, with Driver Turner and Fireman Hodgson in charge, but the running on so momentous an occasion cannot be described as other than pedestrian. They passed Thirsk, 22·2 miles, in 22½ minutes; speed averaged 66 m.p.h. onwards to Darlington, but by Durham there had been a falling off, and the 66·1 miles from York to that point took 66½ minutes. As usual, however, there were some very fast travelling down the Team Valley and a hair-raising run past Gateshead and on to the High Level Bridge. In after years the fireman, Elijah Hodgson, always averred that they had to repeat this sensational act night after night during the race in order to impress their mates at the shed! Thus they contrived to run the last 14½ miles in 12 minutes pass to stop. But the outcome of their leisurely running from York to Durham was that little more than a minute had been gained on the 80-minute schedule, and the arrival in Newcastle at 12.24 a.m. was only about 5 minutes better than that of the previous night.

So far, there had been nothing in the actual running to indicate the very earnest attempt being made that night to lower the West Coast colours. The Great Northern had continued their process of steady improvement; they had reduced the time over the 27 miles from Hitchin to Huntingdon from 23½ minutes on August 19th to 22½ minutes and had run from Peterborough up to Stoke Box in 24 minutes against 25½ minutes two days earlier. Again in making the excellent run of 76 minutes from Grantham to York the improvement on the work of August 19th was one of steady stage-by-stage reductions in the times, *viz*:

Miles		August 19th min.	August 21st min.
0·0	Grantham . . .	0	0
14·6	Newark . . .	14¾	14
33·1	Retford . . .	32	30½
50·5	Doncaster . . .	47¾	46
68·9	Selby . . .	64¾	62
82·7	York. . . .	79½	76

Then at Newcastle Bob Nicholson came on, with the 'M' class engine No. 1620, and according to one newspaper story:

'The smartness displayed in the changing process was heartily cheered by the crowds gathered on the platform. Robert Nicholson relieved George Turner by taking over the duties of driver. Amid enthusiastic cheering and waving of handkerchiefs the next stage of the journey was resumed.'

It was soon evident that a phenomenal change had come over the character of the running. No longer was there a staid, dignified acceleration over the previous best; the train was not 20 miles out of Newcastle before it was clear they were in for a piece of stark, undisguised 'hell-for-leather' racing. Of Bob Nicholson it was said that he was safer on the ground than on a locomotive footplate, and the way he took the curves at Morpeth and Alnmouth Junction that night would seem to bear it out! Alnmouth, 34·8 miles, was passed in 33½ minutes; Belford, 51·6 miles, in 48 minutes, and despite the lateness of the hour a crowd had gathered at Berwick to see the flyer come through. At the time there was a speed restriction right down to 5 m.p.h. through the old station, but when that excited throng saw the train come tearing round the curve from Tweedmouth and up over the Royal Border Bridge they scattered for their lives.

Nicholson was through Berwick in exactly 1 hour from Newcastle, 66·9 miles, and he pressed on up the long bank to Grantshouse and thence down to the sea at Cockburnspath in such style as to average over 60 m.p.h. from Berwick to Dunbar. Then over the final stretch, along the Lothian coast, he ran to such purpose as to yield the highest point-to-point average speeds of the whole race, including 74 m.p.h. over the 12·8 miles from Drem to Portobello, and a flying average of 78·8 from Drem to Longniddry; and although there were no Macdonald, no Scott, no Rous-Marten to enjoy it, the passage through Portobello must have been almost as fast as on the memorable run of two nights earlier. So the amazing time of 113 minutes, start to stop, was made over the 124·4 miles from Newcastle to Edinburgh. This showed an average speed of 66·2 m.p.h., but more important still, it was faster by *eighteen minutes* than the run of the previous night, and brought the train into Edinburgh at an unprecedented time of 2.19 a.m., and at an overall average speed of 62·2 m.p.h. from Kings Cross. The North British were able to get away at 2.21 a.m., twenty-three minutes earlier than on the previous night. Thanks to Nicholson, his fireman Tom Blades, and the N.E.R. engine 1620, the East Coast had the job practically in the bag. The

North British, with engine 293 to Dundee, and 262 from there onwards, improved fractionally on their previous best, taking $101\frac{1}{2}$
minutes for the $92\frac{1}{2}$ miles to Kinnaber, against 102 minutes, and so
passed the junction at $4.2\frac{1}{2}$ a.m. The West Coast train was not away
from Perth until 3.30 a.m. and although John Soutar ran in his best
style he did not pass Kinnaber until 4.17 a.m.

The night's running was a great triumph for the East Coast
companies; for although Nicholson and Blades stole most of the
limelight and made by far the biggest cut in time over the previous
record, the North British men made an outstanding contribution in
repeating their very fast work between Edinburgh and Dundee, and
their exceptionally smart performance between Arbroath and Kinnaber. A little hesitance, a little reluctance to run right up to the
limit round curves, and over junctions, and ten minutes might
easily have been lost; but in actual fact the running between Edinburgh and Dundee was faster than ever, in 59 minutes start to stop.
The train was at the Aberdeen ticket platform at 4.38 a.m. and
arrived in the station at 4.40 a.m. – 523·5 miles in 520 minutes. That
morning the West Coast train also made its fastest run to date,
arriving at 4.54 a.m., in 534 minutes for the 539·8 miles from Euston.
The average speeds by both trains were thus almost exactly the same,
both over 60 m.p.h., and the margin of superiority registered by the
East Coast reflected their advantage in distance.

The sparks were scarcely down that morning before intense
diplomatic activity began between the respective East Coast
managements. Conacher was in Aberdeen, Sir Henry Oakley at
Kings Cross, and George S. Gibb was on holiday, staying at the new
Highland Railway Hotel at Dornoch, Sutherlandshire. It was
Conacher who set the ball rolling. No later than 9 a.m. he wired Sir
Henry Oakley:

'After this morning's achievement I think we ought tonight to revert
to advertised time, making another effort later on if West Coast do better.
There is a feeling here that rivalry has gone far enough already and I
think we might rest on the position gained unless again challenged when
we can choose our own time for another effort. Have wired Gibb also.
Shall be here all day.

CONACHER.'

One can scarcely realize today how cumbersome the means of
communication were at that time, and how difficult it was to gather
such a concensus of opinion that would enable a quick decision to be
made. Apparently, also, neither of his fellow General Managers

appreciated from his first telegrams that Conacher was in Aberdeen, for their replies were sent to the North British headquarters offices in Edinburgh, and fresh telegrams had to be sent forward to Aberdeen. These were not despatched until past noon, and the first reactions were against Conacher's evident desire to stop. The two telegrams, as received in Aberdeen, read:

'Oakley wires I think we ought to continue to shew our friends the hopelessness of their effort. Stopping now would be commented on. Please reply.'

'Gibb wires from Dornoch Having made record this morning my opinion in favour of confining racing to this week. Best policy to be able to prove that except this week we have worked our trains not as racers but under ordinary traffic conditions.'

But Conacher persisted in his view, and almost at once he wired back to Sir Henry Oakley:

'You were repeated from Edinburgh. There are so many chances against our repeating last night's performance tonight and tomorrow night, especially as everything depends on reaching Kinnaber first, that I hesitate to risk spoiling it. If however you think otherwise I agree, but if you can do even better it ought to be done as West Coast will be sure to make great efforts tonight.

CONACHER.'

It is difficult to see what Conacher was getting at here; the North British locomotives had done most consistent work since the final acceleration, and the real question was surely whether the North Eastern could repeat their astounding performance of August 22nd. In the meantime, however, there had evidently been some telegrams exchanged between Gibb and Sir Henry Oakley, while Oakley had been in touch with his Chairman and other Great Northern directors; at 1.50 p.m. a further telegram, in a changed tone, was sent off from London:

'To Conacher, Palace Hotel, Aberdeen.
'Gibb suggests we continue this week. Have told you propose ceasing tonight. Feeling of directors here that we should cease having shewn what we can do. Reply now.

OAKLEY.'

Conacher and the Great Northern directors had turned the scale, and at 2.50 p.m., in evident satisfaction Conacher wired back:

'Your second telegram received. Am glad your directors agree to view expressed in my first telegram. I think it the safest course and most dignified. Wire here whether it is the 6.25 arrival going back to and I will instruct our people. Details can be settled by Superintendents.

CONACHER.'

Gibb also approved, and so in this series of telegrams was brought to an end the greatest contest in speed that the world had then seen. It was some little time before the news leaked out. As each stage of the race, up to that time, had not been completed until around 5 a.m. the public had to wait for news until the following morning. This is how the *Yorkshire Post* of August 23rd presented the story of the great East Coast triumph:

THE GREAT RACE TO SCOTLAND

'The rivalry of the East and West Coast Railway Companies which has become keener day by day, culminated yesterday morning, after arousing an extraordinary amount of interest throughout England and Scotland in the struggle of supremacy. Neither of the competing groups of companies show the least disposition to yield the palm to its rival, and the breaking of records on one route only strengthens the determination of the officials on the other to eclipse all previous achievements. On Tuesday the victory was won by the West Coast companies (the London & North Western and Caledonian), who beat the world's record. Yesterday morning it was the turn of the East Coast companies (the Great Northern, North Eastern, and North British) to bear off the laurels, and to create yet another record. The officials of the latter companies braced themselves up for a gigantic effort on Wednesday night, and gave the word that the journey was to be done in the shortest time possible. Even the most sanguine official, however, scarcely believed that the time occupied on the previous night by the West Coast express – 8 hours and 58 minutes – would be much improved upon. But so well did the drivers acquit themselves, and so expeditiously was the exchange of engines performed, that all expectations were exceeded, and the East Coast train steamed into Aberdeen Station at 20 minutes to five yesterday morning, only 8 hours and 40 minutes from leaving Kings Cross. As will be seen from the official record supplied by the North Eastern Railway Company, some parts of the journey had been run at the rate of 66 miles an hour, and the whole distance was accomplished at the speed of more than a mile a minute, the figures being 523 miles in 520 minutes.

'So far as speed is concerned the West Coast companies were no whit behind, but if anything a fraction in advance of their opponents. The whole distance of 540 miles was accomplished in 535 minutes, but the train reached Aberdeen at 4.55, 15 minutes later than the East Coast. The train ran from Euston to Crewe without a stop, six minutes less than three hours sufficing to cover the distance of 158 miles. Spurts of even greater swiftness are said to have been made by the West Coast express on the previous evening, the velocity frequently exceeding 70 miles an hour in the plains of South West Lancashire, and the performance up to that point is declared to have been the greatest triumph in railway running that has yet been accomplished. One of the drivers stated that it was possible for even this speed to be augmented. "Given a clear course" he said, "we can run 80 miles an hour with safety." Whether that can be done remains to be seen, but as will appear later, the London & North Western Company determined to make another great effort to regain the championship.'

On the afternoon of August 22nd, Sir Henry Oakley wrote to Conacher, confirming the decisions taken in such haste by telegram earlier that day.

'Dear Sir,
   'With reference to your telegrams today, I have obtained the authority of my Directors to revert to the advertised time of 6.25, and have instructed Mr Alexander accordingly. I received a telegram from York that the Chairman of the North Eastern wished the published times to be adhered. In the face of such a concensus of opinion, I of course waive my own predilections, which I must confess would have been to have held on until the West Coast abandoned their senseless practice of running a train of 3 or 4 carriages.
   'The speed at which we ran last night was not higher than we run daily with our expresses from Yorkshire and Manchester, the only difference being that the lightening of the train to 6 carriages enabled us to run uphill almost as fast as we could run down. I did not, and do not, feel that there was any risk in the performance. However, as the decision is come to, it shall be loyally carried out.
                                             'Yours faithfully,
                                             (*Signed*) H. OAKLEY.'
'J. Conacher, Esq.,
Palace Hotel, Aberdeen.'

Maybe there was no risk on the Great Northern, but on the North British, running between Edinburgh and Dundee in 'even time', it was another matter altogether. When Conacher wired 'There is a feeling here that rivalry has gone far enough' he was expressing a view that would be echoed by all present-day students of locomotive performances who know that exceedingly difficult road. Naturally there was great disappointment at the East Coast decision, and one of the London newspapers had this comment next morning:

THE EAST COAST SUSPEND THE RACE

'There was a considerable crowd present at Kings Cross last night to witness the departure of the Scotch express which had accomplished the sensational feat of covering 527 miles in 520 minutes, but the interest was somewhat modified when it became known that no attempt to break the record would be made that night by the Great Northern Railway, that company having decided to revert to the scheduled times of running. There was nevertheless much curiosity envinced in the despatch of the train, and the officials and passengers were somewhat hampered by the large crowd that swarmed the platform. The train consisted of twelve carriages, being three in excess of the number that formed the train on the preceding night. The fact that there was to be no more racing seemed to receive general approval, although one young gentleman who had specially booked by this route in the expectation of an exciting journey was loud in his expression of disappointment. The train started punctually to time, and is due in Aberdeen at 6.20 a.m.'

At Euston, however, nothing was farther from the thoughts of Authority than suspension. The East Coast might have called it off, but the North Western and Caledonian were determined to wipe out that single, isolated defeat, and again I quote from *The Yorkshire Post*:

'Euston Station was the scene of much excitement about eight o'clock last night, a considerable number of spectators having arrived to give the West Coast train a "send off". The officials were determined if possible to wipe out the defeat sustained on the previous night, when their rivals won by 15 minutes. The train consisted of three large bogie carriages, which were fairly well filled with passengers, some of whom were visibly suffering from suppressed excitement, as though on the eve of doing great things. The driver of the train had received instructions to make the best time possible, and one facetious youth who was seeing a party of friends off seized upon it as the basis for some lugubrious predictions, and earnest appeal to take insurance tickets. As the clock indicated the hour of departure the whistle was blown, and the Aberdeen express steamed out of the station amid a chorus of hearty wishes for a safe and speedy journey.'

And what a start! *Adriatic* was again the engine, and C. J. Alcock has told me of the amazing sight she made from the old L.N.W.R. station at Chalk Farm. A thunderstorm of terrifying intensity was raging over London, one of the worst Alcock remembers in his long life of eighty years; the torrential rain, the showers of sparks from the engine, the flashes of lightning that lit up that gleaming black compound and her three coaches as she came blazing up Camden bank set a note of high drama as the 'flyer' swept by, and plunged into Primrose Hill tunnel. *The Yorkshire Post* had correspondents stationed at both Crewe and Carlisle, and next morning, under prominent headlines, wrote of 'A Sensational Achievement by the West Coast Express.' The article continued:

'Our Crewe Correspondent telegraphed late last night: The West Coast express beat the record between London and Crewe. Stafford was passed at 10.3 and Crewe – a distance of 158¼ miles – was reached at 10.28, being a mile a minute and ten miles to spare. There was a large crowd at Crewe station. After a stoppage of two minutes for a change of engine the express left for Carlisle in charge of driver Robinson.

'Our Carlisle correspondent telegraphed at one o'clock this morning: To regain the supremacy in the race which was snatched from them by their rivals the West Coast Companies had to reach the critical junction at Kinnaber seventeen and a half minutes earlier than they did on the previous morning, and this necessitated a saving of nine and a half minutes on the North-Western system, and of eight minutes on the Caledonian system. Word was sent to the officials at Carlisle to expect the express at a quarter to one, or nine minutes ahead of its arrival last night, but it actually arrived at 12.35½, the full distance of 300 miles being thus traversed in 275½ minutes. Preston was passed at 11.16, Lancaster at 11.35, and Tebay at 12.4¼. The engines were changed at Carlisle in 2½ minutes and at 12.38 the express was drawn out of the station by the Caledonian locomotive No. 90 amid the hearty cheers of a considerable crowd on the platform.'

From Euston to Crewe the going had indeed been good, with an average speed of 64 m.p.h. from start to stop, but once again when that wonderful trio, Driver Robinson, Fireman Wolstencroft and *Hardwicke* got going, north of Crewe, *The Yorkshire Post* was not exaggerating when it described the results as sensational. To Preston the running was not notably faster than that of two nights before, with a time of 45¾ minutes for the 51 miles, against 46¼ minutes. But then Ben Robinson began to pile it on. Oxenholme, 91 miles, was passed in 81¾ minutes; the average speed was held at over 60 m.p.h. right up to Tebay, and the last 5½ miles to Shap Summit were covered in 6 minutes. And then the descent to Carlisle! With average speeds of 73·7 m.p.h. from Summit to Penrith, and of 74·1 m.p.h. from Penrith to the dead stop in Carlisle, that descent must have been one of the most terrific episodes in the whole race, on either side. One can only guess at the maximum speeds attained, but I will only say here that on a recent run with the 'Midday Scot', a particularly fast one, we ran continuously at 82 to 86 m.p.h. from Calthwaite to the point of slowing for Carlisle, and we took 14¾ minutes in from Penrith against the 14½ minutes of *Hardwicke*!

On the Caledonian line Crooks made a good, though at first sight not an exceptional run to Perth. For the first time the stop at Stirling was omitted, and the fact that a non-stop run as long as 150 miles was being attempted without taking water may have compelled the driver to nurse his engine in the early stages. Carstairs, 73·5 miles, was passed in 74 minutes and Stirling in 116½ minutes – 2½ minutes slower than the time made by Tom Robinson with No. 78 on the previous night, when the load was one coach heavier. By not stopping at Stirling, however, time was saved, and after a run from Carlisle in almost exactly even time Perth was reached at 3.7½ a.m. – 449·9 miles from Euston in the extraordinary time of 427½ minutes. The average speed from the start was 63 m.p.h. and the arrival time 20 minutes earlier than ever before. The stop lasted only 2 minutes and at 3.9½ a.m. John Soutar was away, with the Lambie 4-4-0 No. 17, and he went on to make one of the fastest start-to-stop runs in the whole race, covering the 89·7 miles to the Aberdeen ticket platform in 80½ minutes. Two minutes later the train was in Aberdeen itself, at 4.32 a.m. The 540 miles had thus been covered in the almost incredible time of 512 minutes. The arrival in Aberdeen was made the occasion of an extraordinary demonstration of enthusiasm. *The Sketch* wrote:

'Driver Soutar, who has all along been in charge of this engine, is the railway hero of the moment. Soutar, who is nearly sixty-one, joined the service as a fireman forty-four years ago. He has conveyed the Queen to the North on many occasions with this very engine. There was much excitement at Aberdeen on the great day, the train being waited for by a crowd of spectators. Soutar and his stoker were borne shoulder-high and presented with a couple of blue ribbons. A unique result of the race was that letters which left London by the eight o'clock evening train were sent out in Aberdeen by the first morning delivery.'

And at that astonishing average speed of 63·3 m.p.h. made sixty-three years ago the London–Aberdeen record still stands today.

X

The Aftermath

THE news from Aberdeen on the morning of Friday, August 23rd, must have come as a bombshell to the East Coast managements. When on the previous morning Conacher had urged the cessation of racing he had hinted that the West Coast would almost certainly make great efforts to surpass the East Coast record, but one rather gathers that having established a superiority in minutes equal to their shorter mileage the East Coast authorities felt reasonably secure that, however much the North Western and the Caledonian might try, they would not surpass the time of 8 hours 40 minutes. Perhaps they had been misled by the relatively small improvement in the West Coast times on the Wednesday night as compared with the Tuesday; even the Rev. W. J. Scott was moved to write that: 'It looked now as if the Western allies had almost reached their "possible", for on Wednesday the London & North Western with no pull up at Stafford lost time to Crewe, and were not earlier than before into Carlisle...' Consequently a cut of no less than 23 minutes from their previous best time cannot have come as other than a surprise and a shock. The week-end gave all concerned time for reflection, and Conacher, who had been so eager to give up on the previous Thursday, wrote to Sir Henry Oakley on the Monday morning in quite a different strain. The West Coast record had put a totally different complexion on matters:

Edinburgh
26th August, 1895

'Sir Henry Oakley
Great Northern Railway
Kings Cross
London N.

'My dear Sir Henry,

'I duly received your letter of 22nd inst., the views contained in which are I observe modified by your telegram of the following day. Although I share to the full your opinion regarding the childishness of the whole business, I think we must guard ourselves against an improper use being hereafter made of the West Coast achievement on the night of the 22nd inst., and I am quite prepared to run another train as much like theirs as possible, when I have no doubt we could again shew our superiority.

'I have been comparing their run with ours as described in the newspapers with a view to seeing exactly how they were able to run 17 miles in eight minutes less time, and have put the comparison on the form of the Table annexed. Their advantage, you will see, divides itself into three heads, viz. (1) Lighter load, (2) Fewer stops, and (3) High speed in certain stages of the journey. We could also have a lighter load at this season of the year, but I do not know whether we could also reduce the stops to three. Mr Holmes tells me he might possibly be able to run the 130 miles from Edinburgh to Aberdeen without a stop if the train consisted of three ordinary carriages only, but adds that it would be "risky seeing such high speed has to be maintained". If the Grantham stop were omitted the run would be 105 miles, or 38 more than the longest run on the West Coast route without taking water, and it is for you to say whether your tenders can carry enough water for a run of that length, even if they might for other reasons be allowed to make as long a run. If both stops could be omitted four minutes' standing time at Grantham and Dundee would be saved, with I suppose, another six now lost in stopping and starting, or ten in all. As regards speed, the table shews that you and the North Eastern both run faster in your second laps than your first, and I see no reason why the average speed of 65 miles per hour could not be maintained in them as well as in the second stages, which would save the following times:

London to Grantham at 65 m.p.h. 97 minutes instead of 101 = 4 diff.
York to Newcastle at 65 m.p.h. 74 minutes instead of 79　　= 5 ,,
　　　　　　　　　　　　　　　　　　　　　　　　　　　　 —
　　　　　　　　　　　　　　　　　　　　　　　　　　　　 9
　　　　　　　　　　　　　　　　　　　　　　　　　　　　 —

If to this were added 4 minutes, which it is possible we might save north of Edinburgh, the journey on the 21st having taken 1 minute more than on a previous occasion we should gain a total of 13 minutes.

'The deduction of these 13 minutes from our run of last Wednesday would give our arrival at 4.27 without taking into account the effect of lightening the load. We ought therefore to be able to make the run easily in 8 hours 25 minutes, or 7 minutes less than our friends' "record", leaving for explanation the fact that the omission of our two extra stops necessary to place the two trains on an equality accounts for some ten minutes of our time, the 10 and 7 minutes together representing almost exactly the 17 miles by which our route is shorter than theirs.

'I think we ought to do it unless some strong reason can be urged to the contrary, choosing a night soon when the traffic is likely to be light.

'Yours faithfully,

(*Signed*) J. CONACHER.'

EAST COAST RUN, 21ST AUGUST, 1895
(VEHICLES 6½ OR 101 TONS)

		Miles	Minutes Running	Minutes Stations	Running speed per hour
101 tons	London to Grantham	105	101	2	62½
	Grantham to York	83	77	3	65
	York to Newcastle	80	79	2	61
	Newcastle to Edinburgh	125	115	2	60
56 tons	Edinburgh to Dundee	59	57	2	60
	Dundee to Aberdeen	71	78		54½
		523	509	11	
			520		

WEST COAST RUN 22ND AUGUST, 1895
(VEHICLES 4 OR 72 TONS 10 CWTS)

	Miles	Minutes Running	Minutes Stations	Running speed per hour
London to Crewe	158	148	2	64
Crewe to Carlisle	142	126	2	67½
Carlisle to Perth	150	150	2	60
Perth to Aberdeen	90	82		66
	540	506	6	
		512		

It is certainly easy to follow his reasoning, as to how a faster run might be made by omitting stops, to counteract the advantage from water troughs enjoyed by the London & North Western. But Sir Henry Oakley would not agree to any resumption of racing. On August 28th he wrote to Conacher:

'My dear Sir,

'On my return from Dublin I find your letter of the 26th inst. on the subject of the Scotch arrangements.

'I have had the opportunity of conferring with my Chairman, who has given the gravest consideration to the question. He is strongly averse to any renewal of the racing. I think his opinion coincides with mine expressed in my letter of the 22nd inst. He would not so summarily have put a stop to the competition in speed, but as it has been carried out, he will not revert to the practice.

'We think here, if we were to begin again, the North Western must necessarily follow, and then the competition in speed must be fought out to the bitter end.

'I am much interested in the analysis you have made of the running but I think we must not avoid the conclusion that if we have to race again we must not only reduce the number of stops but lighten the train and run faster.

'I am not much concerned by the empty honour won by the North Western as the fact of their reducing the weight of their train is a practical confession that on equal terms they would be unable to compete with us.

'Our view is strongly that we should continue our present times of running so as to put a steady pressure on the West Coast which they can only sustain at increased cost and for very poor results, while we can practically run an ordinary train, and carry the bulk of the people.

'In general talk here, because people will talk, I invariably reply that we are quite satisfied with our present times, that the North Western advertise 7.0 a.m. and run as near to our time as they can, and that we should adhere to our published timetable.

'Yours faithfully,

(*Signed*) H. OAKLEY.'

'J. Conacher, Esq.,
Edinburgh.'

Apparently Conacher, now that racing had ceased, was anxious to make a treaty with the West Coast, for before Sir Henry Oakley had replied to the Edinburgh letter of August 26th he had wired to secure further consultations. But on his return from Dublin, on the same day that he wrote regarding the resumption of racing, Sir Henry also wrote privately to Conacher:

'My dear Sir,

'ABERDEEN

'Referring to your wire which arrived when I was absent in Dublin, I am *not* disposed to recommend any arrangement with either N.W. or Caledonian. They began and they should finish first.

'My strong conviction is that we should continue to run the 6.25 and use our best efforts to ensure punctuality. The West already feel the pressure. Last night they were behind us, as they must be, if they are to run ordinary trains. When they shew a disposition to retreat I should listen and fix the time of arrival with due regard to our more favourable distance. But I would rather not agree at all.

'Their action has released us from any obligation to run on the same time to Edinburgh, and I should like to let them see more fully the consequence of their hasty action.

'I cannot forget their "try on" at Perth, they may attempt that again or some other plan to outwit us, and only a stern resolve to shew them always that we are neither to be cajoled, nor outrun, will keep them quick.

'I suggest therefore that we propose nothing and agree to nothing, let them do as they please and we will exercise the same privilege.

'Touching Edinburgh, do you know, or can you ascertain, what proportion of London traffic they carry, comparing their share before the last race with what they have now.

'I should very much like to know. The information would help a decision. If they have gained by the concession then made it should be a warning to us. But if they have not succeeded in wresting any of our traffic, we might treat them as harmless, though restive children.

'However, at present I prefer to hold on, shew no symptom of wavering and leave them to their own devices.

'Yours very faithfully,

(*Signed*) H. OAKLEY.'

'J. Conacher, Esq.,
Edinburgh.'

With Sir Henry's homely comments about the august managements of the North Western and Caledonian Railways we leave the official correspondence on the race. There can be no doubt that all operating men were glad to see it at an end. Neele retired at the end of July, and in his reminiscences there is more than a suggestion that he was glad to be out of it:

'Now' [he writes] 'there was really nothing gained by the arrival at 6.25 or 6.30 in Aberdeen. The hotels were not open for their regular work; the discomfort of unprepared breakfast tables, or the accompaniment of dusting damsels in the coffee room, were travellers' annoyances rather than conveniences. The hour earlier into Aberdeen was a drawback rather than a benefit. However, after the end of July it ceased to be any part of my duty, and fell to the lot of my successor, to watch the daily morning reports showing how we had kept our time at Carlisle; how our allies had done their work to Aberdeen and whether our rivals had kept ahead of us or whether we had scored a success.'

Even after the conclusion of the race, however, the North Western had one more shot in its locker, which it duly fired off on Sunday, September 1st. Having made the fastest run ever recorded over such a distance as 299 miles, on the night of August 22nd, when the Aberdeen 'flyer' reached Carlisle at 12.35 a.m., at an average speed of 65·3 m.p.h., they then proceeeed to show that the North Western,

alone among the railways of the world, could run the same distance
non-stop! This run was made with a special train, weighing 151 tons,
leaving Euston at 8.45 a.m. The engine selected was a three-cylinder
compound, No. 1305 *Ionic*, and C. J. Alcock, who saw the train leave
Euston, has told me how astonished he was to see special wire sup-
ports erected on the tender so that the coal could be stacked much
higher than usual. The *Ionic* was manned by the famous crew of
Hardwicke's final racing run, Driver B. Robinson, and Fireman
Wolstenholme. The non-stop run was successfully made at an average
speed of 51 m.p.h., bringing the train into Carlisle at 2.38 p.m.

Reverting to the race itself, a good deal was made of the difference
in load between the East and West Coast trains, but until the final
night they were roughly equal. The East Coast ran six vehicles, five
of which were six-wheelers, and two of these were brake vans.
There were then three vehicles for ordinary passengers, and a bogie
sleeping-car. The West Coast train was composed entirely of bogie
stock and included two brake-thirds, a composite, and a sleeping-car.
There can have been very little difference between the passenger
accommodation. Rous-Marten quoted the West Coast load as about
95 tons, while on the final record-breaking night it was $72\frac{1}{2}$ tons tare,
for three vehicles. The gibes of Sir Henry Oakley about the senseless
practice of running four-coach trains hardly hold water, since the
West Coast were providing as much accommodation in these four
coaches as the East Coast did in six. Scott talks about the final West
Coast record having been made with 'an engine and a hand-cart';
but *Hardwicke* weighed no more than 33 tons, and if one counts the
26-ton tender as part of the load to be hauled the engine was pulling
just three times its own weight. In similar conditions of loading a
modern 'Duchess' class Pacific would be hauling 260 tons behind her
tender, and an 'A4' 245 tons. Neither of these would be called
featherweight loads today.

By way of a last general comment on the race of 1895, a leading
article in *The Engineer* for August 30th, 1895, is worth quoting:

'The graphic articles from the pen of Mr Rous-Marten which we have
published render it unnecessary that we should here say anything concerning the events of the railway race which has just been terminated.
But much remains to be written on certain aspects of the race concerning
which the most extraordinary mistakes have been made by correspondents
of the daily press. There is, too, some reason to believe that a section of
the general public has regarded the race as a dangerous and almost
criminal transaction. Mr John Burns, M.P., has excelled himself in wild
denunciation of the railway companies, and has drawn a lurid picture of

the perils and sufferings of drivers and firemen, which only needed a small substratum of truth to be a really pathetic piece of oratory. It seems that Mr Burns has been riding on an engine in the United States and found it hard work, and a little alarming. We are not surprised. The experience of any man who rides on the footplate of an express locomotive for the first time is rather startling, but it is not necessary that as a result he should rush into print. But Mr Burns is by no means alone. Many other worthy people seem to regard with dread an attempt to accelerate communications with Scotland. It is just possible that a few words from us may tend to reassure and comfort these gentlemen. No lady correspondent of the daily press has yet expressed her fears. Possibly the racing spirit that induced the old lady to give her cargo of hams to the captain of a Mississippi boat to enable him to make more steam and beat a rival still beats in the female breast in this country. We have been repeatedly told that the race to Scotland is dangerous; that the men in charge of the train are over-worked; that the speed is so tremendous that the passengers' health must suffer; that there is no time to avoid collisions; that the risks of running off the line, breaking the rails, bursting up the engine, breaking bridges, and so on are simply enormous. All this is an admirable and instructive example of the way in which history repeats itself. We can almost see some of the correspondents of the daily press copying their letters from old newspapers and reviews. In 1830, and one or two succeeding years, any-thing that has been written during the last couple of weeks was written and printed. The modern terrorist has nothing new to say on the subject. All the fine old crusted stock arguments have been trotted out. We admit there has been one omitted. We have not heard a syllable about the risk of suffocation, of which such capital was once made by the opponents of railways; but this is a small matter. Neither has anything been said about a cow. . . .'

Finally, after commentating upon some of the technical aspects of the contests, *The Engineer* concluded:

'One gratifying result of the race will be perhaps to silence the boasting of the American press. The far-famed Empire State Express has been thoroughly beaten. . . .'

The calendar of the race, noting each successive quickening of the actual time occupied between London and Aberdeen, is tabulated herewith. This begins with the East Coast scheduled times operating until July 15th, 1895, but continues from that time with the times made on individual runs:

Night of the East Coast record: The 8 p.m. from Kings Cross changing engines at York, with G.N.R. 4-2-2 No. 775 just arrived after her last run from Grantham, and the N.E.R. 4-4-0 No. 1621 waiting to take over.

[From a painting by Jack Hill]

NORTH EASTERN EXPRESSES
OF THE 'NINETIES

Above: Up Scotch Express near York. Engines Class
'Q' 4-4-0 No. 1904 and Class 'J' 4-2-2.

Below: The 'Flying Scotsman' leaving York, hauled by
Class 'Q' 4-4-0 No. 1875.

[*Locomotive Publishing Co*

PROTAGONISTS IN AN
ABORTIVE RACE

Above: Caledonian 'Dunalastair' No. 732 at Carlisle.
[*The late W. J. Reynolds*]

Below: Worsdell's 7 ft. 7 in. 4-4-0 No. 1870, with
indicating shelter, outside York.
[*Locomotive Publishing Co*]

The Octocentenary Exhibition at Carlisle, in 1958: *Hardwicke* and the Caledonian 4-2-2 No. 123 stand ahead of the Midland 4-2-2 No. 118.

[*O. S. Nock*

LONDON–ABERDEEN : JULY–AUGUST 1895

Date	Route	Arrival time a.m.	Total time from London min.	Av. speed m.p.h.
Until July 15	East Coast	7.35	695	45·2
,, 15	West Coast	6.47	647	50·1
,, 16	,, ,,	6.21	621	52·2
,, 28	,, ,,	6.14	614	52·7
,, 29	,, ,,	6.06	606	53·5
,, 30	,, ,,	5.59	599	54·1
August 19	,, ,,	5.15	555	58·4
,, 20	East Coast	5.11	551	57·0
,, 20	West Coast	4.58	538	60·2
,, 21	East Coast	4.40	520	60·6
,, 22	West Coast	4.32	512	63·2

Date of departure from London.

Today one would work out various sums, and show how there had been a reduction of 26½ per cent in the total journey time, and an increase, in average speed of 39·8 per cent. The latter figure is, of course, astonishing, but E. L. Ahrons put the case rather more picturesquely. 'By mid-August', he wrote, 'the Aberdonians were rubbing their eyes and wondering if at this rate the granite city was going to become a sort of northern suburb of London!'

Such was the bare calendar of events. In a contest that aroused so much interest and excitement there were, and still are, many who asked: 'Well, who won?' The question does not admit of a definite answer. The West Coast companies trailed their coats for over a month from July 15th, and they capped the carefully prepared East Coast reply of August 19th with a new record of their own. When at last the East Coast companies had cast off the lingering shackles of orthodox railway operating they won a great victory, but instead of staying to consolidate the advantage of their shorter route they cried 'Pax', and quit the field. The West Coast thereupon romped home and were left holding a record that stands to this day, and which is unlikely to be surpassed with steam, if ever! For sheer speed the honours undoubtedly lie with the West Coast; even on their greatest run the East Coast did not achieve an end-to-end average higher than that of their rivals, albeit the difference on that particular night was of no more than decimal points. As to the performances of individual engines and their crews, these will be discussed in the next chapter.

The race left some magnificent daily schedules, particularly on the West Coast route, over which the 8 p.m. Tourist express in the following summer was booked to run the 105·3 miles from Wigan to

I

Carlisle in 112 minutes at an average speed of 56·4 m.p.h. On the Caledonian Railway the going was even more brilliant:

		miles	*min.*	*m.p.h.*
Carlisle–Stirling	.	117·8	125	56·5
Stirling–Perth	.	33·1	35	56·7
Perth–Forfar	.	32·5	32	60·8

Moreover, by 1896 the McIntosh 'Dunalastairs' were on the job, and with loads of 140 to 170 tons they were running from Carlisle to Stirling in less time than the Drummonds had taken with 100 tons, or less. Had there been any resumption of racing in 1896 the Caledonian had a stud of magnificent new engines, ready for any eventuality. No less prepared were the North Eastern Railway. It was characteristic of Wilson Worsdell to obtain authority to build 'racing' locomotives; for how otherwise could his amazing 1869 and 1870 be described? These great, majestic 4-4-os, with cylinders larger than those of the 'M' class, and with larger firegrates, had coupled wheels of no less than 7 ft 7 in diameter – the largest coupled wheels in the world. Five of the class were projected, but when no racing developed in the summer of 1896 no further examples were built; but the fact that 1869 and 1870 were ready for service in the June showed the North Eastern readiness for more record-breaking.

Unfortunately for Anglo-Scottish train services, the West Coast 'racer' came to grief in July 1896 in a most alarming smash at Preston. Taking the curve at the north end of the station at greatly excessive speed the whole train, save the rearmost brake van, was wrecked. Fortunately there was only one person killed, but the mere fact that a fast Scotch express was involved, and moreover, the very train concerned in the racing of the previous summer, caused all the prophets of woe to rise up in chorus. The train had been double-headed, with two 'Jumbos', and the enquiry brought out two astonishing facts, first that neither driver had ever worked the train before, and secondly that neither driver had ever worked on a train booked to pass Preston without stopping. The accident was clearly due to gross misjudgment on the part of two men inexperienced in this particular duty; but from whatever cause, it sounded the death knell of high speed on the Anglo-Scottish services. Quietly, unobtrusively, the schedules were eased out until little remained of that brilliant summer of 1895. The journey times achieved became legendary, until the L.M.S.R. and L.N.E.R. began their programme of acceleration more than thirty years later.

The public and certain sections of the Press were constantly looking for signs of another race, and in 1901 it did seem as though something was brewing up. For the summer service of that year the Midland and North British together booked the 9.30 a.m. express from St Pancras into Waverley at 6.5 p.m., or 10 minutes ahead of the 'Flying Scotsman'. There had been stirrings earlier, which prompted *The Railway Magazine* to publish a quaint and amusing cartoon. But the action of the Midland and North British would probably have evoked no positive response had it not been for the bad running then unhappily too frequent on the Midland Railway. Day after day time was lost south of Carlisle, and to the North Eastern it seemed that if the accelerated train ran true to form it would block the 'Flying Scotsman'. For a short time it seemed that Portobello East might become a second Kinnaber, with the signalman called upon to exercise all his discretion in awarding priorities. To provide against such possibilities the North Eastern determined to run the 'Flying Scotsman' ahead of the rival train, and on the first day of the Midland accelerations the East Coast train reached Waverley at 6.2 p.m. – 13 minutes early, and 4 minutes ahead of the Midland. Some of the daily newspapers seized upon this to try to work up some of the excitement of 1895 all over again. In Newcastle it was perhaps understandable, as there were still vivid memories, and many of the men who had been most actively concerned were still in harness. On July 2nd *The Newcastle Chronicle* carried a headline 'Great Victory of the East Coast', but as that run involved no more than running the 124·4 miles to Waverley in 147 minutes it was not anything very wonderful. But the presence of the redoubtable Bob Nicholson on the footplate brought a host of old memories. In 1901, however, he was riding as an inspector, and with a new 'R' class 4-4-0 No. 2015 and a load of seven bogie coaches the task was simplicity itself compared with what had been done in 1895. The arrivals in Edinburgh during that first week of the Midland acceleration were:

Date	East Coast p.m.	Midland p.m.
July 1	6.2	6.6
,, 2	6.3	6.21
,, 3	6.9	6.15
,, 4	6.7	6.19
,, 5	6.9	6.12
,, 6	6.6	6.14

And in such a minor key the 'race' of 1901 fizzled out of the newspapers.

XI

Locomotive Performance : 1895

THE astonishing engine performances put up towards the end of the 'Ninety-Five' are nowadays often watered down by some comment about the lightness of the loads conveyed. Even contemporary observers were not free from this taint, as witness Scott's jocular remarks about 'an engine and a handcart' in reference to the West Coast epic on the final night. More truly, so far as any portion of the run north of Crewe was concerned, one could amend the Churchillian phrase and reply: 'Some engine; some handcart!' On the most notable runs made at the climax of the 'Ninety-Five' the locomotives were hauling roughly three times their own weight, counting the tender as part of the train, and to see those runs in their true perspective it is interesting to compare them on the same basis with some famous record runs made in later years. It will be seen that on the majority of these great runs the ratio of engine weight to 'train' weight was almost exactly the same, and the comparison is just as striking when the ratios of train weight to tractive effort of the locomotive are set out alongside each other. The historic runs of *Papyrus* (No. 8) and *Princess Elizabeth* (No. 10) compare almost exactly with those of the North Eastern 1620 and of *Hardwicke*. So far as the Great Western 'City' runs of 1903 and 1904 are concerned I have taken only the high-speed parts of each, as running conditions west of Exeter are exceptionally difficult.

Returning now to the racing runs of 1895, a second table has been prepared showing summary details of ten of the most notable runs. Before coming to consider these runs in detail, the differing conditions prevailing need emphasis, and the most important point to bear in mind is that of the competing companies only the London & North Western had water troughs. Runs of 120 to 150 miles were not to be undertaken lightly with non-superheater engines worked as hard as '1620' on the last night from Newcastle to Edinburgh, or on the Caledonian with Beattock summit to be surmounted. The tenders of the North Eastern 'M' class engine had a water capacity of 3,940 gallons, thus providing for a consumption of about 31 gallons per mile on the Newcastle–Edinburgh run. Now in a comprehensive series of trials carried out in 1896 between Newcastle and Tweedmouth a locomotive of the 'M' class, No. 1635, was using roughly

FAMOUS BRITISH RUNS: A COMPARISON

Run No.	Year	Railway	Route	Distance miles	Time min.	Av. speed m.p.h.	Engine No.	Engine wt. tons	Tender wt. tons	Train tons tare	Ratio train-to-engine wt.	Ratio train wt. to T.E. of engine
1	1895	G.N.R.	Grantham–York	82.7	76	65.3	775	45.1	33	101	2.98	22.9
2	1895	N.E.R.	Newcastle–Edinburgh	124.4	113	66.1	1620	50.7	41	101	2.8	18.2
3	1895	L.N.W.R.	Crewe–Carlisle	141.0	126	67.2	790	32.7	25	72.5	2.98	19.4
4	1903	G.W.R.	‡Paddington–Exeter	193.6	173	67.2	3433	55.3	36.7	130	3.02	20.9
5	1904	G.W.R.	†Exeter–Bristol	74.9	64½	69.5	3440	55.3	36.7	148	3.34	23.2
6	1904	G.W.R.	Bristol–Paddington	118.7	99¾	71.3	3065	49.0	36.7	120	3.19	21.9
7	1932	G.W.R.	Swindon–Paddington	77.4	56¾	81.6	5006	79.8	46.7	189	2.95	16.7
8	1935	L.N.E.R.	Newcastle–Kings Cross	268.3	227½*	70.8	2750	96.3	57.0	213	2.81	18.4
9	1935	L.N.E.R.	‡Kings Cross–Peterborough	76.4	55	83.3	2509	103	65	220	2.77	18.0
10	1936	L.M.S.R.	Glasgow–Euston	401.4	344¼	70.0	6201	104.5	55.6	255	2.97	17.2
11	1937	L.M.S.R.	Crewe–Euston	158.1	119	79.8	6220	108	56.5	263	2.96	17.9
12	1937	L.N.E.R.	§Kings Cross–York	188.2	157	72.0	'A4'	103	65	312	3.67	23.8
13	1954	W.R.	Bristol–Paddington	117.6	95	74.4	6015	89	46.7	236	3.18	15.7
14	1935	L.N.E.R.	Leeds–Kings Cross	185.8	176*	63.3	4456	69.6	43.1	277	4.6	41.3

* Net times.   † Pass to stop.   ‡ Start to pass.   § Service schedule of the 'Coronation' express.

THE RACE TO THE NORTH: 189
Summary of best engine performance

Run No.	Railway	Engine No.	Load tons tare	Route	Distance miles	Time min.	Av. speed m.p.h.	Engine weight tons	Load in relation to engine wt.
1	G.N.R.	668	101	Kings Cross–Grantham	105·5	101	62·7	45·1	2·98
2	G.N.R.	775	101	Grantham–York	82·7	76	65·3	45·1	2·98
3	N.E.R.	1621	101	York–Newcastle	80·6	79	61·2	50·7	2·8
4	N.E.R.	1620	101	Newcastle–Edinburgh	124·4	113	66·1	50·7	2·8
5	N.B.R.	293	86	Edinburgh–Dundee	59·2	59	60·2	40·2	2·95
6	L.N.W.R.	1309	72½	Euston–Crewe	158·1	148	64·1	45·5	2·18
7	L.N.W.R.	790	72½	Crewe–Carlisle	141·0	126	67·2	32·7	2·98
8	Caledonian	90	72½	Carlisle–Perth	150·8	149½	60·4	45·0	2·48
9	Caledonian	78	95	Carlisle–Stirling	117·8	114	61·8	45·0	3·0
10	Caledonian	17	72½	Perth–Aberdeen*	89·7	80½	66·8	45·2	2·46

* Ticket platform.

2,000 gallons of water for the run of 65½ miles; the load was 186 tons, and the speed 52½ m.p.h. from start to stop. Judging by modern test figures, the coal and water consumption needed to run a train of 186 tons at 52½ m.p.h. is very nearly the same as that needed for a train of 101 tons at 66 m.p.h., and from this it would seem that the 'M' class engines would have mighty little left in their tenders after a really hard run from Newcastle to Edinburgh. On this account it is easy to understand the nursing of engine No. 1621 from Newcastle to Grantshouse on the night of August 19th.

The Drummond 4-4-0s of the Caledonian had tenders with a water capacity of 3,572 gallons, so that a non-stop run from Carlisle to Stirling needed the most expert of enginemanship if the going was to be hard between Carlisle and Beattock Summit. From July 29th, when the booking became 169 minutes for the 150·8 miles to Perth, inclusive of the Stirling stop, loads up to '12' were taken without assistance up Beattock. In the early hours of August 14th Tom Robinson made the run in 167 minutes with engine No. 78, and 'eleven', and five days later Crooks made what must have been a magnificent run, with engine No. 90 and 'twelve', in 165 minutes. 'Equal to 12' would have meant nearly 200 tons behind the tender. Two days earlier Rous-Marten had been a passenger; on that occasion, unfortunately, the train was heavy enough to be double-headed from Carlisle, with engines 78 and 90 together. The log taken by Rous-Marten is most revealing, for although he was evidently much impressed by the work, even with two engines, the overall time to Perth was 3 minutes *more* than that achieved by No. 90 two nights later when the load was only one coach less. On the run clocked by Rous-Marten, and tabulated herewith, No. 90 was driven by Crooks, as usual, but whether Tom Robinson was on No. 78 I cannot say; probably he was, for the Caledonian engines of that time were nearly all single manned.

The start out of Carlisle was very fast, but after that the two engines together were not appreciably faster than the 'single' No. 123 in the race of 1888. The stop at the summit seems to have been rather protracted, seeing that such haste was needed, and after recording a brisk descent to Carstairs Rous-Marten must have fallen asleep, for his log is blank between Law Junction and Stirling. One can hardly blame him, for he had been recording continuously since leaving Euston, and after this one interlude he carried on without a break till Aberdeen. The total time from Carlisle to Perth on this occasion was 168 minutes 5 seconds. The stops at Beattock Summit, and Stirling lasted 3 and 4½ minutes respectively, giving time to take water; but on non-stop runs to Stirling like those previously mentioned, the tenders would not permit a water consumption of more than 30 gallons per mile. It is small wonder that Crooks was apprehensive when he was asked to run non-stop to Perth on the very last night. Few commentators at the time seem to have given a thought to the water supply. One railway *littérateur*, who should have known better, said that the work of No. 90 was 'poor throughout'; even the Rev. W. J. Scott wrote, 'a Caledonian engine was for once not at its best', while in actual fact Crooks put up a marvellous piece of running. Not until ten years ago was justice done to his work on that night, when J. F. McEwan told how the engine had to be nursed in from Auchterarder and how they arrived in Perth with the tender

CALEDONIAN RAILWAY: 1.43 a.m. CARLISLE–PERTH

Load: 'Equal to 13', 207 tons tare
Engine: Drummond 4-4-0 No. 90 (Driver A. Crooks)
Pilot engine to Beattock Summit, 4-4-0 No. 78

Distance miles							Time min. sec.		Av. speed m.p.h.
0·0	CARLISLE	.	.	.	.	.	0	00	—
4·1	Rockcliff	.	.	.	.	.	5	21	46·0
6·1	Floriston	.	.	.	.	.	6	59	73·3
8·6	Gretna Junc.	.	.	.	.	.	9	10	68·7
13·1	Kirkpatrick	.	.	.	.	.	13	45	58·8
16·7	Kirtlebridge	.	.	.	.	.	17	36	56·2
20·1	Ecclefechan	.	.	.	.	.	20	46	64·3
25·8	LOCKERBIE	.	.	.	.	.	25	58	65·8
28·7	Nethercleugh	.	.	.	.	.	28	30	68·7
31·7	Dinwoodie	.	.	.	.	.	30	58	73·0
34·5	Wamphray	.	.	.	.	.	33	28	67·3
39·7	BEATTOCK	.	.	.	.	.	38	14	65·7
49·7	Summit	.	.	.	.	{ arr.	52	48	
						{ dep.	55	52	—
52·6	Elvanfoot	.	.	.	.	.	59	44	—
55·3	Crawford	.	.	.	.	.	62	07	67·8
57·8	Abington	.	.	.	.	.	64	19	68·2
63·2	Lamington	.	.	.	.	.	69	02	68·7
66·9	Symington	.	.	.	.	.	72	21	67·1
73·5	CARSTAIRS	.	.	.	.	.	78	40	62·8
84·0	Law Junc.	.	.	.	.	.	88	26	64·8
117·8	STIRLING	.	.	.	.	.	125	58	—
0·0							0	22*	
4·9	Dunblane	.	.	.	.	.	6	47	—
7·6	Kinbuck	.	.	.	.	.	11	00	38·5
17·2	Crieff Junc.	.	.	.	.	.	22	33	49·8
23·4	Dunning	.	.	.	.	.	28	02	67·8
26·2	Forteviot	.	.	.	.	.	30	37	65·2
33·0	PERTH	.	.	.	.	.	37	35	—

* Bank engine in rear: Stirling to Kinbuck.

tank absolutely dry. In such straits were Crooks and his mate that they uncoupled, ran ahead, and just waited for a pull to the shed. The water consumption cannot have been more than 22 or 23 gallons per mile.

It is unfortunate that no fully detailed logs were taken of the running on the last two nights of the race. It is understandable that the six enthusiasts who survived the Portobello shake-up on the night of August 19th–20th should have given things a miss on the following night; but none of them appears to have been out with the trains that left London on either the 21st or the 22nd August. As a result we are dependent for data upon other sources. The West Coast train of August 22nd appears to have been logged quite accurately as far as Carlisle, for Mr C. J. Bowen Cooke, later Chief Mechanical Engineer of the L.N.W.R., published details in his book *British Locomotives* giving passing times at principal stations down to the nearest 5 seconds. On the Caledonian, his figures are corroborated and amplified at certain points by a log taken by a certain W. M. Lellan, who appears to have been a North British headquarters' man sent out to 'snoop'; in any case his report and log was in the hands of Mr Conacher twenty-four hours after the end of the run. It was in connection with this run, however, that the most extraordinary error got into print, and into such reputable print that details continued to be wrongly quoted for more than twenty years after the event! Rous-Marten, writing in *The Engineer* of 1895 said: 'It may be observed that there is the greatest difficulty of obtaining trustworthy records of the actual times of the trains.' When he was not on the spot he had to depend upon telegrams and semi-official information for much of the time, and concerning the running on the Caledonian in the early hours of August 23rd, one of his informants let him down with a bang!

A telegram was sent from Scotland to the effect that on this last night the Caledonian had changed engines at Stirling, not Perth, and that a non-stop run had been made from Stirling to the Aberdeen ticket platform. There was logic enough in such an arrangement, for by changing at Stirling the Carlisle–Aberdeen run was divided almost exactly in half, and the very long 150·8-mile non-stop run from Carlisle to Perth would have been avoided. The two runs would therefore have been 117·8 miles and 122·7 miles. This same telegram also contained a delightful piece for a railway journalist, namely that at the very finish of the 'Ninety-Five' the heroine of the 'Eighty-Eight', 4-2-2 No. 123, had been requisitioned and had made a grand run. Again this was quite plausible, for No.

123 was then stationed at Perth. Anyway, Rous-Marten accepted this news and published it in *The Engineer*, of all papers, on the following Friday. And on the very same day the correct story appeared in *The Illustrated London News*, written up by an artist correspondent who had actually travelled on the train. Of course a correction was very quickly made in *The Engineer*, but the original error came up again in 1918 when E. L. Ahrons was contributing his famous series of articles 'Locomotive and Train Working in the Latter Part of the Nineteenth Century' to *The Railway Magazine*. It then transpired that while residing abroad he had seen the original Rous-Marten article, but had never received the issue of *The Engineer* in which the correction was published! There may very likely have been some talk in Perth of using No. 123, and the man who sent the telegram jumped to inappropriate conclusions.

From the information I have been able to gather from a large number of different sources, detailed logs of the more important journeys have been reconstructed. In supplementing existing data I have made careful estimates of certain other intermediate times in order that the character of the running may be more thoroughly assessed. It is, however, important to emphasize that these 'logs' *are* reconstructions. The times at the principal passing points are those handed down to us as authentic, and on this skeleton I have filled in a little more detail, based on a fairly close acquaintance with locomotive running over all the routes in question. As this chapter began with particular reference to Caledonian work it will be appropriate to begin a detailed consideration of the runs with the work of 'Baldie' Crooks, between Carlisle and Perth. The extent to which he was nursing his engine in the early stages is very noticeable when the log is compared with that of No. 123, on August 9th, 1888. Although the 'single' had one more coach she was ahead of No. 90 at Beattock, and dropped only a fraction behind up the bank itself. At the summit both engines were level, but then, surprisingly enough, it was the coupled engine that began to draw ahead. Crooks must have come very hard down the Clyde valley. Very great care had been taken in the design of these engines to secure free running; they had divided slide valves, each with its own exhaust port, and by this Drummond claimed to have reduced back pressure to an infinitesimal amount. No doubt Crooks judged that he could gain a good deal of time by free running on very light steaming downhill, and certainly he was inside 'even time' by the time Holytown was passed.

The time from Carlisle to Stirling was certainly not so spectacular

CALEDONIAN RAILWAY: CARLISLE–PERTH

Load: 3 vehicles (=4½), 72½ tons tare
Engine: Drummond 4-4-0 No. 90
Driver A. Crooks   Fireman R. Smith

Distance miles		Time min. sec.	Av. speed m.p.h.
0·0	CARLISLE	0 00	—
8·6	Gretna Junc.	10 15	—
25·8	LOCKERBIE	27 00	61·6
39·7	BEATTOCK	39 30	66·8
49·7	Summit	53 00	44·4
52·6	Elvanfoot	55 50	61·5
66·9	Symington	68 00	70·7
73·5	CARSTAIRS	74 00	66·0
84·0	Law Junc.	84 30	60·0
89·9	Holytown	89 30	70·8
109·7	LARBERT	109 00	60·9
117·8	STIRLING	116 30	64·8
122·7	Dunblane	121 20	60·8
125·4	Kinbuck	124 20	54·0
135·0	Crieff Junc.	132 50	67·8
146·9	Forgandenny	142 40	72·8
150·8	PERTH	149 30	43·2

as that made by Robinson earlier in the week with No. 78, when the time was 114 minutes start to stop, but Crooks again showed his first-rate enginemanship on the last stage of the long non-stop run. A slow climb up the Dunblane bank would have thrown away much of the advantage he had gained, and so reckoning that he could roll home from Auchterarder, he threw everything he had left into an all-out ascent, and a fast run across the tableland to Crieff Junction. McEwan states that because of the exhaustion of his water supply Crooks came into Perth so slowly as to take nearly 8 minutes for the last 4 miles; had he been assured of ample water 3 minutes might have been cut between Forgandenny and Perth alone. In any case, however, it was a grand piece of running. Mr George Perry has told me that Tom Robinson was terribly disappointed that the race ended when it did, for he was most anxious to try the Carlisle–Perth non-stop with No. 78, and according to Perry had a special technique worked out so as to get through each stage on the least possible water consumption.

The continuation run to Aberdeen, on the final trip, gave the highest start-to-stop average speed of any lap less than 100 miles. It was closely approached by the final Great Northern run from Grantham to York, except that in considering relative difficulty the Stirling 4-2-2 No. 775 had a fine downhill start, whereas the Lambie engine had 7 miles of climbing out to Stanley Junction. Driver

CALEDONIAN RAILWAY: PERTH–ABERDEEN

Load: 4 vehicles, 110 tons tare
Engine: Lambie 4-4-0 No. 17
Driver J. Soutar Fireman D. Fenton

Distance miles		Time min. sec.	Av. speed m.p.h.
0·0	PERTH	0 00	—
7·2	Stanley Junc.	9 15	—
15·8	Coupar Angus	17 38	61·6
20·5	Alyth Junc.	21 55	65·8
26·8	Glamis	27 36	66·4
32·5	FORFAR	33 11	61·2
0·0		0 00	
7·0	Guthrie	7 45	54·2
15·4	Bridge of Dun	16 22	58·7
18·1	Dubton Junc.	18 56	63·2
23·5	Marykirk	24 45	55·8
26·7	Laurencekirk	28 36	49·8
30·0	Fordoun	31 47	62·1
41·2	STONEHAVEN	43 45	56·2
57·2	ABERDEEN (TICKET PLATFORM) .	60 38	56·8

Soutar, on No. 17, made what was probably the fastest running on level track recorded at any time in the whole race. For nearly 11 miles north of Coupar Angus speed averaged 75 m.p.h. The slack through Forfar pulled the average from the start down a little, but after passing Kinnaber both the uphill work through the Mearns country and the speed over the coastal switchback from Stonehaven were really amazing. To have produced such average speeds over

CALEDONIAN RAILWAY: PERTH–ABERDEEN

Load: 3 vehicles (=4½), 72½ tons tare
Engine: Lambie 4-4-0 No. 17
Driver J. Soutar Fireman D. Fenton

Distance miles		Time min. sec.	Av. speed m.p.h.
0·0	PERTH	0 00	—
7·2	Stanley Junc.	8 45	49·4
15·8	Coupar Angus	15 55	72·0
20·5	Alyth Junc.	19 40	75·2
26·8	Glamis	24 40	75·7
32·5	FORFAR	29 30	70·7
41·5	Glasterlaw	39 00	57·0
47·9	Bridge of Dun	44 10	74·3
51·8	*Kinnaber Junc.*	47 30	70·4
59·2	Laurencekirk	54 25	64·3
66·5	Drumlithie	61 00	66·5
73·7	Stonehaven	67 00	72·0
81·6	Portlethen	73 35	72·1
89·2	*Ferryhill Junc.*	79 45	74·0
89·7	ABERDEEN (TICKET PLATFORM) .	80 30	—

G.N.R.: KINGS CROSS–GRANTHAM
Load: 6 vehicles (=6½), 101 tons tare
Engine: Stirling 8ft 4-2-2 No. 668
Driver J. Falkinder

Distance miles		Time min. sec.	Av. speed m.p.h.
0·0	KING CROSS	0 00	—
2·6	Finsbury Park	4 30	34·8
5·0	Wood Green	7 10	54·0
9·4	New Barnet	11 35	59·8
12·7	Potters Bar	15 00	58·1
17·7	HATFIELD	19 30	66·7
22·5	Woolmer Green Box . .	24 15	60·8
31·9	HITCHIN	33 00	64·5
44·1	Sandy	42 50	74·2
51·7	St Neots	49 30	68·2
58·9	HUNTINGDON . . .	55 30	72·0
63·5	Abbots Ripton . . .	60 05	60·3
69·4	Holme	65 30	65·5
76·4	PETERBOROUGH . .	72 00	64·7
88·6	Esscudine	84 30	58·6
100·1	Stoke Box	96 00	60·0
105·5	GRANTHAM	101 00	64·8

the final stages the maximum must have been well over 80 m.p.h. at Stonehaven and in coming down past Cove Bay. The Caledonian Railway was justly proud of this run, and its series of picture post-cards included the one reproduced facing page 64, purporting to show Driver Soutar examining his engine at the end of the journey. The company also published the 'log' as a picture postcard! I cannot recollect that the Great Western, even with their flair for publicity, went so far as this in celebrating the 81 m.p.h. flight of *Tregenna Castle* on the 'Cheltenham Flyer' in 1932.

Turning now to some of the best English achievements in the race, the Great Northern running was perhaps the least sensational of any. The Stirling engines put up good, solid, reliable work, and made their fast end-to-end times by very rapid starts and good hill-climbing. Sir Henry Oakley frequently stressed the point that the maximum speeds did not exceed those regularly run with the Manchester and Leeds expresses, and that it was by lightening the loads that they were able to run uphill at speeds then considered good on the level. As a result there was never quite the dash and fire about the Great Northern work that one saw so often on the L.N.W.R., on the Caledonian, and at times on the North Eastern. Driver Falkinder with the 8-footer No. 668 put up an immaculate performance on the last night of the race, with very fast climbs to both Potters Bar and Stoke Box, and yet no faster average than one

G.N.R.: GRANTHAM–YORK

Load: 9 vehicles (=9½), 146 tons tare
Engine: Stirling 2-2-2 No. 231

Distance miles		Time min. sec.	Av. speed m.p.h.
0·0	GRANTHAM	0 00	—
4·2	Barkston	6 17	40·1
6·0	Hougham.	7 57	64·9
9·9	Claypole	11 05	74·5
14·6	NEWARK	15 00	72·0
20·9	Carlton	20 40	66·8
21·9	Crow Park	21 35	65·7
26·4	Tuxford	26 18	57·3
33·1	RETFORD	32 53	61·0
36·2	Sutton	35 48	63·9
38·4	Ranskill	37 48	66·0
40·3	Scrooby	39 28	68·4
42·2	Bawtry	41 12	65·6
45·8	Rossington	44 55	58·2
—		sigs.	—
50·5	DONCASTER	51 10	45·1
52·6	Arksey	53 50	47·2
57·5	Moss	58 45	59·8
60·5	Balne	61 35	63·7
61·8	Heck	62 50	62·6
64·3	Templehirst	65 17	61·3
68·9	SELBY	69 45	61·8
73·0	Riccall	74 40	50·2
75·6	Escrick	77 15	60·3
78·5	Naburn	79 55	65·3
82·7	YORK	85 10	—

G.N.R.: GRANTHAM–YORK

Load: 6 vehicles (=6½), 101 tons tare
Engine: Stirling 4-2-2 No. 775

Distance miles		Time min. sec.	Av. speed m.p.h.
0·0	GRANTHAM	0 00	—
4·2	Barkston	5 40	44·5
14·6	NEWARK	14 00	73·5
20·9	Carlton	19 15	72·0
26·4	Tuxford	24 30	62·9
33·1	RETFORD	30 30	67·0
38·4	Ranskill	35 10	68·3
42·2	Bawtry	38 25	70·2
45·8	Rossington	41 45	64·8
50·5	DONCASTER	46 00	66·3
57·5	Moss	52 00	70·0
64·3	Templehirst	57 45	71·0
68·9	SELBY	62 00	65·0
73·0	Riccall	66 30	54·7
78·5	Naburn	71 30	66·0
82·7	YORK	76 00	56·0

of 70¼ m.p.h. over the truly racing stretch from Hitchin to Hunting-don. On the second stage of the journey one might imagine that the opening time of 14 minutes for the 14·6 miles from Grantham to Newark was too good to be true; but I have included also a log of a run made at an earlier stage in the race, recorded by a correspondent of *Engineering*.

This log was compiled in careful detail, with the passing times at each station taken to the nearest second. It is of particular interest as showing work of one of the 2-2-2 engines. The start was very brisk, and speed ruled very high between Hougham and Newark; but over the more level stretches of the line the pace was not exceptional, though to be sure the East Coast schedules did not call for anything better at that time. The work of No. 775 on the final night shows the same characteristics, though speeded up proportionately throughout. Sustained speeds on the level north of Doncaster just exceeded 70 m.p.h., while the rapid acceleration from Selby swing bridge slack minimized the effect of this restriction. It would seem, how-ever, that on this occasion at least the flyer must have gone round Chaloners Whin Junction curve 'on one wheel' to achieve such a finishing time into York. On this fine trip all but 67 miles were covered in the first hour from Grantham, a feat equalled later the same night by the North Eastern engine No. 1620, and by the North Western 2-4-0 *Hardwicke* on the following night.

On the L.N.W.R. south of Crewe the work was always sound, and through the entire six weeks of accelerated running the train was only once late into Crewe. One would have liked to have seen more detail of the runs on which *Mercury*, for example, got to Crewe in 167 minutes with a load 'equal to 12', or of that on the Sunday night preceding the final speed-up, when *Hardwicke* was on, with a load

L.N.W.R.: 8 p.m. EUSTON–CREWE

Load: 3 vehicles (=4½), 72½ tons tare
Engine: Webb 3-cylinder compound No. 1309 *Adriatic*
Driver R. Walker   Fireman W. Hammond

Distance miles		Time min. sec.	Av. speed m.p.h.
0·0	EUSTON	0 00	—
17·5	Watford Junc.	17 00	61·8
31·7	Tring	30 30	63·2
46·7	Bletchley.	43 00	72·0
82·6	Rugby	77 00	63·3
97·1	Nuneaton	90 30	64·5
110·0	Tamworth	101 30	70·4
133·6	Stafford	124 00	63·0
158·1	CREWE	147 30	62·6

of '12' and the run from Euston to Crewe was made in 169 minutes. During the last four nights, however, the *Adriatic* had one of the easiest tasks set to any engine in the race, on either side. Although carried on no more than six wheels the 'Teutonic' class compounds were big, heavy engines, second only in weight to the North Eastern 'M' class 4-4-0s, and with the very light North Western standard tender behind them the load on the final night was only 2·18 times the weight of the engine itself. To what extent the North Western were out for a record of records it is not possible to say. The target time for the Crewe arrival was 10.34 p.m., and the train actually ran in at 10.27½. It may not have been practicable to have kept the line clear for more than 5 or 7 minutes in advance, and in such a case harder running would not have been encouraged. But from whatever reasons it may have been, the final run on the night of August 22nd was not especially impressive. The thought inevitably comes to mind that a 6 ft 6 in 'Jumbo', driven hard, would have made much faster times; on the other hand there is no evidence that the *Adriatic* herself was unduly pressed. The average speeds of 63·2 m.p.h. from Watford to Tring and 63·3 from Bletchley to Rugby hardly suggest an all-out effort from a 'Teutonic' with so light a load. They do not compare with *Hardwicke*'s amazing 64·2 m.p.h. from Carnforth to Tebay later the same night. Nevertheless, the run of *Adriatic* must not be disparaged. Only four days earlier the record for the Euston–Crewe journey stood at 167 minutes; to clip off nearly 20 minutes and effect an acceleration of 12 per cent was in itself a splendid feat. Its merit is somewhat obscured because others did so much better.

So we come to the epic achievement of Driver Robinson and Fireman Wolstencroft on *Hardwicke*, when they ran the 141 miles from Crewe to Carlisle in 126 minutes. From earlier chapters in this book it will be realized that this was hardly an isolated effort by this gallant little engine. In the thirty-four days of accelerated running, between July 15th and August 22nd, she had made the Crewe–Carlisle run 18 times prior to the final night, and had in addition worked the racing train 3 times between Euston and Crewe. In all, she made 22 racing trips totalling 3,153 miles, a record that was not equalled even by the Caledonian 4-4-0s 78 and 90, which were among the most regular performers of any during the racing period. Engine No. 90 made 18 racing trips from Carlisle to Perth, totalling 2,710 miles. On the night of August 22nd the running between Crewe and Preston might have been made over a straight and level road for all the effect the junctions, curves and gradients

L.N.W.R.: CREWE–CARLISLE

Load: 3 vehicles (=4½), 72½ tons tare
Engine: 6 ft 6 in 2-4-0 No. 790 *Hardwicke*
Driver B. Robinson   Fireman W. Wolstencroft

Distance miles		Time min. sec.	Av. speed m.p.h.
0·0	CREWE	0 00	—
4·9	Minshull Vernon	5 50	50·5
16·2	Weaver Junc.	15 25	70·8
24·0	WARRINGTON	21 55	72·0
31·0	Golborne.	28 05	68·2
35·8	WIGAN	32 05	72·0
39·1	Standish	35 15	62·5
45·5	Euxton Junc.	40 55	67·8
51·0	PRESTON	45 45	68·3
60·4	Garstang	54 45	62·7
72·0	LANCASTER	64 35	70·8
78·2	CARNFORTH	70 12	66·3
85·6	Milnthorpe	76 27	71·0
91·1	OXENHOLME	81 40	63·3
98·2	Grayrigg	89 05	57·4
104·2	Tebay	94 30	66·5
109·7	Shap Summit	100 30	55·0
111·7	Shap	102 30	60·0
118·9	Clifton	108 05	77·3
123·3	PENRITH	111 30	77·4
128·0	Plumpton	115 15	75·2
136·2	Wreay	121 15	82·0
141·1	CARLISLE	126 00	61·8

had upon the speed. There were then, as now, no serious speed restrictions until Preston itself, though the alignment at Weaver Junction, Warrington, Winwick Junction, and Euxton Junction is such as to demand some slowing at the pace *Hardwicke* was being driven. Whether any appreciable reductions were made it is impossible now to say; but with an engine hauling three times its own weight very rapid recoveries are possible, and the recorded times do not rule out a slack down to 30 m.p.h. or even less through Preston.

To Carnforth, with its average speed of 67 m.p.h. from the start, the run was just about up to the level of the best work of other locomotives in the race, paying due regard to the ratio of engine weight to train weight. North of Carnforth, however, the work was remarkable, for the remaining 62·9 miles to the Carlisle stop were covered in 55 minutes 48 seconds, at an average speed of 67·5 m.p.h. Although the descent to Carlisle was taken very fast it was the uphill work that was so astonishing, including the average of 64·2 m.p.h. from Carnforth up to Tebay that I have already mentioned, and the overall average of 62·4 from Carnforth right up to Shap Summit. The gradient averages 1 in 188 in this 31·5 miles. On the celebrated

L.M.S.R. run with the *Princess Elizabeth* in November 1936, when that engine was hauling 2·73 times its own weight, against 2·98 by *Hardwicke*, the average speed from Carnforth to Shap Summit was 68 m.p.h. This difference between 62.4 m.p.h. in 1895 and 68 in 1936 could be taken as a measure of the improvement in performance, due to improved design and manufacturing technique in the intervening years. I need hardly remind readers that in addition the *Princess Elizabeth* was running non-stop from Euston to Glasgow, whereas *Hardwicke* was working over less than half that distance. But the fact that comparison *can* be made with so outstanding a modern run is enough to show what the men of the L.N.W.R. achieved that night so far back as August 1895. *Hardwicke* ran faster than the *Princess Elizabeth* from Shap Summit to Carlisle, but no faster in from Penrith than the *City of Bristol* on a fairly recent journey of mine with the 'Mid-day Scot'.

	Engine:	790	46237
		min. sec.	min. sec.
Summit–Clifton. . . .		7 35	} 12 35
Clifton–Penrith		3 25	
Penrith–Plumpton . . .		3 45	3 58
Plumpton–Wreay . . .		6 00	5 56
Wreay–Carlisle		4 45	4 51

The maximum speed with the *City of Bristol* was 86½ m.p.h., though the time from Summit down to Penrith was much slower, because of the relatively slow speed at which the Summit was passed. The *City of Bristol* was doing only 24 m.p.h., whereas *Hardwicke* must have been doing between 40 and 45 m.p.h.

Passing now from the North Western to the North Eastern, no time need be spent over the run of No. 1621 from York to Newcastle on the night of August 21st, when little more than strict timekeeping seems to have been attempted. It is, however, another matter altogether with the continuation run to Edinburgh, which set up a record second only in brilliance to that of *Hardwicke*. Here again it is not possible to say how the curves at junctions like Morpeth, Alnmouth, and Portobello were taken, but in piecing together the various fragments of eyewitness information one is inclined to believe that the risks taken were high. It may have been that these risks were more apparent than real, and arose from the rough-riding of the six-wheeled coaches in the train. The 'M' class engines, like the 'Q' class and the 7 ft 7 in 'Q1s', rode most luxuriously and may have tempted the drivers to go harder round curves than was

N.E.R.: NEWCASTLE-EDINBURGH

Load: 6 vehicles (=6½), 101 tons tare
Engine: Class 'M' 4-4-0 No. 1620
Driver R. Nicholson Fireman T. Blades

Distance miles		Time min. sec.		Av. speed m.p.h.
0·0	NEWCASTLE	0	00	—
1·7	Heaton	3	00	—
5·0	Forest Hall	6	45	52·8
9·9	Cramlington	11	45	58·7
13·9	Stannington	15	15	68·5
16·6	MORPETH	18	00	58·9
20·2	Longhirst.	21	15	66·5
25·6	Chevington	25	45	72·0
31·9	Warkworth	31	00	72·0
34·8	ALNMOUTH JUNC. . . .	33	30	69·5
37·5	Longhoughton	36	00	64·9
39·4	Little Mill	38	00	57·0
46·0	Chathill	43	30	72·0
51·6	BELFORD	48	00	74·7
58·6	Beal	53	15	80·0
63·5	Scremerston	57	00	78·5
65·7	Tweedmouth Junc. . . .	58	45	75·0
66·9	BERWICK	60	00	57·6
72·5	Burnmouth	67	00	48·0
74·1	Ayton	68	30	64·0
78·1	Reston Junc.	72	00	68·5
83·2	Grantshouse	77	30	55·7
87·9	Cockburnspath. . . .	81	30	70·5
90·6	Innerwick	83	30	81·0
95·2	DUNBAR	88	00	61·4
100·9	East Linton	93	15	65·1
103·5	East Fortune	95	30	69·3
106·6	DREM JUNC.	98	00	74·4
111·2	Longniddry	101	30	78·8
117·9	Inveresk	107	00	73·2
121·4	Portobello	110	00	70·0
124·4	EDINBURGH (WAVERLEY) . .	113	00	60·0

comfortable for their passengers. The original log gave the passing times at Morpeth, Alnmouth, Belford and Berwick, on the North Eastern part of the journey, and at Reston, Dunbar, Drem, Longniddry, Inveresk and Portobello on the North British; from this the concluding average of 65 m.p.h. from Inveresk to the stop in Waverley suggests another very lively run through Portobello!

So far as engine performance is concerned, as distinct from such resolute and fearless enginemanship as was obviously involved in the making of such a run, the work on the open road can be assessed from the average speed of all but 73 m.p.h. from Longhirst to Tweedmouth, and the later average of 71·8 m.p.h. from Dunbar to Inveresk. By comparison, *Hardwicke* did not get any comparable length of fairly level road on which one could set her averages side by side with those of No. 1620. If the slack at Preston could be considered as balancing that at Berwick we could set the following alongside:

Railway	Section	Miles	Time min.	Av. speed m.p.h.
L.N.W.R.	Minshull Vernon–Carnforth .	73·4	64½	68·3
N.E.R. and N.B.R.	Longhirst–Dunbar . .	75·0	66¾	67·3

Inevitably one draws the conclusion that there was very little in it. Both runs stand for all time among the classics of steam traction, and there is little point in trying to decide which, if either, was the better of the two. The flying averages from Minshull Vernon to Wreay on the North Western, and from Forest Hall to Portobello on the East Coast route, were 68·3 and 67·7 m.p.h. respectively.

So, finally, we come to the North British, and there entirely differ-ent standards have to be applied in judging the extraordinary merits of the work performed during the final week. On most of the other routes concerned the running, although astonishing at the time, has come to be equalled and even surpassed in later years, albeit on exceptional occasions. Between Kings Cross and Newcastle the daily work of the Gresley streamlined high-speed trains eclipsed the fastest work of the 1895 race, while the L.M.S.R. booked an express

N.B.R.: EDINBURGH–DUNDEE

Load: 5 vehicles (=5½), 86 tons tare
Engine: Holmes 4-4-0 No. 293

Distance miles		Time min. sec.	Av. speed m.p.h.
0·0	EDINBURGH (WAVERLEY) . .	0 00	—
3·5	Corstorphine	5 10	—
9·5	Dalmeny	11 00	61·7
11·3	North Queensferry	13 00	54·0
13·2	INVERKEITHING	14 50	62·1
16·1	*Dalgetty Box*	18 05	53·5
17·4	Aberdour	19 15	66·9
20·1	BURNTISLAND	21 35	69·6
22·7	Kinghorn.	24 15	58·5
25·9	KIRKCALDY	27 05	67·8
28·0	Dysart	29 15	52·2
30·7	THORNTON JUNC. . . .	32 00	58·8
34·9	*Lochmuir Box*	36 45	53·1
38·2	Kingskettle	40 45	66·0
39·1	LADYBANK JUNC.. . . .	41 40	59·0
44·6	Cupar	45 30	68·3
50·9	Leuchars Junc.	51 00	68·8
54·6	St Fort	54 15	68·3
56·5	*Tay Bridge South Junc.* . . .	56 00	65·2
58·4	Esplanade	57 40	68·3
59·2	DUNDEE	59 00	—

that frequently loaded to over 500 tons at 64 m.p.h. between Crewe and Willesden Junction. But the North British running between Edinburgh and Dundee stands completely apart. Since the end of World War I there has not been any train over this stretch making a non-stop run in less than 80 minutes, and even when competition with the Caledonian blazed up again in 1906, and a 3-hour schedule was introduced for the 130·6 miles from Waverley to Aberdeen, no timings approaching those of 1895 were scheduled. The running of engine No. 293 in the early hours of August 22nd has been the most difficult to 'reconstruct' of any. Those who travelled by the East Coast trains north of Edinburgh have left us no clues as to the details of the work; there is no mention of whether the curves were taken fast or slow, no comments on the discomfort, or otherwise. The times handed down to us are those at Dalmeny, Kirkcaldy, Thornton and Leuchars; the rest can be no more than conjecture, but I have attempted a reconstruction on the basis that the Forth Bridge was crossed at about 50 to 52 m.p.h., and that the slacks were afterwards 45 to 50 at Inverkeithing, 50 at Burntisland and Thornton, 65 to 70 at Cupar and Leuchars Junction, and about 60 entering upon the Tay Bridge.

Comparison can then be made of probable maximum and minimum speeds with those of a fairly good run on the down 'Aberdonian' that I made in 1935 on the footplate of a Gresley 'A3' Pacific. Booked time was then 81 minutes, which we did not keep because of a permanent-way slack just north of Ladybank; but the comparison of speeds is enough to show how utterly different was the pace set in the 1895 race. If the speed restrictions had been more heavily imposed, the intermediate speeds would need to have been still higher, and that I can scarcely believe. On the night of August 19th–20th, when Macdonald and his friends were on the train, the time to Ladybank was only 1¼ minutes more than on the last night. Yet none of them have told in any detail of their experience. On August 9th Rous-Marten had written, 'I doubt the feasibleness of any material acceleration north of Edinburgh under existing conditions'; but a sensational acceleration there had been, and perhaps the riding had been such that the less those distinguished enthusiasts said about it the better.

Yet it cannot have been too bad, for when later that very morning Macdonald stormed into the North British offices and rated David Deuchars, it was of Portobello he complained and not of any incident on the North British part of the journey. One can only think that the permanent way between Edinburgh and Dundee was very good!

Railway	Engine No.	Load	Ratio Engine weight Train weight
G.N.R.	775	101	2·98
N.E.R.	1620	101	2·8
L.N.W.R. . . .	790	72½	2·95
Caledonian	17	72½	2·46

To sum up, the four fastest runs may be compared as in the accompanying table. Stretches of roughly equal length have been taken over roads that in the aggregate are level and include one severe slack. The comparison is thus fairly even, with the Caledonian coming off best, though the Lambie engine No. 17 was hauling less in relation to her weight than any of the other engines. This table does not include the mountain section of *Hardwicke*'s great run, and it is astonishing to find that instead of the stretch from Minshull Vernon to Carnforth we could take the 75·8 miles from Garstang to Wreay and get precisely the same average – over Shap! It is not merely a case of working out average speeds. When running this train at 68 m.p.h. on level track *Hardwicke* was developing about 370 h.p.

COMPARATIVE SPEEDS: EDINBURGH–DUNDEE

Location	1895 'Racer'	1935 'Aberdonian'
Turnhouse	70	65
†Dalmeny	62	50
†North Queensferry . . .	48	30
—	75	57
*Inverkeithing	50	28
Dalgetty Box	55	23/26
After Aberdour	80	64½
*Burntisland	50	39
Kirkcaldy	71	50
Dysart	58/68	38½
*Thornton Junc. . . .	50	25
Markinch	60	46
Lochmuir Box	52	38
Kingskettle	78	68
†Ladybank Junc. . . .	55	25
Springfield	75	50
†Cupar	65	60
Dairsie	72	57½
†Leuchars Junc. . . .	65	63/39
St Fort	72	57½
Tay Bridge S. Box . . .	60	48
*Before Esplanade. . . .	72	57½

* Severe service slack.   *† Moderate service slack.*

NORTH: 1895

Section	Miles	Time min.	Av. speed m.p.h.	Severe slack included at
Barkston–Naburn	74·3	65¾	67·7	Selby
Longhirst–Dunbar	75·0	66¾	67·3	Berwick
Minshull Vernon–Carnforth	73·4	64½	68·3	Preston
Stanley Junc.–Ferryhill Junc.	82·0	69	71·3	Forfar

in the cylinders. Weight for weight this was equivalent to a modern 'Castle' developing 900 indicated h.p., or a 'Duchess' developing 1,200. But then having put up this excellent performance for over an hour her driver was able to step matters up to such an extent that on the climb from Carnforth to Shap the indicated h.p. of *Hardwicke* went up to nearly 600. E. C. Poultney has related this splendid performance to the heating surface of the boiler, namely 1·8 sq ft per i.h.p. This is a very low figure for locomotives using saturated steam, and a modern 'Duchess' would have to develop fully 2,000 h.p. in the cylinders to equal it. On her climb to Shap *Hardwicke* must have been going very little short of 'all-out': 'an engine and a hand-cart' indeed!

L.N.W.R. RECORDS OF ENGINE WORKING

UNTIL July 14th, 1895, the 8 p.m. night Scotch Express called at Bletchley, Rugby, Crewe and Wigan. It was a heavy train, and ran at the speeds then customary on the North Western. The booked times and average speeds were:

Section	Miles	Booked time min.	Av. speed m.p.h.
Euston–Bletchley . .	46·7	58	48·3
Bletchley–Rugby . .	35·9	45	47·8
Rugby–Crewe . . .	75·5	88	51·4
Crewe–Wigan . . .	35·8	45	47·7
Wigan–Carlisle . . .	105·2	129	48·9

The accompanying tables show details of the running made. Between Euston and Rugby the train engine was always a Webb three-cylinder compound, and one notes that the 'Dreadnought' class took loads up to '18' without assistance. 'Equal to 18' would mean a tare load of about 290 tons. On only one occasion, when there were signal checks, was any time lost in running. On July 2nd, 7th and 9th the pilot engines were not needed, but were working home, while on July 12th, when the 7 ft compound No. 1307 *Coptic* had a load of '20½', the official statement remarks that assistance was not needed after Tring. Certainly *Coptic* continued unassisted from Rugby. Today little is said in favour of the Webb compounds; but this record of day-to-day running on a heavy train shows them to be unfailingly reliable. The load of '20½' taken by *Coptic* would scale about 330 tons tare, and there were few, if any, engines in the country at that time that could have tackled such loads unpiloted.

On July 7th *Achilles*, with the 7 ft 6 in 'single' No. 184 *Problem* assisting, worked through from Euston to Crewe, but on all the other 'Dreadnought' runs engines were changed at Rugby. No. 2056 *Argus* seems to have been a favourite for the Rugby–Crewe run. This engine, it will be recalled, was named after Webb's anonymous opponent who denounced the compounds so vehemently and persistently in the technical press. Although there were losses of time on the Rugby–Crewe section, these were in no cases due to engine, and one would have liked to see more detail of the runs on which *Argus* took 'equal to 19½' unassisted, and no less that with *Coptic* and '20½'. Significantly, however, the fastest run of the whole fortnight was made on the one occasion that a Webb compound was *not* used, namely on July 10th. Because of overtime at Rugby, the train left 6 minutes late, and the two 'Jumbos', 1485 *Smeaton* and 867 *Disraeli*, took their 300-ton train over the 75·5 miles from Rugby to Crewe in 82 minutes, averaging 55·2 m.p.h. from start to stop, and reaching Crewe on time.

North of Crewe the train engines were, with one exception, all of the 6 ft 6 in 'Jumbo' class, and loads up to '20½' were taken as far as Wigan without assistance. The feat of No. 1518 *Countess* on the night of July 12th, in running that initial 35·8 miles in 46 minutes, was a marvellous piece of work with a train that probably weighed, with passengers, luggage and mails, quite 350 tons, behind the tender. The official record states that no pilot at all was taken on the night of July 10th; but I must say that the time of 128 minutes from Wigan to Carlisle takes some believing with a load that would have totalled more than 300 tons with passengers and luggage. I do not say it could not have been done; but if indeed Shap was taken unassisted, *Albion* can be credited with one of *the* runs of the century! The pilots were mostly of 6 ft 'Jumbo' type, or 'Whitworth' class. It was very common to run a 6 ft and a 6 ft 6 in together between Crewe and Carlisle. Because of delays *en route* it is not possible to make a very close assessment of the work of individual engines, and booked time was kept between Wigan and Carlisle on no more than five runs in the fortnight. Also, the train never in this same period reached Carlisle on time. The nearest approach was on July 7th, when the arrival was at 2.22 a.m., yet on this occasion the pilot was one of those most sluggish of North Western engines, the 'Experiment' class compounds.

In this same table is given a summary of the running throughout from Euston to Carlisle. Unfortunately the official record shows the total delays experienced on each trip without reference to the sections on which the incidents occurred. It is evident, however, that a good deal of delay took place at stations, and Rugby, Crewe, and Wigan each took their toll. On July 14th, for example, Rugby kept the train 9 minutes, Crewe 15 minutes, and Wigan 10 minutes, against 4 minutes scheduled in each case. Until July 15th, however, the 8 p.m. from Euston was a veritable 'omnibus' express; it conveyed much parcel and mail traffic, and the long waits at stations can most likely be attributed to this traffic rather than to any operating delays. On other occasions Rugby had no difficulty in changing engines and getting the train away in the 4 minutes allotted, though Crewe never once achieved a smarter stop than 6 minutes. The record of time regained by engine is indeed an impressive one. The North Western had a wonderful reputation for regaining lost time, and many spirited performances lie behind the bare details shown in the table opposite.

From July 15th the 8 p.m. became, virtually, an advance portion of the regular train, conveying passengers for Inverness and Aberdeen. This enabled stops to be cut out, and the load lightened. Furthermore, the intermediate times were not advertised, so that stations could be left as soon as the train was ready to start. At first the locomotives had a very easy task. Up to July 28th the average speed had barely topped 54 m.p.h., with loads of 150 tons, or less. From July 29th, when there was an accelera-

L.N.W.R.: 8 p.m. EUSTON–RUGBY

Date	Train engine			Pilot engine			Load		Times	
	No.	Name	Class	No.	Name	Class	To Bletchley	To Rugby	Euston–Bletchley	Bletchley–Rugby
July 1	513	Mammoth	D	—	—	—	18	18	58	45
,, 2	513	Mammoth	D	883	Phantom	J	17½	19½	57	42
,, 3	2060	Vandal	D	—	—	—	17	17	58	45
,, 4	2058	Medusa	D	—	—	—	17	17	63	45
,, 5	2061	Harpy	D	—	—	—	17	17	58	45
,, 7	511	Achilles	D	184	Problem	L	15	15	58	45
,, 8	2060	Vandal	D	2185	Alma	J	19½	19½	57	45
,, 9	2060	Vandal	D	2186	Lowther	J	18	18	58	45
,, 10	641	City of Lichfield	D	—	—	—	18	18	58	45
,, 11	1307	Coptic	T	—	—	—	17½	17½	58	44
,, 12	1307	Coptic	T	863	Meteor	J	20½	20½	58	44
,, 14	527	Henry Bessemer	GB	—	—	—	14½	14½	58	45

Schedule times = 58 min. Euston–Bletchley. 45 min. Bletchley–Rugby.
Engine classes: D = 'Dreadnought' compound. J = 6 ft 6 in 'Jumbo'.
T = 'Teutonic' compound. L = 'Lady of the Lake'.
GB = 'Greater Britain' compound

L.N.W.R.: 9.50 p.m. RUGBY-CREWE

Date	Train engine			Pilot engine			Load	Time for 75.5 miles
	No.	Name	Class	No.	Name	Class		
July 1	2056	Argus	D	862	Balmoral	J	18	87
,, 2	2056	Argus	D	—	—	—	19½	92
,, 3	2056	Argus	D	—	—	—	17	90
,, 4	2056	Argus	D	—	—	—	17	88
,, 5	2056	Argus	D	—	—	—	16	88
,, 7	511	Achilles	D	184	Problem	L	15	88
,, 8	2059	Greyhound	D	675	Ivanhoe	L	19½	87
,, 9	2059	Greyhound	D	862	Balmoral	J	19	85
,, 10	867	Disraeli	J	1485	Smeaton	J	18	82
,, 11	1307	Coptic	T	—	—	—	18½	91
,, 12	1307	Coptic	T	—	—	—	20½	89
,, 14	527	Henry Bessemer	GB	—	—	—	14½	88

Schedule time: 88 min.

Engine classes: D = 'Dreadnought' compound.
T = 'Teutonic' compound.
GB = 'Greater Britain' compound.

J = 6 ft 6 in 'Jumbo'.
L = 'Lady of the Lake'.

L.N.W.R.: 11.22 p.m. CREWE-CARLISLE

Date	Train engine			Pilot engine (from Wigan)			Load	Time Crewe–Wigan 35·8 miles	Time Wigan–Carlisle 105·2 miles	Arrive Carlisle sch. 2-20 a.m.	Min. late	Total delays Euston–Carlisle	Over-time at station	Time regained by loco.
	No.	Name	Class	No.	Name	Class								
July 1	1520	Franklin	J	35	Talisman	W	18	46	131	2·32	12	34	14	22
,, 2	1518	Countess	J	748	Waterloo	W	19½	47	132	2·37	17	42	12	25
,, 3	1520	Franklin	J	2004	Witch	J	17	47	133	2·32	12	25	4	13
,, 4	1683	Sisyphus	J	738	Terrier	W	17	44	133	2·38	18	30	10	12
,, 5	1305	Doric	T	1685	Gladiator	J	16	49	128	2·35	15	27	12	12
,, 7	396	Tennyson	J	1116	*Friar	E	15	43	127	2·22	2	21	6	19
,, 8	1518	Countess	J	1170	General	J	19½	46	128	2·24	4	26	5	22
,, 9	396	Tennyson	J	814	Henrietta	W	19	46	131	2·27	7	22	7	15
,, 10	1215	Albion	J	—	—	—	18	47	128	2·28	8	28	13	20
,, 11	1520	Franklin	J	1170	General	J	18½	51	129	2·45	25	32	17	7
,, 12	1518	Countess	J	468	Wildfire	W	20½	46	131	2·34	14	24	9	10
,, 14	1518	Countess	J	1215	*Albion	J	14½†	46	134	2·48	28	45	22	17

Schedule times: Crewe–Wigan 45 min.
Wigan–Carlisle 129 min.
* Pilot throughout from Crewe to Carlisle.
† Load '16½' from Wigan.

Engine classes: J = 6 ft 6 in 'Jumbo';
W = 6 ft 0 in 'Jumbo';
T = 'Teutonic' compound.
E = 'Experiment' compound.

tion of the working time, the performance became much finer, though even on the best runs it would seem that the 'Jumbo' still had a good deal in hand. The four best runs were:

EUSTON–CREWE

Date	Engine No.	Load equal to	Approx. tons	Time min.
August 2	749	'12½'	195	170
,, 8	749	'12'	188	169
,, 15	394	'11½'	180	169
,, 18	790	'12'	188	169

In later years the timing to Crewe of the 10.30 a.m. express from Euston to Liverpool and Manchester was 171 minutes. The non-superheater 'Precursors' ran that train regularly with loads of 350 to 380 tons, and if comparison is made on the basis of nominal tractive effort the equivalent load for a 'Jumbo' would be about 220 tons, that is, heavier than anything worked in the race.

North Western engines in the Whale and Bowen-Cooke eras were worked exceedingly hard in relation to their size and nominal tractive effort. In comparison with the heaviest 'Jumbo' loadings in the race, on a timing of 171 minutes from Euston to Crewe later engines, with the same ratio of load to nominal tractive effort, would be hauling:

						tons
L.N.W.R. 'Jumbo' 2-4-0	.	.	.	.		185
L.N.W.R. 'Claughton' 4-6-0		.	.	.		400
L.M.S.R. 'Royal Scot' 4-6-0		.	.	.		560
L.M.S.R. 'Duchess' 4-6-2	.	.	.	.		670

The 'Claughton' rostered load prior to the decelerations of the first world war was 440 tons, whereas the 'Royal Scot' load on L.M.S.R. 'Special Limit' trains was 475 tons. Today, of course, the hardest trains set to the 'Duchess' class engines are timed considerably more sharply than the old L.N.W.R. 171 minutes to Crewe. The running times of the 'Mid-day Scot', for example, add up to no more than 157 minutes between Euston and Crewe, with loads sometimes exceeding 500 tons.

Taken all round, the North Western engines of 1895 were not set an unduly difficult task, even with their heaviest loads, south of Crewe, and on the last four nights the big compound *Adriatic* had some of the easiest tasks of all.

CREWE–CARLISLE: July 15th–August 22nd

From July 22nd onwards, when the working time of arrival at Carlisle was 1.47 a.m. or earlier, some notable work was done on this section. Except on one single occasion, the night of August 18th–19th, the train was never once late at Carlisle despite the fact that delays up to a maxi-

L.N.W.R.: 8 p.m. EUSTON–CREWE

Date	Engine No.	Engine Name	Load equal to	Approx. tons	Time for 158·1 miles min.	Av. speed m.p.h.
July 15	749	Mercury	$8\frac{1}{2}$	134	180	52·7
,, 16	394	Eamont	9	142	179	53·0
,, 17	749	Mercury	9	142	178	53·3
,, 18	394	Eamont	$7\frac{1}{2}$	118	180	52·7
,, 19	749	Mercury	7	110	178	53·3
,, 21	1301	Teutonic	$7\frac{1}{2}$	118	178	53·3
,, 22	394	Eamont	9	142	176	53·9
,, 23	749	Mercury	9	142	175	54·2
,, 24	394	Eamont	$7\frac{1}{2}$	118	176	53·9
,, 25	749	Mercury	9	142	176	53·9
,, 26	394	Eamont	$12\frac{1}{2}$	195	176	53·9
,, 28	1683	Sisyphus	$7\frac{1}{2}$	118	174	54·5
,, 29	749	Mercury	$10\frac{1}{2}$	165	171	55·5
,, 30	394	Eamont	$10\frac{1}{2}$	165	171	55·5
,, 31	749	Mercury	11	172	170	55·8
Aug. 1	394	Eamont	10	158	170	55·8
,, 2	749	Mercury	$12\frac{1}{2}$	195	170	55·8
,, 4	790	Hardwicke	$7\frac{1}{2}$	118	172	55·1
,, 5	394	Eamont	7	110	172	55·1
,, 6	749	Mercury	$8\frac{1}{2}$	134	174	54·5
,, 7	394	Eamont	$7\frac{1}{2}$	118	171	55·5
,, 8	749	Mercury	12	188	169	56·1
,, 9	394	Eamont	13	203	176*	53·9
,, 11	790	Hardwicke	7	110	168	56·4
,, 12	749	Mercury	8	126	168	56·4
,, 13	394	Eamont	11	172	171	55·5
,, 14	749	Mercury	$11\frac{1}{2}$	180	173	54·8
,, 15	394	Eamont	$11\frac{1}{2}$	180	169	56·1
,, 16	1307	Coptic	13	203	173	54·8
,, 18	790	Hardwicke	12	188	169	56·1
,, 19	1309	Adriatic	6	95	157	60·4
,, 20	1309	Adriatic	6	95	156	60·8
,, 21	1309	Adriatic	6	95	155	61·3
,, 22	1309	Adriatic	$4\frac{1}{2}$	72	$147\frac{1}{2}$	64·2

* Stopped 5 min. to attach assistant engine at Rugby (No. 1528 Frobisher).

mum of 22 minutes were experienced on the run from Euston. The official L.N.W.R. record does not sub-divide the delays that occurred south and north of Crewe respectively, but it is evident that a spirit of rare enterprise animated all the engine crews taking part. From the table on pages 160-1 it will be seen that assistance was taken on only six runs out of the total of thirty-four. The maximum load taken unassisted over Shap was 'equal to $11\frac{1}{2}$', or about 180 tons. The run of August 14th, with '$11\frac{1}{2}$', when the overall time was 155 minutes by engine No. 1213 *The Queen*, must have been one of the finest of the whole series. The run of Sunday, August 18th, when Driver Ben Robinson attempted a load of '12' unassisted, was subject to very heavy delay, and eventually he stopped for a bank engine at Tebay. The official record states that the stop at that station lasted 7 minutes, so that it seems as if Robinson's call for assistance caught the shed unawares on that particular Sunday night.

Taking the heavier loadings from July 22nd onwards, the results can be summarized as follows:

Date	Load coaches	Tons	Total time min.
July 22	9	142	163
„ 23	9	142	162
„ 25	9	142	162
„ 29	10½	165	160
„ 30	10½	165	158
„ 31	11	172	159
August 1	10	158	159
„ 13	11	172	160
„ 14	11½	180	155
„ 15	11½	180	160

The above gives an average load on ten runs of 164 tons, and an average time of 160 minutes. By comparison with this the schedule of the 10 a.m. from Euston to Glasgow, until 1917, was 159 minutes with a normal load of well below 300 tons, and in the later years a 'Claughton' to haul it. Again, in the earlier 1930s before the introduction of 'Pacifics', the schedule of the down 'Royal Scot' was 165 minutes with a tare load of 370 to 400 tons. On this basis of comparison the 'Jumbos' of 1895 were having to work relatively hard in contrast to the less severe demands made on them south of Crewe. Moreover, on the above ten runs delays were experienced on every occasion so that the actual performances were undoubtedly a good deal better than the overall times quoted overleaf would suggest.

L.N.W.R.: CREWE–CARLISLE

Date	Engine No.	Name	Driver	Fireman	Load equal to	Load tons	Time for 141 miles	Arrival time in Carlisle	Total delay Euston–Carlisle min.
July 15	790	Hardwicke	Robinson	Wolstencroft	8½	134	163	1·48	10
,, 16	790	Hardwicke	Howman	Harrison	9	142	161	1·45	5
,, 17	790	Hardwicke	Robinson	Wolstencroft	9	142	170	1·52	4
,, 18	790	Hardwicke	Howman	Harrison	7½	118	171	1·55	4
,, 19	790	Hardwicke	Robinson	Wolstencroft	7	110	173	1·55	4
,, 21	790	Hardwicke	Howman	Harrison	7½	118	170	1·52	4
,, 22	790	Hardwicke	Robinson	Wolstencroft	9	142	163	1·45	6
,, 23	790	Hardwicke	Howman	Harrison	9	142	162	1·41	6
,, 24	790	Hardwicke	Robinson	Wolstencroft	7½	118	164	1·44	4
,, 25	790	Hardwicke	Howman	Harrison	9	142	162	1·42	4
,, 26	790	*Hardwicke	Howman	Harrison	12½	195	162	1·42	4
,, 28	396	Tennyson	Phillips	Kay	7½	118	165	1·44	10
,, 29	396	Tennyson	Rowe	Hughes	10½	165	160	1·35	7
,, 30	790	Hardwicke	Howman	Harrison	10½	165	158	1·33	4
,, 31	1213	The Queen	Rowe	Hughes	11	172	159	1·32	7
Aug. 1	790	Hardwicke	Howman	Harrison	10	158	159	1·30	1
,, 2	1213	†The Queen	Rowe	Hughes	12½	195	156	1·34	8
,, 4	2192	Caradoc	Robinson	Wolstencroft	7½	118	157	1·33	9
,, 5	1213	The Queen	Phillips	Kay	7	110	156	1·33	13
,, 6	790	Hardwicke	Robinson	Wolstencroft	8½	134	160	1·38	22
,, 7	1213	The Queen	Phillips	Kay	7½	118	156	1·30	5
,, 8	790	†Hardwicke	Robinson	Wolstencroft	12	188	156	1·29	12

,, 9	1213	†The Queen	Phillips	Kay	13	203	152	1·32	9
,, 11	264	Buckland	Parry	Nicklin	7	110	156	1·29	5
,, 12	1213	The Queen	Rowe	Hughes	8	126	158	1·31	10
,, 13	790	Hardwicke	Howman	Harrison	11	172	160	1·35	4
,, 14	1213	The Queen	Rowe	Hughes	11½	180	155	1·33	9
,, 15	790	Hardwicke	Howman	Harrison	11½	180	160	1·34	5
,, 16	1213	†The Queen	Rowe	Hughes	13	203	152	1·28	5
,, 18	1683	‡Sisyphus	Robinson	Wolstencroft	12	188	175	1·49	20
,, 19	1683	Sisyphus	Phillips	Kay	6	95	140	1·1	6
,, 20	790	Hardwicke	Robinson	Wolstencroft	6	95	134	12·53	7
,, 21	1213	The Queen	Phillips	Kay	6	95	135	12·53	5
,, 22	790	Hardwicke	Robinson	Wolstencroft	4½	72	126	12·36½	5

* Assistant engine throughout 2-2-2 No. 610 *Princess Royal*.
† Assistant engine throughout 2-2-2 No. 622 *Prince Alfred*.
‡ Banked in rear Tebay to Shap Summit by 'DX' 0-6-0 No. 1717.

Working time of arrival (booked)	
July 15–21	2.0 a.m.
July 22–28	1.47
July 29–Aug. 18	1.38
Aug. 19	1.15
Aug. 20	1.0
Aug. 21	12.55
Aug. 22	12.45

L

EAST COAST TRAFFIC CIRCULARS

Circular No. 10,583a.

GREAT NORTHERN RAILWAY
PASSENGER TRAIN ALTERATIONS
COMMENCING MONDAY, 19TH AUGUST, 1895

		616		618		672
		p.m.		p.m.		p.m.
King's Cross	dep.	8.0		8.10		10.0
Hatfield	pass	8.19		8.32		10.23
Huntingdon	,,	9.1		9.15		11.9
Peterborough	,,	9.19		9.33	arr.	11.29
					dep.	11.33
Grantham	arr.	9.49		10.6	arr.	12.9
,,	dep.	9.52		10.10	dep.	12.14
Newark	pass	10.7		10.26		12.31
Retford	,,	10.26		10.45		12.53
Doncaster	,,	10.44		11.3		1.14
Selby	,,	11.3		11.22		1.36
York	arr.	11.18		11.38		1.53
York	dep.	11.23		11.43		2.0
Newcastle	arr.	12.43		1.12		3.37
,,	dep.	12.46		1.17		3.42
Edinburgh	arr.	2.55		3.35		6.12
Edinburgh	dep.	2.58		—		6.25
Dundee	arr.	4.8		—		7.38
Arbroath	,,	4.30		—		8.15
Montrose	,,	—		—		8.39
Stonehaven	,,	—		—		9.20
Aberdeen	,,	5.40		—		9.45
Edinburgh	dep.	—		3.39		6.20
Perth	arr.	—		*4.44		7.40
Edinburgh	dep.	—		4.30		7.35
Glasgow	arr.	—		5.50		9.0
Edinburgh	dep.	—		4.30		—
Larbet	arr.	—		5.13		—
Stirling	,,	—		5.50		—

* The Highland Co. give notice that a train leaves Perth at 5.0 a.m. and arrives at Inverness at 9.15 a.m.

616 will run on weekdays (Saturdays excepted) and on Sundays. Passengers not to be booked by this train for any station south of and including Edinburgh.

The vehicles on this train are for Aberdeen only. AS FAR AS PRACTICABLE THE LOAD OF THIS TRAIN MUST BE LIMITED TO SIX VEHICLES AND MUST NOT EXCEED EIGHT. Tickets must be examined at King's Cross and those of passengers who join the train at Grantham must be examined at that station. 579 down ordinary must be shunted in time to prevent delay to 616 and 618.

618 will run weekdays (Saturdays excepted) and on Sundays. AS FAR AS PRACTICABLE THE LOAD OF THIS TRAIN MUST BE LIMITED TO NINE VEHICLES AND MUST NOT EXCEED ELEVEN. Tickets must be examined at King's Cross and those of passengers who join the train at Grantham must be examined at that Station.

672 – Saturdays and Sundays excepted. Will not run after 30th September. AS FAR AS PRACTICABLE THE LOAD OF THIS TRAIN MUST BE LIMITED TO EIGHT VEHICLES, AND MUST NOT EXCEED TEN. Tickets must be examined at Grantham and those for York collected.

THE GREATEST CARE MUST BE TAKEN THAT A CLEAR ROAD IS KEPT FOR THESE TRAINS.

The 8.0, 8.10 and 10.0 p.m. down expresses from King's Cross will be formed as under.

8.0 p.m. ex King's Cross (6 vehicles)	8.10 p.m. ex King's Cross (9 vehicles)	10.0 p.m. ex King's Cross (8 vehicles)
Aberdeen brake van	Glasgow N.B. Brake van	Edinburgh brake van
,, third (corridor)	,, third	Glasgow compo
,, sleeping car	,, compo (sleeping)	Perth compo (sleeping)
,, compo (corridor)	Fort William compo	
,, third (corridor)	Perth 3rd carriage brake	Aberdeen carriage
,, brake van	,, compo	,, Brake 3rd
	Inverness sleeping car	,, compo (sleeping)
	,, compo	,, ,, ,,
	,, N.B. brake van	,, brake van

A through carriage for Fort William is no longer run in the down express leaving King's Cross at 8.30 p.m.

8.3 p.m. ordinary passenger train King's Cross to Hatfield to run on slow road and follow 618 from New Barnet.

9.30 p.m. express Nottingham to Grantham will run as per working book.

Circular 10,553a is cancelled.

FRANCIS P. COCKSHOTT
Superintendent of the Line.

King's Cross
August 16th, 1895.

(For the information of the Company's Servants only)

NORTH EASTERN RAILWAY

NIGHT SERVICE OF EXPRESS PASSENGER TRAINS
LONDON (KING'S CROSS) TO SCOTLAND

With reference to my circular of the 12th August: The 8.8 p.m. train from London (King's Cross) to Scotland will be discontinued after FRIDAY, the 16th instant.

ON AND AFTER MONDAY, AUGUST 19TH, THE 8.0 P.M. EXPRESS TRAIN FROM LONDON (KING'S CROSS) TO SCOTLAND WILL BE FURTHER ACCELERATED. From the same date also, the 8.16 p.m. Express train from London (King's Cross) to Scotland will start at 8.10 p.m., both trains running at the times given below.

The 10.0 p.m. train from London (King's Cross) to Scotland will be accelerated from Newcastle, and be due to arrive at Edinburgh at 6.12 a.m.

The FULL NIGHT SERVICE from London (King's Cross) to Scotland from August 19th will be as shewn in the following table:

		B	C		D		E		F
		p.m.	p.m.		p.m.		p.m.		p.m.
London (King's Cross)	dep.	8.0	8.10	dep.	8.30	dep.	10.0	dep.	10.40
		a.m.			a.m.		a.m.		a.m.
Doncaster	pass	10.44	11.3	,,	12.2	pass	1.14	,,	2.29
Selby	,,	11.3	11.22	arr.	12.28	,,	1.36	arr.	2.53
,,				dep.	12.29			dep.	2.58
York	arr.	11.18	11.38	arr.	12.52	arr.	1.53	arr.	3.25
,	dep.	11.23	11.43	dep.	1.0	dep.	2.0	dep.	3.35
Alne	pass	11.34	11.56	pass	1.16	pass	2.15	pass	3.50
			a.m.						
Thirsk	,,	11.44	12.7	,,	1.30	,,	2.27	,,	4.2
Northallerton	,,	11.51	12.15	,,	1.40	,,	2.36	,,	4.13
Dalton	,,	12.0	12.25	,,	1.50	,,	2.47	,,	4.25
		a.m.							
Darlington	,,	12.5	12.30	arr.	1.56	,,	2.52	arr.	4.32
,,				dep.	1.59			dep.	4.37
Ferryhill	,,	12.18	12.45	pass	2.18	,,	3.9	arr.	4.57
,,								dep.	4.59
Durham	,,	12.28	12.55	,,	2.30	,,	3.19	arr.	5.13
,,								dep.	5.17
Chester-le-Street	,,	12.34	1.1	,,	2.37	,	3.26	pass	5.25
Gateshead West								dep.	5.41
Newcastle	arr.	12.43	1.12	arr.	2.48	arr.	3.37	arr.	5.44
,,	dep.	12.46	1.17	dep.	2.55	dep.	3.42	dep.	6.0
Morpeth	pass	1.5	1.36	pass	3.19	pass	4.2	pass	6.22
Alnmouth	,,	1.23	1.55	,,	3.40	,,	4.22	,,	6.43
Belford	,,	1.39	2.14	,,	4.1	,,	4.42	,,	7.3
Berwick	,,	1.55	2.30	arr.	4.19	,,	4.59	arr.	7.21
,,		—	—	dep.	4.24	—		dep.	7.26
Reston		—	—	—		—		,,	7.41
Dunbar		—	—	—		—		arr.	8.7
,,								dep.	8.9
Edinburgh	arr.	2.55	3.35	arr.	5.45	arr.	6.12	arr.	8.50

NOTE. The passing times given above are those about which the trains may be expected to pass the various places mentioned.

B runs on Weekdays (Saturdays excepted) and Sundays. It will until further notice convey passengers for Aberdeen and Stations north of Edinburgh via Dundee only, and will not stop to set down passengers at Stations at which it is not timed to do so, *neither will it, from August 19th, convey any fish traffic.*

The train will be made up as shewn below and must not *under any circumstances* exceed eight vehicles.

Brake Van.	for Aberdeen	
Third Class (Corridor) Carriage .	,,	,,
Sleeping Carriage . . .	,,	,,
Composite (Corridor) Carriage .	,,	,,
Third Class ,, . . .	,,	,,
Brake Van (North British) . .	,,	,,

C runs on Weekdays (Saturdays excepted) and Sundays. It will consist of vehicles for Edinburgh, Glasgow and the Highland Railway, and for Oban when necessary. West Highland traffic and the through carriage for Fort William will also be sent by this train.
Fish from Grimsby for places beyond Edinburgh will be attached to this train at Newcastle.

D – No alterations will be made in the working of this train.

E – Saturdays and Sundays excepted. The number of vehicles on this train must not exceed ten.

F – No alteration will be made in the working of this train.

PARTICULAR ATTENTION MUST BE PAID TO THE PROMPT TELEGRAPHING OF THE RUNNING OF THE EXPRESS PASSENGER TRAINS REFERRED TO HEREIN, AND THE MARGINS HITHERTO OBSERVED BETWEEN TRAINS OF LESS IMPORTANCE AND THE 8.0 P.M. EXPRESS TRAIN FROM KING'S CROSS MUST UNTIL FURTHER NOTICE BE *INCREASED* TO THE EXTENT OF NOT LESS THAN *TEN MINUTES*, AND ALL CONCERNED ARE TO UNDERSTAND DISTINCTLY THAT THE LINE MUST BE KEPT ABSOLUTELY CLEAR FOR THESE TRAINS TO RUN.

When the 10.25 p.m. train from York to Newcastle is running not less than ten minutes late, it must be kept at Durham until the 8.0 p.m. train from King's Cross has passed, and the Fish train leaving York at 10.30 p.m. must not be allowed to leave Darlington until the 8.0 p.m. train from King's Cross has passed there.

THE EXPRESS PASSENGER TRAIN SHOWN IN THE TIME TABLES AS LEAVING LEEDS FOR YORK AT 11.0 P.M. WILL ON WEEKDAYS AND SUNDAYS, UNTIL FURTHER NOTICE, LEAVE LEEDS AT 10.45 P.M. AND ARRIVE IN YORK AT 11.25 P.M.

Acknowledge receipt by first train on the form sent herewith.

JOHN WELBURN.
Superintendent of the Line.

York,
August 15th, 1895.

Index

Aberdeen arrivals:
    Summary of best times   .. 129
Accidents:
    Carlisle station   26
    Lockerbie   26
    Preston 130
Accelerations:
    10 a.m. ex Euston   ..   36, 41
    10 a.m. ex Kings Cross 34 et seq., 44
    8 p.m. ex Euston   .. 73 et seq.
    8 p.m. ex Kings Cross   79, 90
Atherstone Level Crossing   44

Brakes:
    Clarke and Webb chain   ..   25
    Non-automatic vacuum   ..   26
    Westinghouse 25, 58

Caledonian Railway:
    Attitude to brakes   26
    Long non-stop runs   .. 135 et seq.
    Operating at Kinnaber   67, 68
    Rapid stops   58
Conacher, summing up of the race
                     122 et seq.
Conferences:
    East Coast at York   90
    East Coast at Edinburgh   .. 103
    L.N.W.R. Director's Committee 41
    L.N.W.R. & C.R. in Glasgow   41
Correspondents, contributing data:
    Alcock, C. J. 82, 119
    Brown, W. H.   82
    Cockman, F. G.   87
    Edwards, W. D. J.   84
    Guild, D. A.   84
    Longley, Cecil W.   82
    McEwan, J. F.   136
    Swaine, T. C. L.   83

Disputes:
    Caledonian versus Edinburgh &
      Glasgow   14
    Manchester, L.N.W.R. versus
      M.S.L.R.   ..   .. 17 et seq.
    Nottingham, engine impounded   17
Drivers:
    Clow (L.N.W.R.)   ..   97, 101
    Crooks (C.R.) 76, 120, 136
    Daynes (L.N.W.R.)   75

Falkinder (G.N.R.)   ..   97, 139
Holt (L.N.W.R.)   75
Howman (L.N.W.R.)   77
Kerr (C.R.) 77, 101
Nicholson (N.E.R.)   .. 45, 114, 131
Phillips (L.N.W.R.)   ..   76, 101
Robinson B. (L.N.W.R.) 76, 120, 127,
                     140
Robinson T. (C.R.) 76, 98, 101, 112,
                     120
Soutar (C.R.) 77, 121, 138
Turner (N.E.R.)   113
Walker (L.N.W.R.)   106

Engineers:
    Bowen-Cooke, C. J.   136
    Drummond, Dugald ..   26, 56
    Fletcher, E. 28, 31
    Holmes, M.   ..   71, 80, 90, 123
    Lambie, J.   69
    McDonnell, A.   29
    McIntosh, J. F.   130
    Ramsbottom, J.   ..   23, 49
    Raven, V. L.   90
    Sacre, C.   31
    Smith, W. M. 32, 71
    Stirling, P.   ..   31, 53, 93
    Webb, F. W. 30, 39, 69
    Whale, G. 31, 41
    Worsdell, T.W.   .. 32, 52, 70
    Worsdell, W. 70, 97, 130
Euston Confederacy ..   .. 11 et seq.

Fife, fast running in   83
Firemen:
    Blades (N.E.R.)   114
    Harrison (L.N.W.R.)   76
    Hewins (L.N.W.R.)   75
    Stinson (L.N.W.R)   75
    Wolstencroft (L.N.W.R.) 75, 120, 127,
                     140
Flying Scotsman   19 et seq., 28, 34 et seq.,
                   54 et seq.
Forth Bridge   62

Gradients:
    Caledonian line   27
    L.N.W.R. Shap   27
    North British   63

Great Northern Railway:
Fight for traffic.. .. 10 *et seq.*
Internal correspondence, loco-
motive department 1895 92 *et seq.*
Locomotive performance 1888 53 *et seq.*
Rivalry with the L.N.W.R. 17 *et seq.*
Speed traditions 28
Veto on double heading .. 36

Kinnaber Junction:
Caledonian practice 67
Close running 68
Exciting finishes 110

Locomotives, individual:
Caledonian,
No. 17 .. .. 77, 110, 121
No. 70 .. .. 77, 101
No. 78 .. .. 76, 112
No. 90 .. 76, 121, 107
No. 123 .. 43 *et seq.*, 56 *et seq.*
G.N.R.,
No. 668 97
No. 775 .. .. 97, 113
L.N.W.R.,
Adriatic .. 97, 101, 112, 119
Eamont 75, 86
Hardwicke 75, 86, 107, 120, 132 *et seq.*
Ionic 127
Mercury 75, 86
Sisyphus 101
The Queen 112
Vulcan.. .. .. 50, 56
Waverley .. .. 42 *et seq.*, 49
N.B.R.,
No. 262 115
No. 293 .. .. 100, 115
N.E.R.,
No. 117 47
No. 1475 52
No. 1620 114
No. 1621 .. .. 99, 113
Locomotive Types:
Caledonian,
Conner singles 26
Drummond 4-4-0 26, 69, 76, 132 *et seq.*
'Dunalastair' 130
Lambie 4-4-0 69
Single No. 123 .. 43, 56 *et seq.*
Great Northern,
Stirling 8ft singles 28, 45, 53, 71
Stirling 7 ft 6 in. 2-2-2 28, 45, 53
L.N.W.R.,
'Dreadnought' compound .. 24

'Experiment' compound .. 24
'Lady of the Lake' 2-2-2 23, 42
'Precedent' 2-4-0 .. 24, 43
'Teutonic' compound .. 69
'Whitworth' 2-4-0 156
North British,
Holmes '633' class 72
North Eastern,
Tennant 2-4-0 .. 29, 51
Worsdell 'F' compound .. 45
Worsdell 4-2-2 singles .. 71
Worsdell 'M' 4-4-0 70
Worsdell 'Q1' 4-4-0 .. 130
Logs of runs:
Caledonian,
Carlisle–Edinburgh, engine
123 59
Carlisle–Perth, engine 90 .. 139
Carlisle–Perth, engine 78 and
90 136
Perth–Aberdeen (stopping at
Forfar), engine 17.. .. 140
Perth–Aberdeen (non-stop)
engine 17 140
Great Northern,
Kings Cross–Grantham, engine
98 52
Kings Cross–Grantham, engine
668 141
Grantham–York, engine 231 142
Grantham–York, engine 775 142
L.N.W.R.,
Euston–Crewe, *Waverley* .. 50
Preston–Carlisle, *Lightning* .. 50
Preston–Carlisle, *Vulcan* .. 50
Crewe–Carlisle, *Hardwicke* .. 107
Euston–Crewe, *Adriatic* .. 143
Crewe–Carlisle (record),
Hardwicke 145
North British,
Edinburgh–Dundee, engine
293 148
North Eastern,
York–Newcastle, engine 1475 52
Newcastle–Edinburgh, engine
1620 147
London & North Western Railway:
Continuous brakes .. 25 *et seq.*
Euston–Carlisle non-stop .. 126
Irish Mail 23
Punctuality 39
Small locomotives 23
Speeds .. .. 23, 36 *et seq.*, 73
Summaries of locomotive
working .. .. 153 *et seq.*
Water troughs 106, 132

Lunch intervals:
  At Preston 21, 43, 44
  At York 45, 47

Midland Railway:
  Abolition of 2nd class   20
  Lowering 1st class fares   ..   20
  Settle and Carlisle line   ..   20

North British Railway:
  Bridgeheads in England   ..   16
  Fife, running difficulties   ..   63
  Forth Bridge, routes north   ..   62
  Running powers   16
North Eastern Railway:
  Engine changing   ..   98, 100
  Speed   29
  Traffic circulars   165

Octuple Agreement   13

Personalities:
  Acworth, Sir W.   40, 56, 81, 96
  Ahrons, E. L.   ..   16, 58, 129, 137
  Alexander, J. 40, 90
  Barker, J. A.   49
  Caldecott, P.   96
  Clarke, S.   11
  Cockshott, F. P.   31, 35, 40, 43, 74 *et seq.*, 103
  Conacher, J.   74 *et seq.*, 111 *et seq.*, 122
  Denison, E.   10
  Deuchars, D.   ..   74 *et seq.*, 90, 102
  Eddy, J.   32
  Farrer, T. C.   39
  Findlay, Sir G.   66
  Foxwell, Prof.   29
  Gibb, Sir G. S.   70, 74 *et seq.*, 111 *et seq.*
  Gilbert, W. M.   96
  Harrison, Sir F.   66
  Hudson, G.   ..   ..   9 *et seq.*
  Huish, Capt. M.   ..   11 *et seq.*, 13

Jackson, Hon. W. L.   ..   78
Kempt, Irvine   32
Lowe, A. C. W.   76
Macdonald, N. D.   40, 43, 81, 96
Matthewman, J. W.   ..   93 *et seq.*
Moon, Sir R. 25, 33, 65
Neele, G. P.   ..   21, 31, 41, 46, 66
Oakley, Sir H.   31, 74 *et seq.*, 111 *et seq.*, 125
Reay, Stephen   65
Rous-Marten, C.   24, 58, 81, 96, 127, 136
Rouse, F.   ..   ..   93 *et seq.*
Scott, Rev. W. J.   40, 53, 76, 81, 96
Stalbridge, Lord   65
Tennant, H. 29, 70
Tweeddale, Marquis of   ..   79
Watkin, Sir E.   44
Welburn, J.   ..   .. 74 *et seq.*, 103
Portobello Incident   99
Press, interest of, 40, 61, 83, 114, 117, 119, 121, 131

Racing Runs analysed, against modern records..   133

Speed competitions in Year:
  1848   12
  1888   ..   ..   ..   34 *et seq.*
  1895   ..   ..   .   74 *et seq.*
  1901   131
Spying, at Euston and Kings Cross   87

Telegrams:
  Conacher to Oakley   74, 75, 78, 115, 116
  Conacher to Tweeddale   ..   79
  Oakley to Conacher   ..   74, 79, 116
  Tweeddale to Conacher   ..   79

Water Supply:
  On Caledonian Railway   ..   133
  On North Eastern Railway   ..   132